Russia's Foreign Policy

Change and Continuity in National Identity

Second Edition

Andrei P. Tsygankov

ROWMAN & LITTLEFIELD PUBLISHERS, INC.
Lanham • Boulder • New York • Toronto • Plymouth, UK

Published by Rowman & Littlefield Publishers, Inc.
A wholly owned subsidiary of The Rowman & Littlefield Publishing Group, Inc.
4501 Forbes Boulevard, Suite 200, Lanham, Maryland 20706
http://www.rowmanlittlefield.com

Estover Road, Plymouth PL6 7PY, United Kingdom

British Library Cataloguing in Publication Information Available

Library of Congress Cataloging-in-Publication Data

Tsygankov, Andrei P., 1964-
  Russia's foreign policy : change and continuity in national identity / Andrei P. Tsygankov. -- 2nd ed.
     p. cm.
  Includes bibliographical references and index.
  ISBN 978-0-7425-6752-8 (cloth : alk. paper) -- ISBN 978-0-7425-6753-5 (paper : alk. paper) -- ISBN 978-0-7425-6754-2 (electronic)
  1. Russia (Federation)--Foreign relations. 2. Soviet Union--Foreign relations.
  3. Great powers. 4. Russia (Federation)--Foreign relations--Western countries.
  5. Western countries--Foreign relations--Russia (Federation)
  6. Nationalism--Russia (Federation) 7. Social change--Russia (Federation) I. Title.
  DK510.764.T785 2010
  327.47--dc22   2009049396

It is the eternal dispute between those who imagine the world to suit their policy, and those who arrange their policy to suit the realities of the world.

—Albert Sorel (Carr 1964, 11)

Contents

Note on the Transliteration

In transliterating names from the Russian, I have used "y" to denote "й," " ' " to denote "ь" and "ъ," "yu" to denote "ю," "ya" to denote "я," "i" to denote "й" and "ий," "iyi" to denote double "и," "e" to denote "э," "kh" to denote "x," "zh" to denote "ж," "ts" to denote "ц," "ch" to denote "ч," "sh" to denote "ш," and "sch" to denote "щ." I have also used "Ye" to distinguish the sound of "E" (such as "Yevropa") in the beginning of a word from that in the middle of a word (such as "vneshnei"). Everywhere, I did not distinguish between "e" and "ё." Original spelling is retained in quotations.

Tables

Chronology of Key Foreign Policy Events, 1985–2009

1985

March	U.S.-Soviet arms negotiations in Geneva
April	Gorbachev announces a unilateral moratorium on deployment of intermediate-range nuclear missiles and proposes a moratorium on all nuclear weapons tests
	Eduard Shevardnadze succeeds Andrei Gromyko as Soviet foreign minister
July	Soviet Union imposes five-month moratorium on nuclear weapons tests, making its extension contingent upon a similar U.S. response
September	Moscow proposes at Geneva negotiations that United States and USSR reduce long- and medium-range nuclear weapons by 50 percent

1986

January	Gorbachev proposes a ban on all nuclear weapons by the year 2000
June	Warsaw Pact meeting in Budapest proposes mutual Warsaw Pact–NATO troops reduction of 100,000 to 150,000 men and the reduction of military capabilities to those "necessary for defense"
July	Gorbachev announces in Vladivostok a five-point plan for cooperation in the Asia-Pacific region and advocates closer ties with China

October   Reagan and Gorbachev meet in Reykjavik, Iceland

1987

May   General Dmitri Yazov is named the new Soviet defense minister
December   Gorbachev and Reagan sign in Washington the INF treaty elimi-
             nating all 2,611 Soviet and U.S. intermediate-range nuclear
             forces

1988

January   Gorbachev announces the need for "innovative policies" in East-
             ern Europe
May   U.S.-Soviet summit in Moscow
December   Gorbachev announces before the United Nations General Assem-
             bly a unilateral reduction of Soviet forces by some 500,000 sol-
             diers, 10,000 tanks, 8,500 artillery pieces, and 800 combat air-
             craft

1989

April   Soviet crackdown on Georgian nationalists in Tbilisi; twenty
             demonstrators killed and two hundred wounded
             Unilateral withdrawal of Soviet forces begins from Hungary
May   Gorbachev before Council of Europe promises not to interfere
             militarily in political events in Eastern Europe
October   Shevardnadze proclaims before the Supreme Soviet that the So-
             viet invasion in Afghanistan in 1979 "violated the norms of
             proper behavior" and that the Krasnoyarsk radar installation is
             illegal under the 1972 ABM treaty
December   "Big Four" (United States, France, Great Britain, and USSR) meet
             to discuss the status of Berlin

1990

January   Soviet troops are deployed to Azerbaijan in the wake of massive
             anti-Armenian demonstrations
February   "Two Plus Four" talks on German reunification announced
March   In response to Lithuania's declaration of independence, Soviet
             paratroopers seize the headquarters of the Lithuanian Commu-
             nist Party

May	U.S.-Soviet summit in Washington
July	Gorbachev and Kohl announce agreement to allow reunified Germany to belong to NATO
November	NATO and Warsaw Pact states sign the CFE treaty and the Charter of Paris at the CSCE Summit
	Gorbachev proposes a new Union treaty
December	Shevardnadze resigns as Soviet foreign minister

1991

January	Soviet troops crack down on pro-independence forces in Lithuania and Latvia; nineteen protesters killed
March	In the Soviet referendum voters choose to preserve the union; Baltics, Armenia, Georgia, and Moldova boycott the vote
July	Warsaw Pact is disbanded in Prague
	Bush and Gorbachev reach an agreement in Moscow on the Strategic Arms Reduction Treaty (START)
	Ten Soviet republics reach an agreement on a new Union treaty to be signed on August 20
August	Coup against Gorbachev
December	Russia, Ukraine, and Belarus establish the CIS in Minsk
	Gorbachev resigns as president of the USSR

1992

February	Foreign Ministry conference "The Transformed Russia in the New World"
March	Kozyrev briefly travels to China
April	Bush, supported by Kohl, announces $24 billion package for Russia
	Yeltsin orders withdrawal of troops from Nagorno-Karabakh and asks for the deployment of NATO troops
	Russia places the Fourteenth Army in Moldova under its control
May	Russia supports the United Nations' sanctions against Yugoslavia
	Russia signs the CIS Collective Security treaty
	Russia joins the IMF and World Bank
June	Russia and United States agree on terms of START II
July	Yeltsin at G-7 summit
	Yeltsin and Moldova's president Snegur sign peace agreement over Transdniestr conflict
December	Yeltsin visits China

Kozyrev acknowledges the need to be more active on the eastern front

1993

January   Yeltsin attends the Civic Union's congress
            Bush and Yeltsin sign START II
April   New Foreign Policy Concept signed into law
May   Russia initiates the CIS Economic Union agreement at Moscow summit
July   The Tokyo G-7 summit declares a $43.4 billion package of assistance for Russia
October   Russia withdraws from the ruble zone
            U.S. secretary of state Warren Christopher promises Yeltsin not to push for NATO expansion immediately and to focus on Partnership for Peace instead
November   Russia adopts new military doctrine
December   Westernizers lose party elections to nationalist Zhirinovski

1994

January   Clinton announces that the question of enlarging NATO is not whether it will happen, but when
July   Kozyrev announces change in his foreign policy course
September   Washington summit; Clinton pledges NATO enlargement will be guided by "three no's"—no surprises, no rush, and no exclusion of Russia
December   Kozyrev refuses to sign up for Partnership for Peace
            Yeltsin warns of "cold peace"
            Russian military launches offensive in Chechnya
            Russia joins G-7

1995

May   Russia begins dialogue with NATO and signs Partnership for Peace
December   In Russian parliamentary elections, Westernizers lose to Communists
            Kozyrev is removed from office
            Primakov replaces Kozyrev as foreign minister

1996

April   Treaty on the Formation of the Russia-Belarus Union State is signed

May   IMF announces $10.2 billion to be disbursed to Russia monthly from March 1996 to March 1999

June   Yeltsin approves the concept of the state nationalities policy of the Russian Federation and states the goal of a multiethnic Russia; he also initiates the search for a new "national idea"

July   Yeltsin is reelected as president

November   Yeltsin and Japanese prime minister meet and commit themselves to signing a peace treaty in 2000

December   Primakov visits Tehran and declares that Russia-Iran relations are "developing along an ascending curve"

Russia is admitted to the Asian and Pacific Economic Council (APEC)

1997

March   Yeltsin meets Clinton in Helsinki and insists that NATO not include former Soviet states

CIS adopts Concept of Economic Integrational Development

April   Russia and China sign the "Joint Declaration on a Multipolar World and the Formation of a New International Order"

May   Yeltsin signs NATO-Russia Founding Act at summit with NATO leaders in Paris

Russia and Ukraine sign the "Big Treaty," which legalizes the borders

June   Peace treaty to end Tajik civil war is signed in Moscow

October   Georgia, Ukraine, Azerbaijan, and Moldova establish a security group to balance Russia

December   Russia adopts new National Security Concept

Primakov responds to the U.S. threat to attack Iraq by entering an alliance with France and negotiating an agreement for the return of the UN inspections to Iraq

1998

February   Russia and Ukraine sign the ambitious Program of Economic Cooperation

May   Yeltsin and Clinton meet in Birmingham; Russia officially joins the G-8

September   Primakov assumes the post of prime minister. Igor' Ivanov becomes foreign minister

December   Russia withdraws ambassadors from London and Washington to protest U.S. and British air strikes against Iraq

Primakov speaks of desirability of Russia-China-India alliance as a "new pole in world politics"

1999

February	Russian Duma narrowly ratifies the Russia-Ukraine "Big Treaty"
March	Russia begins negotiating restructuring of its approaching $17.5 billion foreign debt payment
	NATO's air strikes against Serbia begin; Primakov cancels the upcoming negotiations with the United States and the IMF in Washington
April	Yeltsin appoints Viktor Chernomyrdin as Russia's special envoy on Yugoslavia
	Russian Duma refuses to ratify the START II
May	Sergei Stepashin replaces Primakov as prime minister
June	Chernomyrdin and Finnish president Martti Ahtisaari secure Milošević agreement to NATO terms for ending war
	Russian troops begin participation in the multilateral peacekeeping force in Kosovo
	"Common Strategy of the EU on Russia" is adopted
July	First meeting of Russia-NATO Permanent Council since it was boycotted by Russia in March
August	Russia sends troops to counter Chechen incursions into Dagestan
	Putin replaces Stepashin as prime minister
	Chechen rebels occupy parts of Dagestan; Kremlin resumes military operation
	Bombs explode in Moscow, killing hundreds of residents
October	Russia adopts new military doctrine
December	Yeltsin resigns; Putin becomes acting president of Russia

2000

March	Putin is officially elected president
June	Putin holds summit with Clinton in Moscow
September	Russia, India, and Iran sign an agreement, according to which all signatories will get relief from import tax and customs duties

2001

February	The secretary of the Security Council, Sergei Ivanov, announces the new "pragmatic" course of bilateral relations in the former Soviet region

June   Putin meets George W. Bush in Ljubljana, Slovenia
September   Terrorist attacks on the United States
              Putin announces support for the United States and pledges intel-
              ligence assistance
November   Putin and Bush meet in Crawford, Texas

2002

February   Putin emphasizes Russia as a reliable energy alternative to the
              Middle East; he also proposes creating a "gas OPEC" group
April   Putin proclaims Russia's European foreign policy a priority in the
              Duma address
May   Russia and United States sign a joint declaration on energy coop-
              eration in Moscow
October   Russia-U.S. "energy summit" in Houston
November   At the EU summit Russia proposes to have visa-free arrangement
              in Kaliningrad
December   Russia shuts down the OSCE mission in Chechnya

2003

January   Russia joins the antiwar coalition and argues for the United Na-
              tions as the only legitimate body to sanction the use of force in
              Iraq
April   Russia and Turkmenistan sign a strategic gas agreement
May   Russia and five other ex-Soviet states form the Collective Security
              Treaty Organization for fighting terrorism
June   Putin proposes that visas between EU countries and Russia be
              abandoned altogether by the year 2006
August   Putin seals a joint venture with British Petroleum worth over $6
              billion
              Moscow withdraws its peacekeeping mission from Bosnia and
              Kosovo
September   Russia signs an $800 million deal with Iran and pledges to build
              two more nuclear reactors in Iran
              Russia signs a partnership agreement with Azerbaijan
              Russia signs an agreement with Saudi Arabia pledging cooperation
              in the energy sector and in setting the international price of oil
October   The head of Russia's state electric company, Anatoli Chubais, an-
              nounces that Russia's main goal is to build a "liberal empire" in
              the former USSR

2004

March	Putin is reelected president
May	EU incorporates ten new members
	Russia and EU agree on conditions to extend the Partnership and Cooperation Agreement with EU to the ten new members
September	Terrorist attack in Beslan, northern Ossetia
	Putin announces reform in the political system
November	Orange Revolution in Ukraine; Russia supports Viktor Yanukovich in Ukraine's presidential election

2005

January	Putin-Bush summit in Bratislava
March	Change of power in Kyrgyzstan through a mass protest; Russia takes no side
April	Putin visits Middle East
	Russia and Germany agree to build a gas pipeline under the Baltic Sea
May	Celebration of victory in World War II in Moscow
	Riots and their brutal suppression in Uzbekistan; Russia supports the government
June	Russia-China-India meeting in Vladivostok to discuss prospects of strategic partnership
	Russia and Georgia reach agreement on withdrawal of Russia's military bases
December	Russia-Ukraine dispute over natural gas

2006

June	Russia declares opposition to Ukraine or Georgia joining NATO
September	Russia's economic and political sanctions against Georgia
December	Russia-Belarus dispute over natural gas

2007

February	Putin's speech at the Munich Conference on Security Policy
March	The Foreign Ministry report "A Review of the Russian Federation's Foreign Policy" is released
April	United States announces plans to deploy elements of missile defense system in Eastern Europe

May	Kazakhstan, Turkmenistan and Uzbekistan agree to increase exports of energy via Russia's pipelines
	Putin announces a moratorium on implementing the Conventional Forces in Europe treaty
	Russia-EU summit in Samara
December	Russia announces plans to re-equip its new SS-27 missiles with multiple warheads

2008

March	Medvedev is elected president
April	Russia blocks Georgia and Ukraine from receiving the Membership Action Plan for NATO
June	President Medvedev proposes a new pan-European treaty beyond NATO
	Russia-EU summit in Khanty-Mansiysk
July	Russia and China complete border demarcation
August	Russia-Georgia war
	Russia recognizes the independence of Abkhazia and South Ossetia
December	Russia's new National Security Strategy until 2020 is released

2009

April	Russia expresses concern over the EU's Eastern Partnership project
May	NATO conducts a military exercise in Georgia
	Russia-EU summit in Khabarovsk
June	SCO summit in Ekaterinburg
July	U.S.-Russia summit in Moscow
	Russia conducts a large military exercise in the Caucasus

Partly adapted from: Coit D. Blacker, *Hostage to Revolution: Gorbachev and Soviet Security Policy, 1985–1991* (New York: Council on Foreign Relations, 1993), ix–xviii; Strobe Talbott, *The Russia Hand* (New York: Random House, 2002), 423–29; Karen Dawisha and Bruce Parrott, *Russia and the New States of Eurasia* (Cambridge: Cambridge University Press, 1994), 298–310; Ted Hopf, *Social Construction of International Politics. Identities and Foreign Policies, Moscow, 1955 and 1999* (Ithaca, NY: Cornell University Press, 2002), 212–13.

Preface

Winston Churchill once famously observed that the key to understanding Russia's "enigma" is its national interest. However, he failed to explain what that interest was. It is therefore our scholarly task to uncover what Russians themselves understand to be their foreign policy interests and objectives. In contrast to the direction of Churchill's thought, there has been a great deal of change in Russia's perceptions of its national interest. Thus, President Boris Yeltsin and his first foreign minister, Andrei Kozyrev, defined national interest as that of integration with Western economic and security institutions. The second foreign minister, Yevgeni Primakov, saw the need to restore Russia's great power status and balance hegemonic aspirations of the United States. Finally, President Vladimir Putin adopted his own distinct vision of national interest, according to which Russia's great power status was essential, but not at the expense of special relationships with the West in general and the United States in particular. In the wake of the global economic crisis, Russia is yet again reassessing its interests and relations with the West.

This book seeks to contribute to our understanding of the national interest formation in Russia's foreign policy. Instead of assuming that national interest is about power or modernization, as mainstream international relations theories tend to do, I maintain that we ought to study complex forces behind its formation. Upon closer inspection, we discover that much of Russia's foreign policy and national interest can be understood in the context of the country's relations with the West. Russia's attempts to embrace Western liberalism, as well as its insistence on great power status, make sense when we consider the significance of Western recognition for affirming Russia's actions. Western actions serve to

reinforce or undermine dominant political forces inside Russia. Extending recognition emboldens Russian liberals insisting on their country's belongingness
with the West. Withholding such recognition strengthens Russia's traditionally
strong supporters of greater independence from the West. It is therefore domestic identity coalitions competing for influence in the context of Western actions
that help to make sense of Russia's foreign policy formation. Chapter 1 explains
my approach in greater detail.

The book does not claim to break new ground in empirical research. My
objectives are more modest: to assist fellow academics in their teaching needs
and to suggest a plausible interpretation of Russia's foreign policy. In my own
teaching, I continue to feel a deficit of broadly targeted textbooks appropriate
for senior undergraduate and graduate courses in the field of post-Soviet studies. With the second decade of the post-Soviet changes under way, there is still
surprisingly little written that would meet this criterion. Fortunately, there are
exceptions. There is also a good deal written by specialists on various specific
aspects, issues, and periods in the development of Russia's foreign policy after
communism. In my book, I relied heavily on this literature in attempting to
synthesize it into a relatively broad overview of the subject. In addition to
highlighting in endnotes the impact of some specific sources on my thinking,
I list in an "essential reading" section the readings that influenced this book
the most.

While writing with teaching needs in mind, I have advanced an argument
and taken an explicit analytical perspective. My choice of explaining Russia's
foreign policy turns by changes in the nation's identity, rather than by material
capabilities or leadership's perspectives alone, was a conscientious one. I fully
realize that for the purpose of advancing scholarship, many of the book's as-
sertions would require a much greater documentation. I hope, however, that
my framework is helpful for presenting material, asking interesting questions,
and organizing in-class discussion. After all, no textbook is neutral, and instructors usually try to balance the dominant text(s) by assigning additional
materials with conflicting viewpoints and perspectives. In my own teaching, I
also commonly employ articles and materials by authors holding diverse
views. Provoking thinking and sparking debates in class is essential for learning, as it is through arguing and sometimes only through arguing that we
deepen our understanding. Although this may seem like a challenging way of
teaching, our students deserve nothing less. I therefore intentionally present
material in a somewhat polemical way, as a debate among different social and
political groups in Russia.

I also make an effort to differentiate myself from more common treatment of
Russian foreign policy in the West. My own perspective on the development of
Russia's foreign policy is neither pro-Western liberalism nor anti-Western na-

tionalism. Both of these perspectives have influenced Russian foreign policy formation, but, in my judgment, each has defended views of relatively narrow elite circles and ultimately failed to respond to broader needs of Russian society. I hope that Russia is now closer to having developed an appropriate formula of national interest, which appreciates the value of international cooperation in a globalizing world but is also sensitive to Russia's local conditions and the country's special position in the international system. I also hope that scholars across the world pay close attention to future developments in Russia's foreign policy. Russia is no longer a threat to the West, and that alone has directed some of the sharpest pens away from studying that country's attitudes and behavior. Yet we have not come to understand this nation better just because the iron curtain is no longer in place. Russia also retains its political significance, and engaging it as a legitimate member of world society remains a key to peace and security in the new era. Such engagement requires that we improve our knowledge of Russia's perceived national interests.

The book is divided into eight chapters. The first chapter provides a brief historical overview of Russia's foreign policy and spells out the book's approach to understanding Russia's post-Soviet international behavior. I situate my approach relative to more mainstream international relations theories, realism and liberalism, and I argue the insufficiency of these traditional theoretical perspectives for understanding Russia. The rest of the book is a detailed analysis of several distinct concepts of national interest that guided Russia's international policies in the late-Soviet and post-Soviet years. The latter parts are broken down further in order to cover such stories as the International Monetary Fund (IMF), North Atlantic Treaty Organization (NATO), China, Yugoslavia, Iran, Commonwealth of Independent States (CIS) ties, the United States, the Iraq war, bilateral relations with newly independent states, and others. These are cases that instructors can choose from in order to stimulate a more focused discussion in class. Instructors may elect to assign longer articles or those materials that interpret Russia's actions differently than I do. Chapter 2 analyzes Gorbachev's New Thinking philosophy and what it meant for the country's foreign policy. Chapters 3–6 each explore the formation and consequences of other distinct visions of national interest—Integration with the West (early Yeltsin and Kozyrev), Great Power Balancing (late Yeltsin and Primakov), Great Power Pragmatism (Putin), and Great Power Assertiveness (late Putin and Medvedev). In each of the substantive chapters, I specify international and domestic context of foreign policy formation. I provide a brief overview of domestic debates on national interest and then review Russian policies toward the West, the East, and the former Soviet region. Furthermore, in each chapter, I offer an assessment of each period's foreign policy record. Criteria for my assessment are spelled out in the first chapter. Chapter 7 reflects on the emergence of the post-Western world and the challenges it presents for Russia's enduring quest for great power status with the desire for a special relationship with Western nations.

The final chapter summarizes my explanation of change and continuity in Russia's foreign policy and its implications for Russian and Western policy-makers.

Writing this book would have been impossible without the support of my friends, colleagues, students, and family. Naturally, full responsibility for the book's content is my own. For financial assistance, I wish to thank the Office of the President at San Francisco State University, which granted me an Award for Professional Development of Probationary Faculty and therefore made it possible to complete this book. I owe special thanks to Susan McEachern and Andrzej Korbonski. In the spring of 2002, they each, independently, suggested to me the idea of a textbook on Russian foreign policy. Since then they have been supportive of the project and confident in my ability to finish it. Comments and criticisms by Ronald Linden and an anonymous reviewer have been instrumental in improving the book, and I hope the final version will satisfy some of their expectations. I am also grateful to the University of Chicago's Program on International Politics, Economics, and Security (PIPES) for inviting me to deliver a paper and for providing a stimulating theoretical critique of this book's central argument. I thank especially Charles Lipson, Michelle Murrey, Alexander Wendt, as well as all other program participants for their helpful reactions and suggestions. Sanjoy Banerjee and David Holloway shared their time to discuss central ideas of this book. Julia Godzikovskaya and Anna Radivilova were good enough to provide feedback on individual chapters. Furthermore, I thank many of my students in classes on Russia, post-Soviet states, and United States–Russia relations in Eurasia. The writing process would have been much less rewarding without their reactions to various portions of the book. It has been a pleasure to teach the subject of my own fascination, and to a group of interested and motivated individuals.

Many thanks to Rowman & Littlefield Publishers for smoothing out my prose and to Sheila-Katherine Zwiebel for all her assistance. While revising the book for the second edition, I have greatly benefited from comments and suggestions made by Susan McEachern and anonymous reviewers who have used the text in their teaching. In addition, several years have passed since the book was first published. During these years, I have received many helpful comments from teachers, scholars, journalists, and members of the policy community in reaction to the published book and my other writings on Russia's international policy. Finally, my special debt is to my family for their love and support. I dedicate this book to the youngest members of my family, my daughter Dasha and my son Pasha.

1

Understanding Change and Continuity in Russia's Foreign Policy

When political formulas, such as "national interest" or "national security" gain popularity they need to be scrutinized with particular care. They may not mean the same thing to different people. They may not have any precise meaning at all.

—Arnold Wolfers[1]

This chapter provides analytical tools for understanding the subject of this book. It reviews Russia's international behavior across history and identifies several patterns of change and continuity in the country's foreign policy. Russian traditional foreign policy debates survived the fall of the Soviet system, and Russia's postcommunist behavior should therefore be understood in the historical context. The chapter offers a framework for understanding Russian foreign policy, comparing and contrasting it with some prominent analytical perspectives. My approach focuses on Russia's relations with the outside world, and it views Russia's behavior as particularly influenced by the development and behavior of Western nations. What often determines Moscow's foreign policy choices is whether or not the West's international actions are perceived by Russian officials as accepting Russia as an equal and legitimate member of the world. The chapter also develops standards for evaluating Russia's foreign policy record. Finally, it orients the reader regarding the book's methodology and organizational structure.

1.1. RUSSIA'S FOREIGN POLICY: CHANGE AND CONTINUITY

Russia's foreign policy was formed in different external contexts, while responding to some similar sets of security challenges. This combination provides Russia's historical foreign policy with elements of change and continuity.

Changing Contexts

At least since Peter the Great, Europe and—after World War II—the West in general played an especially prominent role in creating for Russia the system of meanings in which to defend international choices. To many Russians, the West represented a superior civilization whose influences were to be emulated or contained, but never ignored. Yet Western contexts were changing over time, presenting Russia with different policy dilemmas. More specifically, different Wests have been associated respectively with sovereign monarchy, the rise of a liberal political system, and finally the consolidation of a liberal political system.

Sovereign monarchy emerged as a dominant political form in seventeenth-century Europe after the era of religious wars. It was the era of increasingly secular sovereign statehood, and it was in this context that Peter the Great assumed power in 1694. In the context of European secularism, Peter introduced a new ideology of state patriotism, or loyalty to the state—a sharp break with the religious autocratic Russia that had emerged after the two-centuries-long rule by the Mongols. Despite opposition from the Eastern Orthodox Church, the czar decisively turned Russia in the secular nationalist direction. Although religion was still playing an important role, it was increasingly subjected to considerations of the state. European international politics, and with it Russia's international politics, was becoming the politics of accumulating national power rather than affirming religious values.

The liberal and egalitarian ideas of the French Revolution of 1789 further changed Europe by splitting it into progressive and antirevolutionary camps. The era of the rising Europe of Enlightenment, constitutionalism, and capitalism presented Russia with new international dilemmas. Russian rulers had to decide between the old monarch-centered vision of sovereignty and the new popular sovereignty, and this choice was then to shape the nation's international behavior. Some rulers—most prominently Alexander II—attempted to yet again redefine the country's identity in line with the new European ideas of freedom and equality. Their moderate foreign policies reflected the need for Russia to undergo considerable domestic changes. Other rulers were fearful of the new Europe and sought to defend the basic features of the old monarchic regime. Thus, Alexander I insisted on the need to defend status quo in the post-Napoleonic

Europe and embraced antirevolutionary Germany and Austria, rather than progressive France, as his role models. Alexander III also continued policies of siding with European autocracies and repressions at home.

As Europe was fighting its way through the crisis of rising liberal ideas, some Russians began to advocate a break with both old and new Europe. Alexander Herzen, for instance, grew disappointed with European conservative restorations of the 1840s and argued for Russia's own, non-European way of "catching up" economically and socially. The Bolsheviks pushed this line of thinking to its extreme and adopted a fundamentally different political system and foreign policy. The Bolshevik revolution of October 1917 reflected the crisis of European identity and the Russian leadership's inability to choose between the two Europes. The czar failed to prevent the country from the nearing destruction, revolution, and civil war. The rule of Nicholas II was symbolic in this respect. In 1904, he dismissed his finance minister, Count Sergei Witte, a proponent of the new Europe and an economic reformer, and chose to sacrifice domestic reforms to the goals of foreign policy expansionism by going to war against Japan. By then entering World War I, Nicholas further brought the European crisis closer to home and made it impossible to prevent the spread of extremist Marxist ideas in Russia, a move which brought his downfall in the Bolshevik revolution of 1917. In recognition of the West's world role, however, even the Bolsheviks sought to engage Western nations and related to their technological and material power. The Bolsheviks' concept of the Soviet power and proletarian democracy was also a response to egalitarian ideas of the French Revolution. Furthermore, Bolsheviks' foreign policy, after the early efforts to overthrow the "bourgeois" governments in Europe, was that of rapprochement and pragmatic cooperation with the West.

As Europe reemerged as a consolidated liberal-democratic continent after World War II, the Soviet rulers sought to preserve a connection with the new West. The intercourse with the West grew stronger under Nikita Khrushchev and then Mikhail Gorbachev. Soviet leader Nikita Khrushchev's famous de-Stalinization speech at the XXth Communist Party congress broke many taboos of the old thinking and meant, among other things, to bring Soviet Russia closer to Europe.[2] Despite Khrushchev's removal, the impact of de-Stalinization proved to be irreversible—a considerable part of a new intellectual generation now referred to themselves as the "children of the XXth party congress" and worked within and outside the establishment to bring Soviet Russia closer to the West. The post-Stalin period saw, in particular, growth of specialized institutions in which researchers carefully analyzed Western viewpoints, such as those generated by American international relations (IR) scholars.

Ultimately, the new Western influences contributed greatly to the discourse of human rights and democracy in the Soviet Union, creating the environment for reformers and helping Gorbachev come to power. Although he never meant for the socialist system to be replaced by that of Western liberalism, Gorbachev proclaimed a new era in relationships with the West and therefore greatly contributed to the new fundamental change. In addition to Khrushchev's policies of de-Stalinization and peaceful coexistence, Gorbachev drew from ideas of Russian liberal-minded scientists, such as Vladimir Vernadski, Pyotr Kapitsa, and Andrei Sakharov—all long-term advocates of developing relationships with the West. The leader of perestroika was also building on European social-democratic ideas, as well as American theories of transnationalism and interdependence. The Soviet collapse of 1991 completed the process of the country's difficult adjustment to the new international context and laid the groundwork for the establishment of Russia's liberal foreign policy orientation. The new liberal context continues to be highly contested in Russia and will be shaped further by the country's interaction with Western nations. If the West remains a relatively consolidated liberal entity with a clear and unambiguous message to the world, the new liberal identity has good chances of taking stronger roots in post-Soviet Russia.

Continuous Schools

Although Russia's foreign policy was a response to various international contexts, it also displayed a remarkable degree of historical continuity. Across the eras of monarchy and liberalism, Russia's engagement with the world followed several persistent patterns of thinking and behavior. As a borderland nation in an uncertain, often volatile external environment, Russia had to continuously respond to similar challenges to its security. These challenges included unrests in neighboring territories, threats of external invasion, and difficulties in preserving internal state integrity. Over time, the country has developed three distinct traditions, or schools, of foreign policy thinking—Westernist, Statist, and Civilizationist. Throughout centuries, Westernizers, Statists, and Civilizationists sought to present Russia's international choices in ways consistent with the schools' historically established images of the country and the outside world.

Westernizers placed the emphasis on Russia's similarity with the West and viewed the West as the most viable and progressive civilization in the world. The early Westernizers sought to present Russia as a loyal member in the family of European monarchies. Historically the emergence of this school of thinking can be traced back to Peter the Great's military Westernization. Peter was the first to admire the West for its technological superiority and to raise the possibility of borrowing Western technology to overcome Russia's backwardness. Alexander I was more consistent in defending the values of the old Europe and vigorously opposing the spread of French egalitarian ideas. After the defeat of Napoleon, Alexander championed the so-called legitimist policies and established the Holy Alliance with Germany and Austria in order to suppress revolutionary activities on the Continent.

Liberal Westernizers identified with the Western values of constitutional freedoms and political equality. After the era of great reforms and Russia's shifting its relations from Germany to France and Britain under Alexander II, the czarist government seemed more willing to embrace the new European values of constitutionalism. Pavel Milyukov, once a foreign minister and a leader of Russian liberals, took the most active pro-European position by insisting that Russia must stay in World War I as an active member of the anti-German coalition. To Milyukov, support for the European allies—despite all the devastations that the war had brought to Russia—was a matter of principle and the country's identity orientation.

Westernizers within the Soviet system saw Russia as not standing too far apart from European social democratic ideas. For instance, one of Gorbachev's favorite lines of thinking was that the Soviet Union had to "purify" itself of Stalinist "distortions" and become a democratic, or "human," version of socialism (*gumannyi sotsializm*). In his foreign policy, Gorbachev pursued the notion of mutual security with the West and presided over a series of revolutionary arms-control agreements with the United States, as well as over the Soviet military withdrawals from Europe and the third world. By introducing the idea of "common European home," Gorbachev meant to achieve Russian-European integration based on the principles of European social democracy.

Finally, the liberal Westernizers in post-Soviet Russia argued the "natural" affinity of their country with the West based on such shared values as democracy, human rights, and a free market. Liberal Westernizers warned against relations with former Soviet allies and insisted that only by building Western liberal institutions and joining the coalition of what was frequently referred to as the community of "Western civilized nations" would Russia be able to respond to its threats and overcome its economic and political backwardness. Andrei Kozyrev and Boris Yeltsin's vision of "integration" and "strategic partnership with the West" assumed that Russia would develop liberal democratic institutions and build a market economy after the manner of the West.

Statists have emphasized the state's ability to govern and preserve the social and political order. This is, arguably, the most influential school of Russia's foreign policy thinking. It is explicit in choosing values of power, stability, and sovereignty over those of freedom and democracy. Critical to Statism is the notion of external threat to Russia's security. Ever since the two-centuries-long conquest by the Mongols, Russians have developed a psychological complex of insecurity and a readiness to sacrifice everything for independence and sovereignty. Multiple wars in Europe and Asia further reinforced this mentality and provided Statism's supporters with extra justifications for their reasoning. For instance, when justifying the need for a rapid industrialization, the leader of the Soviet state, Josef Stalin, famously framed his argument in terms of responding to powerful external threats.

> The history of the old Russia was the continual beating she suffered because of her backwardness. She was beaten by the Mongol khans. She was beaten by the Turkish beys. She was beaten by the Swedish feudal lords. She was beaten by the Polish and Lithuanian gentry. She was beaten by the English and French capitalists. She was beaten by the Japanese barons. All beat her—for her backwardness. . . . We are fifty or a hundred years behind the advanced countries. We must make good this distance in ten years. Either we do it, or we shall be crushed.[3]

The Statists, however, are not inherently anti-Western; they merely seek the West's recognition by putting the emphasis on economic and military capabilities. The Statists of the monarchical era valued Russia's autocratic structure of power, partly because such were the structures of European monarchies as well. In foreign policy, Statists often trace their intellectual and policy origins to Prince Alexander Gorchakov. Gorchakov labored as Alexander II's foreign minister to recover Russia's lost international positions after the defeat in the Crimean War. He pursued the policy of "concentration" by developing a system of flexible alliances and limiting Russia's involvement in European affairs.[4] Other Statists trace their roots to Peter the Great. Unlike Westernizers emphasizing Peter's Europeanness, Statists relate to Peter's military competitiveness. It is state security and military competitiveness, they argue, that brought about the czar's notion of getting closer to Europe.

The socialist Statists insisted on the importance of the Communist Party's firm control over the society for the purpose of maintaining political order and averting external "capitalist" threats. Within the Soviet leadership, this school was always suspicious of efforts to activate political institutions outside the party and opposed Gorbachev's democratization reform. In foreign policy, some Statists advocated relative accommodation with the West, while others favored balancing strategies. Maksim Litvinov, for instance, supported a "collective security" system in Europe in order to prevent the rise of fascism. Nikita Khrushchev, too, wanted to break taboos of isolationism and to bring Soviet Russia closer to Europe. He also called for a return to Lenin's principles of "coexistence" with the capitalist world, although he later slipped into several incidents of confrontation with the West. Both Litvinov and Khrushchev saw themselves as supporters of the late Lenin's course to give up the idea of the world revolution and learn to live and trade with the potentially dangerous capitalist world.

On the other hand, Stalin's pact with Hitler, as well as Leonid Brezhnev's "correlation of forces" strategy, reflected the will to balance perceived dangerous influences from the outside world. By signing the treaty of friendship with Nazi Germany, Stalin hoped to isolate Russia from World War II or at least to buy enough time to prepare for it. His successors operated on a world scale and, with the "correlation of forces" doctrine, they meant to respond to the perceived growing global influence of the West. Both strategies meant to preserve Russia's independence in world affairs and had some elements of Gorchakov's described strategy of concentration.

The liberal Statists of the post-Soviet era no longer supported a single-party state, and they agreed with the importance of building a market economy and political democracy. However, they were not ready to sacrifice to these new values the historically tested notion of a strong state, and they argued that liberal values should be established to strengthen, not weaken, the state. The liberal Statists believed that Russia continued to be exposed to external threats and must remain a great power capable of responding to those threats anywhere in the world. Yet they proposed different strategies to achieve the great power status. The distinction between Primakov's and Putin's policies is a case in point. Both camps have at one point or another referred to Gorchakov as their inspiration, and both viewed Russia's greatness and strength as key goals of their foreign policies. In their domestic policies, both wanted to bring more order and control to the social and political life. Primakov sought to control big business. Putin continued in the same vein, but also tightened his grip over the legislature, party building, regions, and electronic media, while at the same time declaring his commitment to the newly established political institutions and economic liberalization. The critical foreign policy difference between the two, however, is that Primakov was trying to rebuild the former Soviet Union and contain the United States through a strategic alliance with China and India, whereas Putin emphasized bilateral relations in Russia's periphery and was ambitious to develop partnership with the United States to deter terrorism.

Finally, Civilizationists have always seen Russian values as different from those of the West, and they have always attempted to spread Russian values abroad, outside the West. Their response to Russia's security dilemmas has been more aggressive than that of the more status quo–oriented Statists. As a foreign policy philosophy, Civilizationism dates back to Ivan IV's ("Ivan the Terrible's") "gathering of Russian lands" after the Mongol Yoke and to the dictum "Moscow is the third Rome," which was adopted under Ivan. Unlike Westernizers and Statists, Civilizationists have sought to challenge the Western system of values, insisting on the cultural distinctiveness of Russia and Russia-centered civilization. Some representatives of this school advocated a firm commitment to values of Orthodox Christianity, while others viewed Russia as a synthesis of various religions.

The early Civilizationists advocated the identity of the "Russian empire." They recognized the constraints set by the West-centered external context and recommended that Russia expand beyond its eastern and southern borders. Yet they were eager to defend what they saw as a cultural unity of their outer area. For instance, in the nineteenth century, Civilizationists defended the notion of Slavic unity, and their ideology of Pan-Slavism affected some of the czar's foreign policy decisions.

The socialist Civilizationists went further and challenged the West in a most direct fashion. The Lenin-Trotski doctrine of the world revolution was the Soviet version of Civilizationist thinking. Although it had died in 1921 as an official philosophy with Lenin's commitment to coexistence with capitalism, many in the official and social circles remained convinced of the virtues of the thinking. For example, in the late Soviet and the post-Soviet context, some hard-line political and intellectual movements often defend a widespread external expansion as the best means of ensuring Russia's security. The so-called Eurasianists view Russia as a constantly expanding land-based empire in a struggle for power against sea-based Atlanticism, associated especially with the United States.[5] Born out of the agony of two Europes, Soviet Russia saw itself as superior to the "decadent" and "rotten" Western capitalist civilization. Yet even the Soviet Civilizationists sought to justify their foreign policy expansionism by the need to respond to the "global imperial expansion" of the West. The expansionism therefore was seen by Russian rulers as legitimate and permissible in the international context. It remains to be seen which forms Russia's post-Soviet liberal Civilizationism might take.[6]

The continuity of Russian schools of foreign policy thinking in different external contexts is summarized in table 1.1.

1.2. EXPLAINING CHANGE AND CONTINUITY IN RUSSIAN FOREIGN POLICY

This section introduces various explanations of Russian foreign policy and argues the insufficiency of traditional approaches. In attempting to address the shortcomings of these approaches, I offer a framework for understanding Russian behavior as shaped by the nation's interaction with the West.

The Insufficiency of Traditional Explanations

The most influential tradition of international thinking commonly referred to as realism has focused on historical patterns and continuity in Russia's foreign policy. In particular, scholars have sought to explain Russia's consistent com-

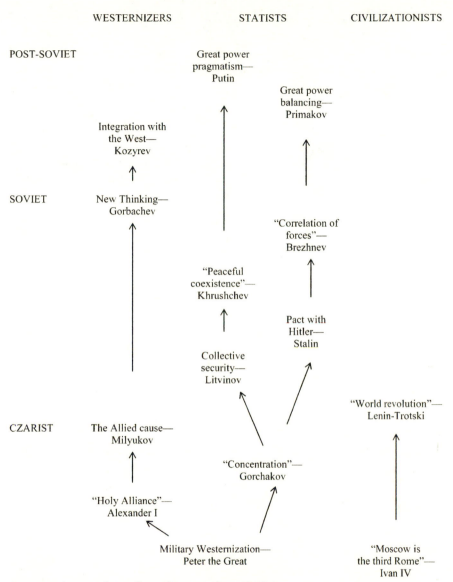

1.1:   Russia's Foreign Policy: Change and Continuity

mitments to status quo, as well as foreign policy expansionism. Scholars in this tradition have often emphasized Russia's national interest as the driving force behind its international behavior. Defining it as a preservation and enhancement of power within the existing international system, many scholars and statesmen alike saw national interest as a geopolitically enduring reality, rather than something open to interpretations. Other factors, such as ideology, nature of government, and political culture, mattered, too. Yet their role was to specify, and sometimes to cover for, but never to contradict "genuine" national interest. Realists have typically argued that the Soviet leaders, while employing a revolutionary ideology and acting under a totalitarian system of government, defended Russia's traditional interests.

> Soviet leaders did not act as though the demands of ideology and those of the Russian national interest were in conflict. Lenin, in negotiating the Treaty in Brest-Litovsk, and Stalin, in negotiating the Nazi-Soviet Pact and in the wartime summit conferences, were constantly aware that their first priority was to ensure the survival of the Russian state and to seek ways to enhance its security. . . . When they had opportunities to expand, the territories that interested them were identical to those that the tsars had sought, for identical strategic reasons.[7]

Others have pointed to underlying consistencies in Soviet policy. For instance, Nathan Leites, in his seminal study of Bolshevik ideology, identified three rules guiding the Soviet behavior: "never risk already conquered major positions for the sake of uncertain gains," "anything less than the exertion of maximum pressure is ineffective," and "mastery in the skill of retreating is as necessary as mastery in the skill of advancing."[8] For Western policymakers, realist studies implied the need to stay firm in resisting Russia's power aspirations, rather than to keep searching for common solutions, and apply what during the Cold War would be called "containment." As Winston Churchill put it in his famous "iron curtain" speech, "There is nothing they [Russians] admire so much as strength, and there is nothing for which they have less respect than for . . . military weakness."[9]

More recent developments in realist thinking point to the structure of the international system, namely, the absence of a legitimate authority (anarchy) as the central force that affects Russia's international behavior. For example, some realists have explained Russia's liberal momentum of the late 1980s–early 1990s and the searches for active accommodation with the West by the Soviet defeat in the Cold War and the need to respond to the emergence of an America-centered global unipolar system. In this perspective, Russia's hegemonic policy in the former Soviet area and a nonconfrontational engagement with the West is the only rational strategy given the fundamental weakness of Russia's post–Cold War capabilities.[10] The new or structural realists continue to view power and national interest as the underlying force of Russia's international behavior. Even when they employ factors other than power, such as perceptions and domestic politics,[11] they assign to these factors secondary roles relative to the role attributed to the structure of the international system. Introducing perceptions and domestic politics therefore does not change the overall thrust of the realist analysis, according to which the international environment is anarchic in nature and states have a constant drive for security and power (national interest).

By focusing on the foreign policy continuity, realists employ a very narrow perspective on "change," limiting it to fluctuations of available power capabilities. In the realist tradition, there is little room for foreign policy patterns as shaped by considerations other than power, such as indigenous ideas or cultural beliefs. As a result, realists typically overlook and wrongfully interpret some far-reaching changes in Russia's foreign policy that are potent for cooperation with Western nations. Realism seems to work when the actual policies at play are of a zero-sum nature, but it errs when the zero-sum reality is not in place. For example, in his engagement with two leading realists, Robert English pointed to the inaccuracy of presenting Gorbachev as the overseer of the Soviet strategic retreat. He argued that the origins of Gorbachev's New Thinking dated back to the late 1950s and 1960s and had to do with domestic changes and the revival of cultural links to the West, not defense calculations and economic needs.[12] If this criticism is correct, realism is unable to account fully for Russia's liberal changes. It has a built-in tendency to misrepresent the scope and the origins of Russia's foreign policy changes. It follows that it is simply unfit to fully understand Russian liberal-minded statesmen, such as Pavel Milyukov, Mikhail Gorbachev, or Andrei Kozyrev. Even when realists are able to correctly identify the direction of Russia's "realist" policymakers, such as Primakov and Putin, their excessive emphasis on the international structure of power makes them neglectful of important domestic/local sources that often shape Russia's foreign policy.[13]

A less prominent, but still influential, tradition in international relations concentrates on understanding foreign policy changes. Western scholars working in this tradition have challenged the realist notion of foreign policy continuity by pointing to such episodes as Khrushchev's early arms control efforts, the Soviet policies of détente, and Gorbachev's sweeping international initiatives. Frequently referred to as liberals, these scholars have also sought to undermine the concept of national interest as something objective and geographically defined. In particular, they have pointed to considerable disagreements among state elites regarding Russia's international priorities and interests. They have also identified multiple coalitions and interest groups with different foreign policy agendas and ways to influence the policymaking process. Furthermore, they identified some learning curves in Russian/Soviet foreign policymaking.[14]

The end of the Cold War produced the new expectations of increasing policy convergence across nations and pushed liberals toward developing theories of foreign policy that would be more sensitive to the structure of the international system. The liberal view of the international system is principally different from that of the realists. Unlike realists, who emphasize international anarchy and cyclical development, liberals have argued the global and progressive ascendancy of Western political and economic values. Francis Fukuyama pioneered the claim and insisted on the arrival of "the universalization of Western Liberal democracy as the final form of human government."[15] In this spirit, many scholars and policymakers took the end of the Cold War as the opportunity to assert that economic and political modernization, rather than geopolitically defined national interest, should serve as the primary foreign policy goal. Theories on the transition to free-market economy and pluralistic democracy became dominant in academic and political discourse. Behind those theories lay a deep conviction in the progressive nature of international relations and the ability of the market democratic institutions to turn the world into a more peaceful and prosperous place.

Three different schools emerged in the liberal community to challenge the realist outlook. One school promoted economic globalization and the growing "common marketization" of international relations as a guarantee of the diminution of the likelihood of large-scale conflict between states. Its supporters questioned the realist belief in the primacy of states by insisting that in an increasingly "borderless world," the state role will be reduced to providing the necessary infrastructure for competitive behavior in the global market.[16] Another school concentrated on democracy building as a guarantee for peace in international relations. In line with the old ideas of the German philosopher Immanuel Kant and U.S. president Woodrow Wilson, this school embraced the proposition that democracies are essentially peaceful in relations with one another, and therefore democracy promotion will keep the peace in the world.[17] Yet another group argued the significance of various transnational ties—transnational expert communities, political ideas, and social movements—for challenging the realist notion of international anarchy.[18] It is the transnational ties, the scholars insisted, that had become especially important in foreign policy formulation. The case of Mikhail Gorbachev's leadership has become especially important to liberals.[19]

The power of the liberal outlook was reflected in policy actions. Policymakers, such as U.S. president Bill Clinton, committed themselves to transforming the world in line with the liberal internationalist ideas of Kant and Wilson. The democratic peace theory became the official justification of the United States' foreign policy actions in the 1990s. Clinton's 1994 national security strategy stated,

> Our national security strategy is based on enlarging the community of market
> democracies while deterring and containing a range of threats to our nation, our

allies and our interests. The more that democracy and political and economic liberalization take hold in the world, particularly in countries of geo-strategic importance to us, the safer our nation is likely to be and the more our people are likely to prosper.[20]

In their speeches, Clinton and his advisers were arguing, just as Clinton's senior adviser and top Russia expert Strobe Talbott did, that "democracy . . . is the one big thing that we must defend, sustain, and promote wherever possible, even as we deal with the many other tasks that face us."[21]

Despite the increased sophistication of its foreign policy analysis, liberalism is a limited guide in understanding Russia's foreign policy. It cannot offer a comprehensive theory of foreign policy because of its unrealistic assumptions and selective focus. While rejecting the anarchy-based perspective as inaccurate, liberals produced the vision of an international system that is restrictive in its own way. Unlike that of realists, the liberal vision of foreign policy change is progressive and cumulative. However, this vision does not account fully for conservative turns in Russia's foreign policy. Such turns are normally viewed as "setbacks" that imply Russia's future "return" to the track of progressive liberal changes. For instance, in acknowledgment of scholars of Clinton's Russia policies, "for the Clinton team, Yeltsin the man *was* reform, while his enemies represented regression and the possible return of communism."[22] It is not surprising that the Clinton White House miscalculated many of Russia's developments and often did not want to admit some obvious facts. For instance, as late as the second half of 1993, the American officials believed that Russia's transition was on track and, as a result, they were completely unprepared for the nationalist victory in Russia's December 1993 parliamentary election. When the extreme nationalist Vladimir Zhirinovski did win the election, Clinton's officials attributed the win to economic hardship under reform, never questioning the principal applicability of pro-Western democratization and marketization to Russia's inherent conditions. Even after Russia's financial default to the International Monetary Fund (IMF) in August 1998, Washington did not believe in the failure of Russia's liberal experiment and pointed instead to the "imperatives of the global marketplace." Rather than try to understand Russia's specific conditions, the Clinton team explained the nation's shift "away from the unabashedly pro-Western reformers and toward nationalistic bureaucrats who had been waiting in the shadow" in terms of insufficient financial aid for the Russian reform.[23] Just as realists view Russia's liberal shifts as an anomaly, liberals consider the country's conservative shifts as tenuous and short term. Some larger assumptions seem to be in play here: while realists study zero-sum interactions, liberals are interested primarily in positive-sum changes. It seems symptomatic and hardly accidental that liberals, who devoted so much energy to explaining the New Thinking and Russia's liberal "revolution," have produced no systematic accounts of Russia's return to great power thinking in the post-Soviet era. As a result, liberals have failed to fully understand the changes that Yevgeni Primakov and Vladimir Putin brought to Russia's foreign policy.

Social Constructivism and Its Promise

Overall, there are two problems with realist and liberal accounts of foreign policy. First, both theories tend to emphasize one aspect of the international system at the expense of others. Rather than acknowledging the validity of both power and modernization/democratization imperatives in foreign policy formation, they choose to highlight one or the other. In so doing, the two approaches refrain from developing a comprehensive and complex explanatory framework. In such a framework, realism would need to be modified to account for liberal changes in Russia's foreign policy, whereas liberalism should be revised to explain Russia's periodical retreats to great power thinking. The second problem is that both realism and liberalism are ethnocentric in the sense that they view Russia's foreign policy through similar Western cultural lenses and do not pay sufficient attention to Russia's indigenous history and system of perceptions. While realists are committed to the notion of Western power and dominance in the world, liberals advocate economic and political modernization by making little effort to apply any but the Western definition of the notion. Developed in the West, by the West, and for the West, these two approaches are increasingly problematic in a world that is multicultural and multimeaningful. In order to address their limitations, they both need to be sensitized to social conditions in which various changes of Russia's foreign policy take place. If we are to understand diversity of national foreign policies, we ought to first understand what "national" is.

In the field of international relations, the perspective that begins the analysis by asking what "national" is and that exposes the "nation" to various meanings and interpretations is called social constructivism. Constructivists are different from realists and liberals in viewing the international system as a social or cultural phenomenon. In addition to military and institutional constraints or facilitators of state actions, as emphasized by the other two theories, constructivists concentrate on cultural contexts and meanings in which these actions take place. From this perspective, the international system is not merely a terrain for applying available military, economic, and diplomatic instruments; rather, the role of the international system is in assisting states in their socialization and understanding of interests in world politics. The international environment constructs state actions and interests. Such actions and interests are not rationally uniform, and they differ depending on individual state experiences with the international system and its parts. Constructivists argue that because particular social contexts define national interests, the formation of such interests should be carefully studied, rather than merely assumed as rational or irrational. In the words of a leading constructivist, "It is striking how little empirical research has been done investigating what kind of interests state actors actually have."[24]

The central category of the constructivist theory of international politics is identity. Before nations figure out how to best defend their interests with available material and diplomatic means, they first seek to understand what these interests in the international society are. By interacting with other members of international society, nations develop affiliations, attachments, and—ultimately—their own identities. Historically, some nations or cultural communities emerge as more important than others, and it is through these significant Others that national Selves define their appropriate character and types of actions. The very existence of the Self becomes difficult without recognition from the Other. National identity therefore is a system of meanings that expresses the Self's emotional, cognitive, and evaluative orientations toward its significant Other. The significant Other establishes the meaningful context for the Self's existence and development and therefore exerts decisive influence on the Self. Through its actions, the Other may reinforce or erode the earlier established sense of national identity. Depending on whether these influences are read by the Self as extending or denying it recognition, they may either encourage or discourage the Self to act cooperatively. (Table 1.2 summarizes the constructivist perspective on foreign policy, relative to those of realism and liberalism.)

At the same time, one must not privilege international social practices at the expense of those of local origins. Local conditions, such as the state of the economy, relations among different social groups, or the type of political regime, are just as important in shaping national perceptions. These and other conditions have long been part of foreign policy analysis, and the initially international system-oriented constructivism is now moving toward incorporating

Table 1.2.   International Relations Theories and Their Perspectives on Foreign Policy

	International Influences	Foreign Policy Actor	Foreign Policy Objective
Realism	Anarchy	State	State power
Liberalism	Western economic and political progress	Individuals, groups	Modernization and democratization
Constructivism	Significant Other	National Self	Self's acceptance by the Other

domestic-level variables.[25] Foreign policy begins when a state manages to transcend the dichotomy of internal/external pressures and develops multiple strategies of responding to world challenges.[26] With distinct social conditions in place, nations have distinct concerns and therefore view the world in their own way. For instance, perceptions of reality by rich nations will differ from those that are considered poor. Some local concerns are more historically stable and are formed across a relatively long time, while others are more immediate and emerge in response to short-term developments. But in both cases, they serve as cultural lenses through which a nation views the outside world.

A nation, however, is not a homogenous entity. Different traditions or schools of thinking about the world develop in response to international and local conditions, and these schools compete for political influence. They hold different images regarding a nation's identity, the nature of the external world, and appropriate policy response. In a relatively open society, they compete openly for the dominant position and are supported by various social groups or coalitions. Constructivists do not view foreign policy as a product of a unitary state's advancing power, as in realism, or as a particular group's pursuing modernization interests, as in liberalism. Rather, the role of a coalition is to put forward a particular image of national identity that will speak to the existing local conditions and be recognized by the significant Other. Identity coalitions are broader and more fundamental than interest coalitions, and they seek to achieve social recognition, rather than to maximize wealth or power.

To summarize, both international influences and local conditions are critical in understanding the processes of foreign policy formation and change. International influences by the Other create the meaningful context in which the national Self evolves and then shapes foreign policy. Past interactions with external environment, as well as local conditions, establish identity as a relatively stable system of meanings with a well-consolidated context in which to act. Therefore, a nation has relative autonomy in influencing foreign policy, and that autonomy is historically established. On a more contemporary level, however, identity is a product of discursive competition among different groups and coalitions, drawing on different actions of the Other and interpreting contemporary international and local influences in a way that suits the groups' interests. The process that links international and local conditions, national identity and foreign policy, is a complex one, and it includes vigorous debates over the nature of national identity and national interests. Because international society contains multiple norms and influences, some of them may conflict in influencing the Self. For instance, realists emphasize the need to be strong, while liberals insist that the world revolves around values of free economy and society. Both strength and liberty can serve as powerful normative messages the modern West sends to the outside world. However, just as realists and liberals disagree, the norms of strength and liberty can conflict in shaping the identity of the Self.

At this point, identity becomes highly contested. Different identity coalitions form to promote their visions. Promoted by various identity groups in both public and private spaces, identity contestation is especially intense until one of the available visions becomes predominant. Activities of political entrepreneurs, appropriate material and ideational resources, conducive institutional arrangements, and historical practices can considerably facilitate this process of persuading the general public and elites. When this persuasion part of the process is complete, the state appropriates the dominant national identity vision as a guide in policymaking (national interest). Foreign policy, then, is a highly political phenomenon. It evolves with the rise and fall of various identity visions, as advocated by different social and political groups. Other factors and influences may interfere with a decision-making process, yet if all the other factors are equal, one can expect a reasonable degree of foreign policy consistency based on an adopted image of national identity. (Table 1.3 spells out the causal influences on foreign policy as viewed from the constructivist perspective.)

The Social Construction of Russia's Foreign Policy

In Russia's case, Europe and the West in general played the role of the significant Other and prominently figured in debates about national identity. It was Europe and the West that created the meaningful environment in which Russia's rulers defended their visions of national identity and national interest. Russia has historically sought to be recognized by the Western Other and to modernize after the manner of the West. In 1917—partly because of the West's own agonizing split between autocracy and liberalism and partly because of the special local conditions and the leadership's errors—Russia went through the experience of a social revolution and ceased experimenting with liberal reforms. The liberal

Table 1.3.   Constructivist Explanation of Foreign Policy: A Causal Process

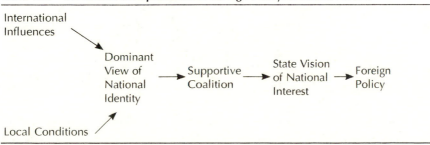

West therefore rejected Russia as its own, and Bolshevik leaders sought to be recognized for their strength, rather than for the nature of their domestic institutions. Statist thinking prevailed in the Soviet discourse, reflecting the desire to maintain the balance of power with the West. As the West consolidated its liberal institutions after World War II, liberal thinking returned to the Soviet Union, paving the way for possible future changes. Gorbachev's arrival signaled that the Soviet liberalism had grown strong enough to challenge the tenets of the old Statist and Civilizationist thinking.

However, Gorbachev was unable to stay his course. Under the conditions of extreme polarization between the old Statists and Civilizationists and the new liberal Westernizers, Gorbachev lost his initial support among elites and the general populace and subsequently had to resign. Although he never meant for Russia's socialist identity to be replaced by that of pro-Western liberalism, Gorbachev undoubtedly greatly contributed to the rise of domestic Westernizers. The 1991 collapse of the Soviet Union presented Russia's new liberals with an opportunity to fashion a pro-Western course of foreign policy. President Boris Yeltsin and his foreign minister Andrei Kozyrev pursued policies of strategic partnership and Integration with the West and its institutions. Externally, they were inspired by the Western promises of support, and they expected to "join" the West within a few years. They saw the West's victory in the Cold War as the promise and the opportunity of the new liberal era. Domestically, the Westernizing coalition included—in addition to liberal-minded leadership—intellectuals, human rights activists, and new procapitalist elites, particularly those with export interests in the West. The new identity coalition pursued a revolutionary agenda of transforming the old Soviet institutions into those of a pro-Western nation-state. It seemed as if the new liberal identity was finally to be established in Russia.

But Soviet disintegration did not end the old identity debates. In fact—partly because of the Soviet breakup—the new post-Soviet identity became deeply contested, and the liberal momentum did not last. Soon the pro-Western policies were met with a formidable opposition, in which the new Statists played the key role. The new Statists were different from their Soviet counterparts in acknowledging the necessity to build a market economy and democratic institutions. At the same time, they shared the old line of Statist reasoning, according to which all reforms had to be subjected to the main objective of strengthening the state. The new Statist coalition included military industrialists, the army, and the security services—those who saw only marginal benefits in adopting the Western model. Led by presidential adviser Sergei Stankevich and then the chief of foreign intelligence Yevgeni Primakov, the new Statists insisted that the national interest had not changed significantly and still had to do with defending Russia's great power status. Over time, this reasoning proved to win the support of the elites and masses, and the state had to adopt the Statist concept of national interest. Primakov—now Russia's newly appointed foreign minister—argued for more restrained relations with the West and for a more "balanced" and "diverse" foreign policy. Primakov believed that Russia's new liberal values did not erase the need to maintain the status of a distinct Eurasianist great power and to balance Western influences. One of his prominent proposals was that Russia develop a strategic alliance with China and India.

Statists were able to defeat Westernizers because of the power of the old Statist identity, the establishment of which could be traced as far back as the 1920s. The Statists were also successful in using the weakness of the new liberal state and mobilizing various informal channels for influencing policymaking. In particular, they benefited politically from the failure of Westernist radical economic reform. Externally, the identity struggle between Statists and Westernizers took place in the changed context. Looking to protect Russia's security, Statists were soon able to identify several threatening developments. Newly emerged instabilities and conflicts in the former Soviet republics and inside the country (Chechnya) in the early to mid-1990s made it extremely difficult for Westernizers to sustain their policies of disengagement from the periphery. Importantly, the West—Russia's significant Other—greatly strengthened the Statist discourse by making a decision to expand the North Atlantic Treaty Organization (NATO) eastward and exclude Russia from the process. This strengthened the sense that the West was not accepting Russia as one of its own. All these developments provided the context for constructing the sought image of external threat and solidified the influence of the new identity coalition. On the other hand, Westernism did not have sufficient public support in order to be able to reduce the power of the Statists.

The arrival of Vladimir Putin as the new president signaled yet another change in policies and a renewed interest in engaging the West. In a stunning strategic reversal, the state adopted another distinct view of national interest—different from those of Westernizers and Primakovites. Although Putin insisted on Russia's priority to preserve great power status, his strategy of achieving this objective differed considerably from Primakov's. Instead of continuing the policy of balancing against the West, Putin explicitly sided with Europe and the United States and insisted that Russia was a country of European and Western, rather than Asian, identity.

Why such a modification in the previous Statist thinking? The unresolved identity question, the shifting balance in the Statists-Westernizers debate, and the new international context help to explain Putin's strategic innovation. Domestically, Putin's course of "pragmatic cooperation" with the West was the project of a mixed-identity coalition that included both Westernist and Statist interests. Sometimes referred to as the alliance of oligarchs and chekists,[27] the new domestic coalition brought Putin to power and gained strength in the new world context, which held both threats and opportunities for Russia. Opportunities came from domestic economic stabilization and cooperation with the United States after the September 11, 2001, terrorist attacks, and threats were defined by the new leadership as being of a terrorist nature and emanating from both inside and outside of Russia. The public strongly supported Putin's approach. His vision of the national interests, which included the preservation of Russia's security and identity, socioeconomic development, and the strengthening of political institutions,[28] resonated with the domestic public better than the security-underplayed Westernism of Kozyrev or the security-overplayed Eurasianism of Primakov. In response to the colored revolutions and perceived Western pressures, Russia's Great Power Pragmatism obtained a more assertive dimension. The Kremlin sought to consolidate Russia's position by challenging the Western nations to open their markets to Russian business and not expand their military infrastructure closer to Russia's borders.

Neither realism nor liberalism is fully satisfactory in explaining the identified changes and continuity in Russia's foreign policy. Realist arguments that post-Soviet Russia was merely looking to consolidate its great power capabilities fail to acknowledge the socialist Westernist nature of Gorbachev's policies and the liberal Westernist vision of Russia's first post-Soviet foreign minister. Both Gorbachev and Kozyrev were thinking in terms of priority of cooperation and engagement with the world, rather than preserving or reviving Russia's material power. They had roots in domestic international thinking, but were also motivated and encouraged by the West's liberal developments. Because of the failure to acknowledge the true origins of the identified liberal foreign policy developments, realists also misrepresented the scope of changes resulting from these developments. Both changes implied fundamental breaks with the Statist past and went far beyond strategic adaptation to the grown military power of the West. Liberals, on the other hand, have difficulties with making sense of Russia's retreat to great power thinking. To them, this retreat does not seem rational, since in the world of globalization, preoccupation with great power status may be an impediment to development and, ultimately, survival of the country.

Ultimately, both theories are inadequate in identifying the genuine nature and origins of various concepts of national interest guiding Russia's international behavior. In particular, they miss the fact that national interest is not about power or modernization. Instead, it is about social adaptation to the constantly changing international and local conditions, and it is about recognition by the identified significant Other. For both Westernizers and Statists, the West is a key point of reference, although each school understands its nature differently. Even Civilizationists, who rarely held a prominent position in domestic discourse, aspired to be respected by the West. What matters in national-interest formation is how debate about national identity is shaped by (1) a population's most pressing local concerns and (2) contemporary behavior of Western nations toward Russia that vindicates or erodes the earlier established images of the West. In addition, as I try to show in the following chapters, each school must work hard to make use of available material and institutional resources in the society. Ultimately, it is the described local conditions combined with considerations of international recognition and respect, rather than a position in the international economy or balance of power, that determine the concept of national interest adopted by the state as a foreign policy guide. Russia's post-Soviet concepts of national interests and their formation are summarized in table 1.4. The remaining chapters of the book further develop the above-suggested explanation of Russia's foreign policy.

1.3. EVALUATING RUSSIA'S FOREIGN POLICY

In addition to describing and explaining Russia's foreign policy, one should also attempt to evaluate the record of its efficiency. This section introduces the evaluative standards adopted in this book and briefly illustrates their application with examples from the post-Soviet era. The remaining chapters offer a more detailed assessment of accomplishments and losses of each of the described foreign policy courses.

Evaluative Standards

Four criteria deserve to be carefully considered in evaluating foreign policy record—security, welfare, autonomy, and identity. Security typically refers to

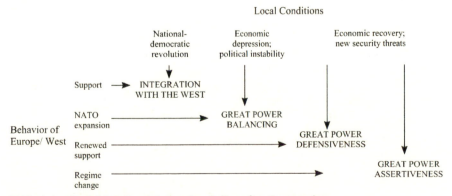

Table 1.4:   Explaining Russia's Foreign Policy after Communism

the absence of military threats to the nation, particularly (but not limited to) from outside. The welfare criterion implies that foreign policy assists the nation in creating external conditions for the improvement of standards of living that may have to do with economic growth, new jobs, and social services. Autonomy has to do with the state's ability to make decisions by withstanding possible pressures of special interests from inside and outside the country. Finally, a successful foreign policy is not fundamentally disruptive to the existing system of cultural values. Rather, such policy relies on these values by reshaping and mobilizing them in the manner that would further the nation's interests and assist the nation in accomplishing its principal goals.

In general, a foreign policy is about protection of a nation's external security, economy, and social lifestyle. Each of these criteria or objectives can be measured by a variety of indicators. A more secure nation, for example, is one that has relatively few military threats from outside and therefore can afford to reduce its military expenditures. A more prosperous nation has stable growth and improving living standards for the general population. A more autonomous nation has a state that is capable of defending the interests of the people as a whole and is not hostage to some powerful influences at home, such as big business or military, or from abroad. Determining the state's foreign policy autonomy requires comparing how the proclaimed goals of defending the interests of the national majority stand against specific international actions of the state, as well as to what extent these actions represent interest groups at the expense of the rest of the society. Finally, a culturally sensitive foreign policy reflects the already-established historical patterns and usually has the population's support with regard to the asserted relationships with the nation's significant Other. Approval of the society in each of these categories expressed through public opinion polls (should such polls be available) may serve as additional evidence for evaluating a foreign policy record.

The foreign policy of each time period can be evaluated using these criteria as they apply during a specified period. Foreign policy is successful if at a given time it has provided a balanced defense of all the listed objectives using the available resources.

From New Thinking to Great Power Pragmatism

Overall, Russia has pursued a balanced foreign policy adequately responding to the imperatives of transition from the Soviet era. Without resorting to an imperialist course, Russia has defended its security, and it has done so with limited foreign policy resources available to its leadership. After the collapse of the economy in the early 1990s, it began a difficult process of recovery, and the society on the whole has begun to feel the difference of the post-Yeltsin era. Under

Putin, the state has restored a good measure of policy autonomy, and recent key international decisions have become more reflective of the social consensus than those of the early to mid-1990s. Finally, as a result of a more moderate foreign policy course, Russia has been able to strike a better cultural balance between the necessity to rethink the old Soviet legacy and the need to respect some traditional values, such as the defense of Russian-language speakers abroad. Geopolitically, Russia's foreign policy reflects the nation's desire to think of itself as a part of European, or Western, civilization, while attempting to preserve special relations with Muslim and Asian neighbors.

In none of the specified areas, however, has Russia's foreign policy been perfectly efficient. For instance, terrorism continues to pose a serious challenge to the nation's internal and external security. The economic improvement is still more of a product of the 1998 currency devaluation and favorable world oil prices than of competitive domestic restructuring. In a number of areas, interest groups have preserved their influence on state policy. And the crisis of Russia's post-Soviet identity has not yet been fully resolved. The transition to a relatively balanced foreign policy course has also not been easy or straightforward. Rather, it has emerged as a result of zigs and zags of different strategies different leaders pursue in concert with their views of Russia's national interest. Nevertheless, the overall improvement in foreign policy efficiency has been evident if one examines the record over the past fifteen years. Polls of the general public on some pressing international issues during the past two years or so consistently demonstrate that people on the whole are satisfied with the country's foreign policy. What follows is a brief assessment of four distinct periods in Russia's international activities.

Gorbachev's foreign policy course was based on innovative understanding of national interest that called for rethinking the Soviet system and its international environment (New Thinking). Its most important accomplishment was a radical improvement of Russia's national security, which resulted mainly from fundamentally changed relationships with the West. Thanks largely to Gorbachev's personal leadership and commitment, several key arms-control agreements were concluded, and the whole era of highly adventurous arms races was gone forever. The disappearance of the threat from the West liberated a great deal of resources that had been previously spent to feed one of the most powerful military machines in the world.

The New Thinking record is not as impressive in areas outside security. Gorbachev's preoccupation with matters of arms control did not assist him in reforming the Soviet economy or improving people's standards of living. From 1988 to 1989, polls began to register growing disappointment with reforms and a lack of trust in the central leadership. While Moscow was busy negotiating with Western nations over security matters, such as thresholds of nuclear sufficiency and withdrawals of troops from the third world and Eastern Europe, the economy was increasingly losing control, eventually collapsing in 1990. This development severely handicapped Gorbachev in his ability to pursue the originally designed international course. Already in 1990, this course was on its way to changing from the Soviet one in terms of initiative and design into a largely West-controlled one. The leader of New Thinking was weakened and had to make many more concessions to Western leaders than he had envisioned. He no longer had the initiative or policy autonomy required for sustaining his course, and U.S. president George H. W. Bush was therefore correct to proclaim the West's "victory" in the Cold War in his 1992 State of the Union address. In addition, Gorbachev's foreign policy failed to mobilize Russian cultural identity. Introduced to reinvigorate the country's social energy and initiative, New Thinking left the nation's citizens deeply divided and unsure about their future. Already in 1989, 34 percent of the public felt that the Soviet Union could not serve as an example to the outside world, compared with only 5 percent in 1988.[29]

The course of Integration with the West, pursued by president Yeltsin and his foreign minister Kozyrev, meant to capitalize on the already-achieved security and improved relations with Western nations. The post-Soviet leaders went much further than Gorbachev in their proclaimed convergence of the interests of new Russia with those of the West. Whereas Gorbachev saw the Soviet Union and the West as culturally distinct entities, the new leadership proposed that Russia become a full-fledged member of the Western civilization by borrowing key Western values, such as individualism, market economy, and political democracy. Partly, the new concept of national interest, which emphasized rapid economic and political modernization, was designed to attract Western economic assistance and therefore address the welfare criterion of foreign policy. Yeltsin and Kozyrev hoped that after proclaiming their commitment to Western values and adopting principles of rapid marketization, or the so-called shock therapy, private investments and financial assistance would quickly revive the half-alive and continuously deteriorating economy.

The reality was different. Western investments remained scarce. Through the use of IMF and World Bank loans, the economy was stabilized, but at the heavy price of stagnation, collapsed social services, and skyrocketed poverty. The failure of shock therapy to bring Russia into the family of rich Western nations alienated a considerable portion of the elites and general public, making it difficult to defend the foreign policy record of the pro-Western leadership. Increasingly, the populace felt that strategic partnership with the West was not working, and many developed resentment toward Western nations, particularly the United States. For instance, during 1993–

1995, the number of those viewing the United States as a threat increased from 26 to 44 percent among the general public and from 27 to 53 percent among the elites.[30] In addition, many had judged that Russia was effectively ceding its policy autonomy to the West in economic and other affairs. In 1995, 75 percent of the population believed that the economy was essentially in foreign hands.[31] The number of those perceiving the West as seeking to weaken Russia also increased. The increased dependency on the West in economic affairs went hand in hand with loss of autonomy in security affairs, as Washington was often dictating Moscow's foreign policy in such critical areas as the Balkans and Iraq.

Perhaps worst of all, security issues returned to the agenda. Partly the result of Kozyrev's overconcentration on the Western direction, the security threats reemerged in the form of ethnic and military conflicts in the former Soviet Union and even inside Russia (Chechnya). All these developments further exacerbated the sense of Russian hurt pride and identity. The pro-Western foreign policy course did little to address those feelings. Accompanied by failures to protect the nation's security, economy, and policy autonomy, this course in fact deepened the sense of cultural loneliness among Russians. Shrunken in size after the Soviet Union's disintegration and confronted with NATO's decision to expand eastward, Russia was bound to seriously rethink the assumptions of its pro-Western foreign policy.

When the leading critic of the West-oriented course Yevgeni Primakov replaced Kozyrev as foreign minister, Russia's foreign policy changed greatly. As much as it was possible under Yeltsin's leadership, the new foreign minister pursued policies of restoring great power status. He addressed the new security threats through intense diplomatic involvement in the former Soviet region, particularly in the areas of military confrontations and civil wars (Tajikistan, Moldova), and through the initiation of economic and security projects aimed to tighten the ties among the former Soviet republics under the leadership of Russia. Primakov was also successful in restoring some measures of foreign policy autonomy. While Russia's dependence on Western lending agencies continued, the new course was pursued with greater respect for public perception of national interest, and it was considerably less tolerant of Washington's attempts to shape Russia's policies toward the Balkans, Iraq, and the former Soviet region. Both elites and the general public expressed their strong support for the new course, welcoming its greater independence and concentration on solving security issues in the former Soviet Union. In line with the new course, the public was supportive of strengthening the army and relations with the former republics.[32]

The strategy of Great Power Balancing was not as successful in improving the welfare of Russians. The project of integrating the former Soviet region

proved to be excessively geopolitically driven and not as founded on economic grounds. The economy continued to stagnate, not bringing any foreign investments and increasing the burden of foreign debt. The new foreign
policy strategy was also dubious with respect to the criterion of identity. Primakov addressed the new cultural fears of the West by attempting to pragmatically defuse the crisis in relations with NATO and by proposing to build
a strategic triangle of Russia, China, and India to balance American hegemonic growth in world politics. NATO's military intervention in Yugoslavia
in 1999 further pushed Russia away from the West. Yet the Westernist component of Russia's cultural identity is a well-established reality, and the strategy of Eurasia-oriented Great Power Balancing failed to address this part of
the Russian national psyche.

Vladimir Putin's course of Great Power Pragmatism has been more successful in terms of meeting the criteria of security, welfare, autonomy, and identity.
Creatively borrowing from both Westernist and Statist thinking of the post-
Soviet era, the president forcefully responded to the new security challenge of
terrorism in Chechnya, the Caucasus, and central Asia, simultaneously improving somewhat damaged relations with the West. On Chechnya and the
Caucasus, the improvement remained marginal, with terrorist attacks continuing and the Russian public expressing reservations about the effectiveness
of Putin's policies. Great Power Pragmatism proved to be more effective in
Russia's relations with the former Soviet republics and the outside world, and
the public backed Putin in those areas. Apart from the conflict with Georgia,
Russia did not experience any major threats to its security. While pressing for
preserving and strengthening security ties with Western countries, Russia
sustained good relations with Middle Eastern nations and China.

The economy and social welfare have also improved. This has been the
result partially of high oil prices, but Russia has also signaled its renewed
interest in joining Western institutions, such as the World Trade Organization (WTO). Modernizing the economy is very high on the new leadership's
agenda, but—in the best tradition of Statist thinking—the emphasis is on
preserving Russia's own independence and economic reform that does not
come at the expense of the loss of policy autonomy to the West or domestic
commercial groups with Western exporting interests. Finally, Great Power
Pragmatism seems to best respond to the current needs of Russia's national
psychology. It preserves both Westernist and Statist components of Russia's
identity, and it successfully orients Russians to adjust to the West while preserving their own cultural legacy. At the moment, such emphasis seems
highly appropriate for the country that relates to the West as its significant
Other, but has long-standing relations with non-Western nations in Asia and
the Muslim world.

1.4. METHODOLOGY AND ORGANIZATION OF THE BOOK

This study combines two methods. In order to explore the indigenous system of Russian perceptions, I explore the content and intensity of Russian foreign policy debates by comparing arguments made by the identified schools of thinking. For understanding the process of contestation of national interests, I employ the method of "schools of thought" analysis. Following Martin Wight's conceptualization,[33] I identify three distinct schools of thinking about national interest that existed in Russia before and after Gorbachev's perestroika (Westernism, Statism, and Civilizationism). Careful exploration of the arguments made by various schools and participants in Russian discourse allows me to identify existing foreign policy alternatives and to present a comprehensive picture of the country's international thinking.

For understanding changes in Russia's post-Soviet foreign policy, I employ a method of "over time comparison." Beginning with the next chapter, I offer a detailed analysis of the rise and fall of five distinct concepts of national interests—New Thinking, Integration with the West, Great Power Balancing, and two versions of Great Power Pragmatism—as well as policies that stemmed from each of these concepts. I trace how each of these visions first emerged outside the state and the process through which it then came to define leadership's perceptions and adopted international policies. The book's central argument is that it is these visions of national interest, rather than Russia's position in the international economy or balance of power, that have determined the country's foreign policy after communism. During the 1990s through the early 2000s, neither structural power conditions nor the international economic position of Russia has changed sufficiently to fully account for its foreign policy choices.

The book's organization is straightforward. The chapters that follow study national interests and foreign policy formation through four distinct periods from the late 1980s until the late 2000s. In each chapter, I describe the international and local contexts in which Russian debates about national interest took place. I analyze the process through which one of the foreign policy visions prevailed and obtained the status of state vision. I then review specific international policies pursued by leaders toward the former Soviet Union and outside world in attempting to satisfy their visions of national interest. Finally, I attempt to evaluate the accomplishments and losses of each of the pursued foreign policy courses. The concluding chapters reflect on future choices of Russia's foreign policy and summarize the analysis by comparing the diverse concepts of national interest and evaluating their relative performance. The final chapter also draws lessons for Russian and Western policymakers.

NOTES

1. Arnold Wolfers, "'National Security' as an Ambiguous Symbol," in *Classics of International Relations*, 2d ed., ed. John A. Vasques (Englewood Cliffs, NJ: Prentice Hall, 1990), 135.

2. Khrushchev's Europeanism was limited, and it pursued the objective of a greater European independence in the context of a power struggle with the Americans. Yet his position that the European Economic Community became a reality emboldened those in domestic politics who wanted to improve relationships with Bonn and other European nations. See Iver B. Neumann, *Russia and the Idea of Europe: A Study in Identity and International Relations* (London: Routledge, 1996), 140–41.

3. As cited in Richard Sakwa, *The Rise and Fall of the Soviet Union, 1917–1991* (London: Routledge, 1999), 187–88.

4. See Yevgeni Primakov, "Rossiya v mirovoi politike"; I. Ivanov, *Vneshnyaya politika Rossiyi*, 313–30; *Strategiya dlya Rossiyi: Povestka dlya prezidenta—2000*. Russian Westernists, on the other hand, are often critical of Gorchakov's diplomacy (see, for example, Yuri Fedorov, "Krizis vneshnei politiki Rossiyi," *Pro et Contra* 6, no. 1–2 [2001]).

5. Aleksandr Dugin, *Osnovy geopolitiki* (Moscow: Arktogeya, 1997); Aleksandr Mitrofanov, *Shagi novoi geopolitiki* (Moscow, 1998).

6. Interestingly enough, Yeltsin's former privatization czar and current head of Russia's state electric company, Anatoli Chubais, recently wrote that Russia's main goal in the twenty-first century should be to build up a "liberal empire" through the strengthening of its position in the former Soviet Union. "EES Head Calls for Russia to Become a 'Liberal Empire,'" *RFE/RL Newsline*, September 26, 2003; Anatoli Chubais, "Missiya Rossiyi v XXI veke," *Nezavisimaya gazeta*, October 1, 2003.

7. Robert H. Donaldson and Joseph L. Nogee, *The Foreign Policy of Russia* (Armonk, NY: M. E. Sharpe, 1998), 59.

8. Nathan Leites, *The Operational Code of the Politburo* (New York: McGraw-Hill, 1951), as cited in Celeste A. Wallander, "The Sources of Russian Conduct," in *The Sources of Russian Foreign Policy after the Cold War*, ed. C. A. Wallander (Boulder, CO: Westview Press, 1996), 5.

9. Sakwa, *The Rise and Fall of the Soviet Union*, 295.

10. Neil MacFarlane, "Realism and Russian Strategy after the Collapse of the USSR," in *Unipolar Politics*, ed. Ethan B. Kapstein and Michael Mastanduno (New York: Columbia University Press, 1999); Allen Lynch, "Realism of Russian Foreign Policy," *Europe-Asia Studies* 53, no. 1 (2001).

11. Gideon Rose, "Neoclassical Realism and Theories of Foreign Policy," *World Politics* 51, no. 1 (1998).

12. Robert English, "Power, Ideas, and New Evidence on the Cold War's End," *International Security* 26, no. 4 (Spring 2002): 78–82.

13. In fact, both Primakov's and Putin's foreign policies can be understood in terms of Russia's responses to new domestic challenges, such as economic poverty and insecure borders. As some scholars have argued, outside the Western Hemisphere, states' international responses often explain the need to stabilize political regimes internally.

See, for example, Mohammed Ayoob, *Third World Security Predicament: State Making, Regional Conflict, and the International System* (Boulder, CO: Lynne Rienner, 1995).

14. For a more detailed overview of Russia's foreign policy studies, see Wallander, "The Sources of Russian Conduct."

15. Francis Fukuyama, "The End of History?" *National Interest* (1989): 4.

16. See, especially, Kenichi Ohmae, *The Borderless World: Power and Strategy in the Interlinked Economy* (New York: Harper Perennial, 1991); and Thomas L. Friedman, *The Lexus and the Olive Tree* (New York: Farrar, Straus and Giroux, 1999).

17. For overviews, see Michael E. Brown, Sean M. Lynn-Jones, and Steven E. Miller, eds., *Debating the Democratic Peace* (Cambridge, MA: MIT Press, 1996); Fred Chernoff, "The Study of Democratic Peace and Progress in International Relations," *International Studies Review* 6 (2004).

18. George W. Breslauer and Philip E. Tetlock, eds., *Learning in U.S. and Soviet Foreign Policy* (Boulder, CO: Westview Press, 1991); Peter Haas, "Introduction: Epistemic Communities," *International Organization* 46, no. 2 (1992); Thomas Risse-Kappen, ed., *Bringing Transnational Relations Back In* (Cambridge: Cambridge University Press, 1995); M. E. Keck and Katherine Sikkink, *Activists beyond Borders: Advocacy Networks in International Politics* (Ithaca, NY: Cornell University Press, 1998).

19. Liberal scholars have linked Gorbachev's policies to principal economic and political changes in the West, as well as to activities of transnational expert communities, ideas, and social movements. See, for example, Celeste A. Wallander, "Opportunity, Incrementalism, and Learning in the Extension and Retraction of Soviet Global Commitments," *Security Studies* 1 (Spring 1992); Mathew Evangelista, *Unarmed Forces: The Transnational Movements to End the Cold War* (Ithaca, NY: Cornell University Press, 1999); Robert D. English, *Russia and the Idea of the West: Gorbachev, Intellectuals and the End of the Cold War* (New York: Columbia University Press, 2000).

20. As cited in James N. Goldgeier and Michael McFaul, *Power and Purpose: U.S. Policy toward Russia after the Cold War* (Washington, DC: Brookings Institution Press, 2003), 11.

21. Goldgeier and McFaul, *Power and Purpose*, 90.

22. Goldgeier and McFaul, *Power and Purpose*, 11.

23. Strobe Talbott, *The Russia Hand: A Memoir of Presidential Diplomacy* (New York: Random House, 2002), 367, 407–8; Goldgeier and McFaul, *Power and Purpose*, 133–34.

24. Alexander Wendt, *Social Theory of International Politics* (Cambridge: Cambridge University Press, 1999), 133.

25. As one scholar suggests, "Identity explanations are likely to become 'foreign policy-ized' by connecting identity to other factors and theories that have long been part of the FPA agenda." Juliet Kaarbo, "Foreign Policy Analysis in the Twenty-First Century: Back to Comparison, Forward to Identity and Ideas," *International Studies Review* 5 (2003): 160. International relations scholars have recognized the internal/external bind by referring to it as a "two-level game." Robert D. Putnam, "Diplomacy and Domestic Politics: The Logic of Two-Level Games," *International Organization* 42, no. 2 (1988).

26. For additional hypotheses about international influences and their interaction with local conditions, see Jack Snyder, "International Leverage on Soviet Domestic Change," *World Politics* 42, no. 1 (1989); James Richter, *Khrushchev's Double Bind: International Pressures and Domestic Coalition Politics* (Baltimore: Johns Hopkins University Press, 1994).

27. *Chekist* originates from the Russian *CheKa*, the original name of the Bolsheviks' security service. It was led by People's Commissar Feliks Dzerzhinski. Oligarchs are, of course, superrich captains of Russia's newly privatized economy.

28. See Vladimir Putin, "Rossiya na rubezhe tysyacheleti," *Nezavisimaya gazeta*, December 2, 1999.

29. Yuri Levada, ed., *Est' mneniye! Itogi sotsiologicheskogo oprosa* (Moscow: Progress, 1990), 284.

30. William Zimmerman, *The Russian People and Foreign Policy* (Princeton: Princeton University Press, 2002), 91.

31. Zimmerman, *The Russian People*, 92.

32. Zimmerman, *The Russian People*, 91; Fond Obschestvennoye Mneniye, at www.fom.ru.

33. Martin Wight, *International Theory: The Three Traditions* (Leicester: Leicester University Press, 1991).

2

The Cold War Crisis and the Soviet
New Thinking

> Taking into account the new situation in the world, the problem of interests
> must be addressed in a new way.
>
> —Mikhail Gorbachev[1]

With Gorbachev, Russia's story of engagement with the West took a sharp
turn. While being a convinced socialist, Gorbachev pursued a radically different interpretation of Russia's socialist identity, which he viewed as distinct yet
compatible with Western ideas of democracy and which eventually collapsed
under the heavy weight of Western modernity. Before we analyze the leader of
perestroika's worldview and perceptions, we must, however, review the context in which Gorbachev formulated his foreign policy vision. For it was this
context that shaped Soviet Russia's new understanding of national interest.

2.1. THE COLD WAR AND SOVIET FOREIGN POLICY

During the Cold War, the Western Other changed in some fundamental ways.
These changes, as well as their influences on the Soviet Union, can be viewed
in at least two different lights. On the one hand, the West has emerged as a
more unified civilization committed to values of democracy, liberal capitalist
reconstruction, and human rights. The success of the Marshall Plan in post–
World War II Europe, as well as a considerable improvement in living standards, made a positive impression on some officials in Soviet Russia and encouraged reformers inside the country. On the other hand, the Cold War

warriors in the West pushed for increased military expenditures and a tougher stance toward Russia, which made it more difficult for the Soviet reformers to advocate change and rapprochement with Western nations. As the logic of confrontation was gaining the upper hand in Russia-West relations, the two sides were increasingly losing sight of many other important international issues, such as poverty and environmental degradation. In this context, everything was progressively viewed through the lens of who gains more power and who manages to more successfully weaken the opponent.

In this contradictory context, the Soviet schools of foreign policy thinking drew their inspiration from different developments in the West. The Soviet Westernizers emphasized the West's democratic consolidation and policies of détente. They sought to acquire Western recognition by conducting domestic reforms and advocating a more robust international cooperation. In Europe, it was social democratic ideas that most closely resembled this group's views. Through support of détente, European social democrats made it easier for the Soviet reformists to press on with their international and domestic agenda.[2] Gorbachev, as well as his reformist predecessors, such as Nikita Khrushchev, did not see the West as inherently evil. They identified with the West of reform and moderation, rather than with that of containment or defeat of the Soviet "evil empire" in an arms race competition. Outside the political class, this nonconfrontational vision appealed to the Soviet middle class—the highly educated social strata that were eager to break the taboos of Soviet isolationism and develop mutually beneficial relationships with the West.

A more nationalist group within the Soviet establishment, the Statists, made a note of détente, but also saw the West's militarism and policies aimed at preventing the Soviet Union from influencing world affairs. Many in the Soviet bureaucratic and military establishment, therefore, did not believe in any far-reaching changes and instead advocated limited reforms and coexistence with the "world of capitalism." This group was not closed to changes in world politics, but was prepared to cooperate with the West in a reciprocal manner only. Continuation of détente was viewed to be possible, but only to the extent that the West itself was committed to it. Similarly to Western realists insisting on reaching a balance of power between the Soviet and Western poles, this group advocated the notion of "correlation of forces" between socialism and capitalism. Members of the group saw the goal of achieving international status and acceptance in terms of preservation of strength, both military and economic.

Finally, there were also some die-hard Bolsheviks committed to the ideology of winning the competition between socialism and capitalism. Unlike Westernizers and pragmatically oriented nationalists, this group stood for the authentic "socialist values" that were deemed to be superior to those of capitalism. The supporters of such views, or Civilizationists, had zero trust in détente and rapprochement with the West and associated all the Western activities with aggressive "imperialist" intentions. There could be no middle ground in the struggle with imperialism, and the Cold War was ultimately a competition between the two systems' cultural values, rather than merely economic or military systems. It was through the spreading of values that the group planned to achieve the appropriate recognition of the Soviet Union by the outside world. This group included some leading Communist Party ideologists and eventually emerged as the main opposition to the future New Thinking.

It was Statists who were primarily in control of the actual foreign policymaking during the Cold War era. Immediately after the 1917 revolution, the Bolsheviks were conducting two foreign policies—one was aimed at stabilizing relations with the Western leaders and conducted by the Commissariat on Foreign Affairs, whereas the other sought to undermine the West through the activities of Comintern. That duality receded into the past as Stalin took charge and shifted the effort away from the highly ideological communist rhetoric and toward winning recognition of Soviet Russia as a "Great Power" and, later, a "Superpower."[3] Stalin's Statism therefore won over the Comintern-like Civilizationism in foreign affairs. Only during the so-called second Cold War of the late 1970s through the early 1980s did the Soviet Civilizationists regain some of their former prominence, partly in response to the rise of hard-line thinking toward Soviet Russia in the West. The arguments about the need to expand into Afghanistan and other third world countries were partly provoked by the West's own military buildup, opposition to the ratification of the Strategic Arms Limitations Talks (SALT II), and the decision by the North Atlantic Treaty Organization (NATO) to deploy American missiles in Europe. In addition to aiding Afghanistan, the Soviets supplied communists in Vietnam and Angola. When in 1983 U.S. president Ronald Reagan announced the Strategic Defense Initiative, also known as the Star Wars program, the Soviet leaders were divided between the more status quo–oriented Statists and the more expansionist Civilizationists. Westernizers were hardly in the picture; they occupied much less prominent positions and could not be taken very seriously given the extent of tensions with the West. After the death of Konstantin Chernenko, Gorbachev was elected general secretary of the Communist Party for his vigor and youth rather than his policy beliefs. At the time, his worldview and policy beliefs were hardly known to his comrades in the Politburo.

2.2. GORBACHEV AND THE CONCEPT OF NEW THINKING

In the mid-1980s, Gorbachev was not known for his radical international ideas. After being elected general secretary, he moved cautiously and first proposed the strategy of accelerating scientific and technological progress as a way to improve the state of the Soviet economy. The idea, although well received by the ruling establishment, brought little practical results, and the new leader used the momentum to advance his more radical vision of economic, political, and international changes known as perestroika. Gorbachev also insisted that perestroika could take place only if accompanied by New Thinking, or radical transformation of the traditional outlook on world affairs.

The New Vision of World Politics

By introducing New Thinking, Gorbachev did not mean to replace the Soviet system with one similar to that of the West. He was a product of the system and a firm believer in the Soviet Union's principal viability. At the same time, Gorbachev was highly critical of how the system had performed in the past and he wanted to renew it in some fundamental way. In particular, he dreamed of releasing human potential and social creativity that, in his opinion, were suppressed under the Stalinist regime. Eventually Gorbachev meant to bring the system closer to the model of Scandinavian societies, in which democracy was combined with strong egalitarian principles in the economy.

Yet Gorbachev proved to be especially innovative in the area of world politics. Seeking to break the Cold War hostilities and be accepted by the Western nations as an equal member of the world, Gorbachev proposed a vision that required the Cold War enemies to cooperate.[4] The new vision sought to present the old enemies with a notion of a common threat leaving them little choice but to abandon their old hostilities. At the heart of the vision lay the notion of a global and principally nondivisive world, which was argued to be in danger of annihilation. The Cold War, with its arms races and power struggle, put humankind on the verge of nuclear, ecological, and moral catastrophe. New Thinking diagnosed the catastrophe as one that was global in nature and could be resolved only through global efforts. To quote from the author of New Thinking,

> For all the contradictions of the present-day world, for all the diversity of social and political systems in it, and for all the different choices made by the nations in different times, this world is nevertheless one whole. We are all passengers aboard one ship, the Earth, and we must not allow it to be wrecked. There will be no second Noah's Ark.[5]

It was therefore critical to acknowledge the primacy of values "common to all humankind" and to understand that security could be only mutual. The reasons for this were the threat of mutual destruction in a nuclear war, as well as an increased level of economic and ecological interdependence in the world.

Table 2.1.   GNP for USSR and USA, 1960–1985

	1965	1970	1975	1980	1985
USSR	4.8	4.9	3.0	1.9	1.8
USA	4.6	3.0	2.2	3.4	2.5

Source: David Kotz and Fred Weir, *Revolution from Above: The Demise of the Soviet System* (London: Routledge, 1997), 42.

The origins of New Thinking therefore had little to do with the necessity of a strategic retreat in the face of the growing economic and military strength of the West—the argument often advanced by realists.[6] To argue this is to neglect Gorbachev's domestic intellectual roots. It is true that the Soviet economy was in decline by the time of Gorbachev's arrival (see table 2.1). Yet the new leader did not make sense of the world in terms of economic or military capabilities. He was not a member of the Statist school, and his entire thinking about international politics was shaped by a desire to reach out to a liberal and social democratic West. This thinking also had a distinct domestic tradition stretching back at least to Nikolai Bukharin's and Nikita Khrushchev's foreign policy liberalizations.

Achieving recognition by Western nations was extremely difficult given the legacy of the Cold War. For at least a decade, conservatives were in power, and they originally received the arrival of Gorbachev and his ideas of perestroika and New Thinking with suspicion. Such recognition was all the more difficult because Gorbachev was not a believer in the primacy of the Western values of political democracy and market economy. Instead, he envisioned some global unity from contributions of both capitalist and socialist systems. He was prepared to learn from other systems and other nations,[7] while remaining a socialist and a believer that the whole world would continue to be influenced by the socialist experience and "socialist values."[8]

The Domestic Appeal

The new vision of world politics was designed to appeal to all the main groups of the Soviet political class. Westernizers were to be attracted to ideas of democratization, reform, and rapprochement with the West. Gorbachev himself was influenced by the ideas of European social democrats, as well as liberal-minded scientists, such as Vladimir Vernadski, Pyotr Kapitsa, and Andrei Sakharov. His concept of a "common European home" also had its roots in Nikita Khrushchev's efforts to bring Soviet Russia closer to Europe. Khrushchev saw Russia as culturally close to Europe, and at one point he even proposed the concurrent disbandment of NATO and the Warsaw Pact. New

Thinking also sought to appeal to at least some of the Statists, who understood the necessity to respond to Western military pressures by reducing diplomatic tensions and moving in the direction of a new détente. Finally, Gorbachev's vision meant to engage some of the most forward-thinking members of the Civilizationist school, because it offered a new, admittedly very unorthodox, way of capitalizing on "socialist values." The leader of perestroika traced his origins to the late Lenin's notion of coexistence with capitalism, and he kept emphasizing that his project was a development, not an abandonment, of socialism. As utopian as it was, the vision had global ambitions and even elements of a moral messianism. It was therefore a creative synthesis that attempted to engage representatives of the entire political class.

But Gorbachev's vision was never a purely elite product. Socially, it reflected the worldview of the Soviet middle class that grew stronger during the 1960–1986 period. The proportion of highly educated and qualified urban specialists had increased during the indicated period fourfold. The overall number of urban dwellers in the total population had grown by over two-thirds, by some calculations.[9] The Soviet middle class was dissatisfied with Brezhnev's unwillingness to initiate change, and increasingly expected reforms in the rigid economic and political system. Many representatives of this class were also in touch with the outside world's technological developments, and their perceptions of the world began to conflict with those of Brezhnev's *nomenklatura* and hard-line military. Increasingly, Soviet society supported accommodation, not confrontation, with the outside world. Although the Soviet system's resources were far from exhausted, the anticipation of and the eagerness for its change were already in the air.

Redefining National Interest

The above-described vision left little room for national interest as pursued independently of the interests of other members of the global society. Gorbachev did not expect the Soviet Union or any other nations to give up what they perceived to be in their interests. Yet he called for acknowledging the futility of class and narrowly viewed national gains and for developing a globally integrated approach based on the notion of mutual responsibility and "balance of interests." Practically speaking, he proposed compromises and multilateral negotiations as a way to implement the new vision.

For the Soviet Union, New Thinking implied the necessity to formulate its national interest and foreign policy objectives in a way that would be respectful of world opinion and nonthreatening toward others. In particular, Gorbachev proposed to rethink the nature of capitalism. The old ideological vision assumed that the Soviet Union had to contain the influence of world capitalism, because at its highest stage of development, imperialism, capitalism was intrinsically related to expansion and war. Without containing imperialism, the Soviet Union would be destroyed. As Josef Stalin said in a slightly different context, "Either we do it, or we shall be crushed."[10] The Gorbachev vision posited something very different. In February 1988, he criticized the very notion of imperialism as being no longer accurate. He argued that capitalism had developed domestic democratic mechanisms for resisting expansion and war and was therefore self-containing. Such criticism had its roots in the Soviet postwar debates. Already in the late 1940s, Yevgeni Varga, director of the Moscow Institute of World Economy and World Politics, began arguing that postwar capitalism could regulate its contradictions and had relatively stabilized. After Stalin's death, those emphasizing the depth of imperialist contradictions and the inevitability of the capitalist decline gathered around Richard Kosolapov, the editor in chief of *Kommunist* and member of the Central Committee of the Communist Party, while those opposing this hard-line view assembled at the Institute of World Economy and World Politics.[11] Siding with supporters of the anti-imperialism view of capitalism allowed Gorbachev to present the notion of military sufficiency in an entirely different light and to call for a reevaluation of Soviet defense expenditures. It provided the basis for terminating the arms race in which the Soviet Union had been previously heavily involved. Clarifying the new approach, the foreign minister Eduard Shevardnadze argued that attempts to reach military parity with all the potential enemies were in fact against the Soviet national interests.[12] (Table 2.2 summarizes the New Thinking view of national interest.)

The introduction of the notion of "national interest" was partly strategic and was designed to preempt possible criticism that New Thinking was nothing but a series of concessions to capitalism. Multiple withdrawals from Eastern Europe and the third world, as well as proposals to eliminate entire classes of nuclear missiles, could now be presented as something that was part of a long-term strategy. For example, the "loss" of Eastern Europe after the 1989 fall of the Berlin Wall could now be presented as a net "gain" in a general calculus of creating a favorable international environment. In February 1990, Shevardnadze insisted along these lines, "Our national, as well as historic and

Table 2.2.   New Thinking: View of National Interest

What?	Global responsibility and "balance of interests"
How?	Military sufficiency Multilateral negotiations Diplomatic compromises

everyday, interest is that our neighbors are stable and prosperous. We will only benefit from this."[13]

2.3. DOMESTIC CRITICS OF NEW THINKING

Despite Gorbachev's efforts to be a consensus builder, his New Thinking was soon attacked from two different directions. Conservative forces charged that Gorbachev was "selling out" the Soviet interests to the West, whereas liberals saw him as indecisive in abandoning the "outdated" Soviet outlook. Revolutionary changes in the country further polarized the process of foreign policy formation, making it impossible to sustain the originally devised plan with appeal to all main social groups. The original coalition of New Thinkers was fairly broad, representing the industrial, military, party, and academic establishment. Over time, however, that coalition began to fall apart, and the struggle of ideas around New Thinking suggested in which directions some future social and politicoeconomic groups were to emerge.

Conservative Opposition

Conservative opposition to Gorbachev consisted of some representatives of Statist and Civilizationist schools. Intellectually heterogeneous, conservatives were united in their hatred of New Thinking, perceiving it as leading to the Soviet Union's social and political disintegration. Conservative Statists remained highly skeptical of the ideas of détente and domestic reform and were prepared to discuss only military modernization. Conservative Civilizationists put their emphasis on what they saw as key socialist values, such as economic and political centralization of the system. Both groups had much to agree on and enjoyed sufficient support in the military and party establishments, as well as in the wider society.

Conservatives rejected the idea that the West had made a considerable contribution to world development and insisted that Soviet Russia had little to learn from Western modernity. To them, the moral authority in the world lay unquestionably outside the West, whereas the West was viewed as an inferior community united by the aspiration to become rich at the expense of the world. The global crisis diagnosed by Gorbachev could therefore not be solved by appeals to the West itself. Nor could there be dialogue with those who exploit the world economically and corrupt it morally. To Statists, New Thinking was to result in destroying the Soviet military capabilities, and to Civilizationists, it was to erode the very spirit of the Soviet society. Religious nationalists, who followed the philosophy of the nineteenth-century Slavophiles and viewed Russia as a holder of Orthodox religious beliefs not to be corrupted by Western Christianity, reinforced the position of the latter.[14]

Not tempted by New Thinking's emphasis on common human values, conservatives recommended that the Soviet Union stay firm and preserve its own historical and cultural tradition. They insisted on the need to continue to resist the influences from the West. Some proposed to accumulate power through economic and technological development, and to abstain from global military conflicts, while others suggested an offensive strategy of expansion to fill the geopolitical vacuum between the Soviet Union and the West.[15]

Liberal Opposition

Conservative perspectives initially remained marginalized in Soviet society. As Gorbachev's reforms were failing to live up to rising expectations, there was still little in Western behavior that could have justified the conservative fears of attempting to destroy Russia. On the contrary, a number of successful negotiations with Western leaders made Russians trust the West more and attracted them even more to its values.

This situation improved the position of liberal-minded Westernizers in the national discourse and provided conditions for the consolidation of a Westernist coalition. Originally sympathetic to Gorbachev's agenda, members of the new coalition now felt that he was too slow and inconsistent in his policies. The coalition included representatives of the Soviet middle class, liberal intellectuals, and some party *nomenklatura*, all of whom were growing impatient with the pace of Gorbachev's domestic and external changes. Eventually Boris Yeltsin, a former provincial party secretary, emerged as the leader of the Westernist coalition. Supported by some ethnic republics, liberals were attracted to the "Western" model of development and disappointed in Gorbachev's "socialist" character of reform.

Liberal critique of New Thinking was just the opposite of that of conservatives. It insisted that Gorbachev's philosophy failed to attribute most common human values to Western civilization. In the view of one scholar, common human values are those "that are based on the criteria of the Western civilization, with its liberal-democratic values and the level of scientific-technological development."[16] Whereas Gorbachev was proposing a globally integrated approach based on the notion of mutual responsibility, liberals viewed the West as the ultimate moral authority and the model to follow. With the nineteenth-century thinker Petr Chaadayev, who believed that "we [Russians] are placed somewhat outside of the times,"[17] the Soviet liberals had little faith in the national tradition of development. In their view, the dilemma before Soviet Russia was either modernization-Westernization or autarchy and backwardness.

Any alternative ways of development were no longer available, and Gorbachev's renewed socialist project was nothing but a harmful utopia.

Table 2.3 summarizes contending views on the New Thinking.

2.4. NEW THINKING ABROAD: BANKING ON THE WEST'S RECOGNITION

It follows that both conservative and liberal critics of New Thinking had a tendency to view national interest in zero-sum terms. While conservatives saw the Soviet national interests as anti-Western, liberals tended to equate them with those of the West. Gorbachev's complex and dialectical perspective on the Soviet Union in world politics was hardly acceptable to either one of his opponents. To stay his course at home, he needed major support from the West. Obtaining such support in response to New Thinking initiatives could have improved Gorbachev's domestic credibility and assisted him in keeping together his fragile coalition of support. Banking on recognition from the West became a crucial part of the new Soviet strategy. The inadequacy of Western reciprocity, along with Gorbachev's own errors in reforming the economic and political system, ultimately contributed to his failure.

Promises and Disappointments

Gorbachev's ambitious foreign policy agenda included far-reaching disarmament measures, particularly in the area of Soviet-American relations, withdrawal of military assistance and troops from the external imperial territories in Eastern Europe and the third world, and strengthening of global institutions (see the chronology earlier in this book for a summary of key events during Gorbachev's tenure). The latter was crucial for fighting militarization, poverty, and environmental degradation across the world, and Gorbachev placed a high premium on the United Nations in accomplishing these goals. The New Thinking vision assumed the emergence of a new global community, in which diverse socioeconomic systems would cooperate in the spirit of mutual trust and reciprocity.

Table 2.3.   New Thinking (NT): Contending Views

Conservatives:		Liberals:
NT weakens the Soviet state	VS.	NT fails to the change the Soviet system

Initially, Gorbachev planned to engage the West through multiple disarmament and demilitarization initiatives. Already in 1985 he argued that military doctrine should become more defensive; announced a unilateral moratorium on nuclear tests; insisted on the need to dissolve military blocs; and made known the Soviet readiness to make disproportionately large cuts in conventional forces.[18] He followed up by proposing more far-reaching changes during several summits with Western leaders. In January 1986, Gorbachev proposed to eliminate all nuclear weapons by 2000, and he offered some major cuts in strategic weapons. He then made several significant concessions on the issue of intermediate nuclear forces, and at the end of 1987, he traveled to Washington to sign the agreement that dismantled the whole class of medium-range and short-range missiles (see table 2.4 for a summary of Gorbachev's security record). No less crucial were decisions to withdraw military assistance and troops from Eastern Europe and the third world. In 1987, the Eastern European leaders were informed that the Soviets were considering troop withdrawal, which was fully consistent with New Thinkers' beliefs in freedom of choice and noninterference in Eastern European domestic affairs. In early 1988, Gorbachev announced the decision to withdraw from Afghanistan, as well as from other third world countries. Gorbachev himself had made these decisions much earlier; indeed, he came to office convinced of their necessity.[19] Finally, in the spirit of strengthening global institutions, the leader of New Thinking took to heart the idea of reforming the United Nations. He supported more extensive resources for peacekeeping forces, proposed to renounce the use of force by the permanent members of the Security Council, and argued for a number of new agencies and agreements. Consistent with these proposals, the new Soviet leadership paid the United Nations $200 million for peacekeeping operations that the old leaders had refused to support since 1973. It also contributed to mediating political resolutions of conflicts in Africa and Latin America.[20]

Despite all these efforts, the Western leaders were not as cooperative as Gorbachev had hoped. Although Ronald Reagan and British prime minister Margaret Thatcher liked Gorbachev personally, they did not feel convinced by his arguments against nuclear deterrence and nuclear weapons as an "absolute evil." During 1985–1987, they were also not persuaded that the Soviet Union was sincere about renouncing the "Brezhnev doctrine" in Eastern Europe or withdrawing its troops from the third world. The core of the mistrust had to do with the uncertain nature of the Soviet reform and a fear of a conservative comeback to power. As a result, many of Gorbachev's initiatives were met with skepticism. For instance, the Geneva Summit in November 1985 produced nothing but a declaration of inadmissibility of nuclear war. Reykjavik, too, failed, as the Soviet proposals were left unreciprocated. Gorbachev also found

Table 2.4.   Gorbachev's Legacy in Security Policy

The INF Treaty (December 1987). U.S. and USSR agreed to eliminate 1,600 intermediate-range missiles. Also eliminated were approximately 1,100 shorter-range missile systems (500–1,000 km) deployed in Europe.

The CFE Treaty (November 1990). Signed by sixteen NATO states and six members of the Warsaw Pact, the Treaty on Conventional Armed Forces in Europe placed restrictions on the number of conventional weapons within the agreed zone. The treaty deprived the USSR of the ability to mount a credible attack against NATO in Europe.

START (July 1991). The Strategic Arms Reduction Treaty limited each side to a total of 1,600 long-range ballistic missiles and heavy bombers.

Withdrawals of troops from Eastern Europe. Gorbachev decided not to interfere in Eastern Europe before or after anticommunist revolutions there and began to withdraw the Soviet troops in April 1989.

The unification of Germany. Gorbachev endorsed the "Two Plus Four" formula to produce the final settlement on Germany to acquiesce in Western Germany's virtual absorption of its eastern neighbor (largely on Western terms), and to accept that a united Germany become a full member of NATO.

The radical upturn in U.S.-Soviet relations. By the time of the Bush-Gorbachev summit in December 1989, the two sides converged on many international issues, such as the desirability of a negotiated peace in Nicaragua and El Salvador and a reduction of the Soviet assistance to Cuba. Bush was even at first reluctant to accept the reality of the December 1991 Soviet breakup when the leaders of Ukraine, Russia, and Belarus announced the creation of the Commonwealth of Independent States.

Adapted from: Coit D. Blacker, Hostage to Revolution: Gorbachev and Soviet Security Policy, 1985–1991 (New York: Council on Foreign Relations, 1993), 184–89.

no support on the issue of nonuse of force and nonintervention in the internal affairs of other states,[21] which was crucial for him to reciprocate his "freedom of choice" principle with regard to the former outer empire of the Soviet Union. Increasingly, he was left in a difficult position to respond to conservative critics at home.

Conservatives in the party and military establishment opposed New Thinking with a growing vigor. Initially, Gorbachev's coalition was a fairly broad one and even included the chief of the general staff Sergei Akhromeyev and the Politburo member Yegor Ligachev, who agreed with a number of military cuts and withdrawals. In particular, both supported Gorbachev's decision to withdraw from Afghanistan. Yet the more radical the New Thinkers were in their proposals, the more vigorous was the opposition. The military was critical of Reykjavik and of the notion of defense "sufficiency," which meant to make military doctrine more defense oriented and prepare the ground for future military cuts. Party officials objected to the principle of "freedom of choice" with regard to Eastern Europe. For instance, Oleg Rakhmanin, head of the Central Committee department for relations with socialist countries, publicly defended the Brezhnev doctrine of limited sovereignty and denounced any changes in bloc relations.[22] Gorbachev fought back by pushing for more military cuts and concessions to the West. He took advantage of the system's failures, such as Chernobyl's nuclear accident and a foreign private aircraft's landing in Red Square, using them as a pretext for replacing hard-liners with those more loyal to his course. In addition, although there was initially no direct connection between his foreign policy initiatives and the state of the Soviet economy, the leader of perestroika was constantly making this connection to maintain conservative support for his course.

Decline and Capitulation

After 1988, the domestic situation took a sharp turn. An economic slowdown, a dramatic worsening of people's living standards, and political separatism of some of the Soviet republics severely affected Gorbachev's ability to stay the course that had already been undermined by the West's reluctant cooperation. The economy was especially important. Although it was growing at the rate of 2.2 percent after the cyclical decline of the early 1980s, it began to decline again during the 1987–1989 period and then collapsed after 1989[23] (see table 2.5). The collapse of the economy was a likely reaction to the vacuum of power resulting from the abolition of state orders. The "law of state enterprise" that came into effect in 1988 replaced state orders with nonbinding control figures. The economy that for decades had been state regulated had not yet developed market-based incentive and was now in a free fall.

As a result, domestic politics was growing increasingly polarized, with conservatives and liberals pulling in opposite directions. Conservatives feverishly tried to restore control over the system and argued for preservation of the class perspective in international relations. But with the Eastern European revolu-

Table 2.5. Growth Rates for the Soviet Economy, 1985–1991

	Western Estimates (GNP)	Official Soviet Data (NMP)
1985	1.8	3.2
1986	4.1	2.3
1987	1.3	1.6
1988	2.1	4.4
1989	1.5	2.5
1990	−2.4	−3.9
1991	−12.8*	−15*

*Estimate excludes Georgia and the Baltic republics.
Source: David Kotz and Fred Weir, *Revolution from Above: The Demise of the Soviet System* (London: Routledge, 1997), 75

tions under way, the reality was slipping away. The spring 1989 elections in Poland and Hungary brought to power anticommunist forces, and November 1989 saw a key symbol of the Cold War, the Berlin Wall, falling. As the old system was largely discredited, the political attention was turning to liberals, who attacked Gorbachev for his indecisiveness and unwillingness to follow the West's model of development. As the leader of New Thinking was losing control, liberal forces were consolidating around Boris Yeltsin, who was soon elected president of the Russian Federation. Even Gorbachev's closest supporters, such as Aleksandr Yakovlev and Eduard Shevardnadze, were now leaving him disappointed. Finally, the general public, too, grew dissatisfied with the results of reform. For instance, in 1989, 39 percent associated the difficulties of reforms with the government's indecisiveness, while only 22 percent of the public attributed such difficulties to the activities of conservative forces.[24]

These domestic changes affected the course negatively. Initially designed as a middle ground between Western capitalism and Stalinist socialism, New Thinking was now seriously endangered and increasingly looked like a failure. After 1988, as Gorbachev was losing ground at home, his foreign policies toward the West were losing their momentum and originality. Symptomatically, in November 1989, the foreign minister Eduard Shevardnadze publicly admitted a lack of "conceptual ideas" and "deficit of counterarguments" in responding to conclusions about the coming triumph of Western liberal ideology.[25] In the meantime, the general public was losing its faith in the country. While in 1988 only 5.3 percent of respondents had felt that the Soviet Union could not serve as an example to the outside world, in 1989 the share of those expressing that feeling reached the level of 34 percent.[26] Western leaders understood Gorbachev's inability to sustain his originally globalist course and pressed for more concessions, without offering much in return. Yegor Ligachev, Gorbachev's powerful conservative opponent, had reasons to charge that certain forces in the United States were "linking perestroika with the dismantling of socialism."[27] Gorbachev still tried to save what was left of his course by resisting unified Germany's membership in NATO and insisting on diplomatic solutions to the Persian Gulf crisis. But the Cold War was over, and after having initiated the change, the Soviet Union had little say in negotiating its outcomes. Banking on the West's recognition proved to be a flawed strategy.

On balance, Gorbachev contributed greatly to improving his country's security by relieving an extremely heavy burden of military expenditures that by the time of his arrival had reached the share of some 16.5 percent of the gross national product (GNP).[28] Yet, even if judged by Gorbachev's own standards and expectations, New Thinking was a failure and a capitulation before the West. As an identity project, it did not serve the formulated purposes. Few of Gorbachev's hopes matched the reality. One of them was that far-reaching disarmament initiatives would break down the old Western mistrust and produce some global commitments to demilitarization. Convinced of the viability of socialism, Gorbachev also declared the "freedom of choice" principle with regard to Eastern Europe and the third world. He hoped that these areas would remain neutral and might eventually turn social democratic. He expected the old bipolar security system to be gradually replaced by that of nonconfrontation and cooperation. The old military blocs, such as the Warsaw Pact and NATO, were to recede into the past, and European security would have been organized around the inclusive Organization for Security and Co-operation in Europe (OSCE), the origins of which had been in the 1975 Helsinki Accord signed by the Soviet Union. Finally, the United Nations was expected to develop enough muscles to successfully deal with the possible vacuum of power and rising instabilities in the third world after the Soviet withdrawals.

Such were the hopes. The reality, however, was different. Western leaders expressed a willingness to negotiate arms control agreements, but showed no desire to go as far as Gorbachev expected them to. Neither Margaret Thatcher nor Ronald Reagan shared Gorbachev's vision of complete demilitarization and denuclearization. Eastern European states had their own memory of being a part of the Soviet outer empire and, once the opportunity presented itself, rushed to join Western economic and security institutions, first and foremost NATO. Germany reunited. The Warsaw Pact disappeared, but NATO persisted and even decided to expand all the way to the Russian borders. The United Nations remained relatively weak and unable to adequately deal with growing violence in the third world. Afghanistan in particular is a case in point. The Soviet withdrawal from there ultimately resulted in that state's collapse. Afghanistan's leader Najibulla was executed, while the new regime of the Taliban became a safe haven for terrorists and their training camps.

2.5. THE CRISIS FOR NATIONALITIES AND THE REVENGE OF NEW THINKING AT HOME

The Soviet Union was an empire, in which the center effectively controlled the sovereignty of the peripheral republics. The Kremlin, rather than Russia and the Russians, played the role of the center—in many ways, Russia was just as heavily exploited by the authorities for the sake of maintaining the empire's economic and political cohesion. Although the Soviet authorities maintained the principle of representation of indigenous nationalities in the power structures, they also relied on political coercion, economic redistribution, and forceful migration—all the traditional tools of empire building. Yet the principle of the nationalities' representation developed and reinforced the sense of peripheral distinctiveness from the empire. Historically, it paved the way for nationalist mobilization during imperial decline, particularly among those republics that had developed a sense of national Self before incorporation into the Soviet empire.

Given this nature of relationships between Moscow and the Soviet republics, changing the Soviet territorial power structure should have been high on Gorbachev's list of priorities. If, externally, the Soviet national interests were to be pursued in balance with interests of other nations, that principle should have applied internally as well. Yet until the early 1990s, Gorbachev failed to address the problem, and his way of dealing with the imperial decline and nationalities crisis presents us with another illustration of how naïve and divorced from power considerations New Thinking ideas were. Gorbachev failed to recognize the Soviet Union as an empire and simply did not see the need for major power changes. By not reacting to national uprisings in a timely and systematic manner, he lost some valuable time (table 2.6 summarizes the rise of ethnonationalism in the Soviet Union). Only in March 1990 did he raise the question of a new union treaty as a way to avoid a political disintegration. By that time, nationalists in the Baltic republics and elsewhere had been active for more than three years. Six republics—the Baltic ones, Georgia, Moldova, and Armenia—announced their intent of nonparticipation in the new union treaty, and Russian liberal critics of Gorbachev were already debating the idea of confederation. Later, the leader of perestroika himself admitted that he had "underestimated the strength of national feelings and aspirations."[29]

By the time Gorbachev had formulated his concept of revived union, he had to defend it against well-elaborated positions of conservatives and Westernizers. Conservatives advocated the idea of empire. Some popularized the essentialist notion of Soviet Eurasia as a new continental empire and a distinct civilization, and recommended the use of force in preserving territorial integrity. Liberal Westernizers around Yeltsin and his supporters criticized the Soviet Union as a hypercentralized state, attacking it from a colonial nationalist perspective. Increasingly, they saw the solution in separating Russia from the center and building Russia's own state institutions. Gorbachev's perspective was not an essentialist one. Rather than advocating an empire or a nation-state, he argued for the Soviet Union as a reformed federation and a community of various peoples. Culturally, he saw this community in transnational terms. A European in his social and political outlook, Gorbachev saw the need to maintain a cultural balance. After 1987 he upgraded his "common European home" formula by adding the Asian dimension and more frequently referring to the Soviet Union as an Asian, as well as a European, country. His foreign minister Eduard Shevardnadze also touted this vision. For example, in October 1988 in his welcoming message to foreign guests attending the Asia-

Table 2.6.   The Rise of Ethnonationalism in the Union Republics, 1989–1991

Union Republic	Main Ethnonationalist Movement (date of foundation)	Sovereignty Declaration (rank)
Armenia	Karabakh Committee (Feb. 1988)	July 1990 (8)
Azerbaijan	Azeri Popular Front (July 1988)	Sept. 1989 (4)
Belarus	Renewal (Andradzhen'ne) (June 1989)	June 1990 (7)
Estonia	Estonian Popular Front (July 1988)	Nov. 1988 (1)
Georgia	Committee for National Salvation (Oct. 1989)	Nov. 1989 (5)
Kazakhstan	Nevada Semipalatinsk Movement (Feb. 1989)	Sept. 1990 (9)
Kyrgyzstan	Openness (Ashar) (July 1989)	Nov. 1990 (10)
Latvia	Latvian Popular Front (July 1988)	May 1989 (2)
Lithuania	Sajudis (June 1988)	July 1989 (3)
Moldova	Moldovan Popular Front (Jan. 1989)	May 1990 (6)
Russia	Democratic Russia (1990)	May 1990 (6)
Tajikistan	Openness (Ashkara) (June 1989)	July 1990 (8)
Turkmenistan	Unity (Agzybirlik) (Jan. 1990)	July 1990 (8)
Ukraine	Popular Front (Rukh) (Nov 1988)	June 1990 (7)
Uzbekistan	Unity (Birlik) (Nov 1988)	May 1990 (6)

Adapted from: Graham Smith, *The Post-Soviet States: Mapping the Politics of Transition* (London: Arnold, 1999), 39; Ann Sheehy, "Factsheet on Declarations of Sovereignty," *Report on the USSR*, November 9, 1990.

Pacific region conference in Vladivostok, he stressed the Soviet Union as a "great Eurasian space" and a "world of worlds" (*mir mirov*), and argued that Russia had to live in a complex world of both European and Asian nations.

That vision had broad popular support. For example, even as late as during the March 1991 referendum on the future of the new union—a referendum that was conducted in all of the Soviet republics except the Baltics, Armenia, Georgia, and Moldova—147 million people voted and 76.4 percent approved the preservation of the union. The wording of the question was: "Do you support the preservation of the union as a renewed federation of sovereign republics in which the rights of a person of any nationality are fully guaranteed?"[30]

Yet it was a struggle of elites, rather than involvement of the general public, that was about to determine the future of the Soviet Union. The referendum for a renewed union took place in the context of Gorbachev's struggle against liberal elites on the one hand, and conservatives on the other. Yeltsin's umbrella organization, Democratic Russia, openly called for the dissolution of the Soviet Union and even tried (unsuccessfully) to convince Yeltsin to campaign for a "no" vote in the referendum. Liberals turned nationalists presented the Soviet Union as an "empire" that was to be dismantled for the sake of Russian prosperity. Throughout the political campaigns of 1990 and 1991, Yeltsin had advanced the "Russia-victim" argument, and it was his advisers who eventually wrote a scenario of dissolving the union. Conservatives, too, did what was in their power to sabotage Gorbachev's efforts. In early 1991, Soviet troops cracked down on the rebellious Lithuania and Latvia. Gorbachev denied responsibility by putting the blame on his defense minister, Dmitri Yazov. Yet liberals in Russia widely associated the crackdown with Gorbachev, and this association worsened the problem. The conservative coup in August meant to prevent the scheduled signing of the new union treaty between the center and nine republics, but it only made the Soviet disintegration inevitable. The nationalism of the republics' political leadership then reached its highest degree, with Russia and Ukraine playing a particularly important role. On December 25, 1991, after Russia-Ukraine-Belarus had concluded a separate treaty creating the Commonwealth of Independent States (CIS) without consulting the center, Gorbachev resigned.

Paradoxically, New Thinking contributed to the breakup of the Soviet Union. By aiming for the West's support and recognition, it inserted itself into the arena of the Western modernity of nation-states, making it increasingly difficult to discourage the Soviet ethnic republics from embarking on nationalist projects. Soon after the beginning of perestroika, nationalists were openly referring to the Soviet Union as the last empire in the "age of decolonization." By announcing glasnost and democratization, New Thinking also provided nationalists in Russia and other republics with the required channels for political mobilization. The organization of mass demonstrations in the Baltic republics and then elections to national parliaments of those who saw the future only in terms of complete independence greatly facilitated the undermining of the Soviet Union. Finally, Gorbachev's own vision made little room for timely changes in nationalities policy. Despite mounting evidence of strong secessionist sentiments displayed by several republics, he kept insisting that the republics formed a natural historical unity and that they should be "grateful" to the Soviet Union for their social and economic development. Such "New Thinking" undoubtedly stimulated peripheral nationalism. Although public support for the preservation of the union was sound, the extreme polarization of the political space by elites deprived Russia of a chance to reformulate its transnational identity.

2.6. UTOPIA AND REALITY: ASSESSMENT
OF GORBACHEV'S FOREIGN POLICY

Gorbachev's New Thinking project was introduced to renew the Soviet national identity and to save it as the idea of a reformed socialism open to an outside world yet loyal to some of the already-developed social values. Over time, however, the project of saving the national idea regressed into a national defeat. Most of New Thinking's expectations regarding the outside world failed to materialize. The Cold War ended on terms that Gorbachev himself found difficult to accept. The Soviet Union unilaterally withdrew from most areas of the world where it had been present, and it did so without receiving the satisfaction of strengthening global institutions, such as the United Nations, or being given credit for changing the world's thinking. Instead, it was widely accepted that the Soviets lost the Cold War to the West, and it was the West that emerged as the triumphant civilization and the guarantor of peace and security in the world. As if this were not enough, the forces of nationalism in Russia and several other republics added to Gorbachev's domestic defeat. He acknowledged the defeat and resigned as president of a country that was no more. His overall project of external openness and domestic liberalization had been initially widely supported in Soviet society and among elites, who felt ready to move away from the stiffening bureaucratic and militaristic system. But in the process of being implemented, New Thinking lost the appeal both externally and domestically, and it contributed to the loss of governance in the country. This section offers a more detailed assessment of Gorbachev's foreign policy record. It reflects on causes of what happened and draws lessons from the failure of New Thinking.

The Record: Accomplishments and Losses

Gorbachev and his team should be given great credit for initiating a new progressive thinking about the future of the country and the world. Liberals worldwide have been appreciative of the intellectual effort to reactivate the social initiative and put a human being in the center of state policy. It is highly misleading to view New Thinking as driven by some power necessities or as an ideology meant to cover the Soviet system's prime desire to rebuild its economic and military capabilities. Gorbachev might have been naïve in his expectations and strategic design, but he certainly was not a cynical power calculator whose main concern was to save the Soviet economic and military machine from defeat in the Cold War. In fact, he did not need to be a New Thinker for power purposes, as the old system could have survived for another generation or so.[31] Nor did he believe, when he came to power, that the Soviet economy was in serious trouble. Gorbachev could have continued to enjoy power without introducing any changes, or he could have introduced limited measures to reform the economy and fight corruption, as favored by his predecessor Yuri Andropov and the majority of the leadership. Instead he initiated what he himself liked to refer to as a "social revolution."

One undisputed accomplishment of New Thinking has been a break with the old Soviet-style isolationism and a radical improvement in military security (see tables 2.4. and 2.7. for summaries). It is only thanks to major theoretical innovations and subsequent arms control agreements that the Soviet leadership was able to avert the threat of war and move to a realistic military budget. After the 1987 agreement with Washington about the elimination of an entire class of nuclear forces, the very idea of a war with Western countries seemed anachronistic. The state could now concentrate on what it declared as its major tasks—improving people's lives and making the system more accountable to society.

Yet it is in the areas outside military security that the state failed to deliver. Gorbachev's foreign policy failed when judged by the three key criteria of social welfare, policy autonomy, and cultural identity. First, New Thinking did little to improve living standards at home, and it did not result in the expected active participation of the West in reforming the domestic economy. In some ways, Gorbachev's active foreign policy even harmed the domestic reforms, as it precluded the leader of New Thinking from concentrating on what required his full attention at home. Although Gorbachev visualized partial privatization of the economy, he never seriously tried it. Partly, he was too busy with his revolutionary foreign policy. But he was also fearful that private property would lead to a capitalist system at home subverting what he saw as accomplishments of socialism. For instance, in September 1990, several Soviet and Western economists developed the plan "500 days," which included economic restructuring, privatization, and active involvement of foreign capital. Gorbachev backed away from the plan, viewing it as leading to a restoration of capitalism. But even before then he missed many opportunities to introduce a more decentralized system and economic incentives. Unlike his more pragmatic teacher Vladimir Lenin, who was not afraid of large foreign concessions and a "dual economy" with a relatively large private sector during the post–civil war reconstruction, Gorbachev proved to be a much less flexible reformer. As a result of

Table 2.7.   Limits on Arms Accepted or Proposed by Gorbachev, 1983–1991

Delivery Systems (warheads)	START, 1983	START, 1991*
Strategic nuclear delivery vehicles	12,580	6,000
Ballistic missiles	10,180	4,900
Heavy ICBMs	3,080	1,540
Sea-launched ballistic missiles	3,080	Limits
Bombers	2,400	1,100

*As proposed in 1987
Adapted from: Michael McGwire, *Perestroika and Soviet National Security* (Washington, DC: The Brookings Institution, 1991), 79.

his hesitancy, even a mixed economy, in which only small and medium-sized businesses are in private hands, never appeared. The economy remained heavily centralized, and it was unrealistic to expect a considerable Western participation in the process of economic reform. It was even less realistic to expect such participation after the Soviet economy had collapsed.

As a result of the collapsing economy, Gorbachev was increasingly perceived abroad as weak and unable to sustain his foreign policy course. Western leaders pressed for more concessions, as in negotiations over Germany's reunification and its role in European security, and the leader of New Thinking was surrendering one position after another. Increasingly, the West, in its own policy calculations, successfully used him. Although this did not yet amount to a loss of Soviet foreign policy autonomy or ability to make independent decisions, it might have created preconditions for future diminished autonomy. Finally, Gorbachev's foreign policy failed to deliver what New Thinking saw as perhaps the most important of its promises—reformulation of the Soviet cultural identity. Isolation from the world and the West was to be replaced by an image of a more open, democratic, and yet socialist nation confidently looking forward and even providing the world with an example to follow. Instead, Russia found itself a deeply divided nation, with an identity crisis extending well into the post-Soviet era.

Table 2.8 summarizes the record of the New Thinking.

Lessons of New Thinking's Failure

New Thinking failed to achieve its objectives abroad and at home not because it had developed a wrong vision for the world's future, but because it had chosen a wrong course to implement that vision by largely divorcing itself from domestic and international power considerations. No grand idea can materialize if it is promoted without a due consideration for the existing political context. Although Gorbachev had started his reforms supported by a relatively broad coalition, which included intellectuals and members of the mid-

Table 2.8.   The Record of New Thinking

Security	New arms control agreements
	End of the Soviet isolationism
Welfare	State disintegration
	Collapsed economy
Autonomy	Voluntary concessions
	Growing dependence on the West
Identity	A culturally divided nation

dle class, the military, and party bureaucracy, he was ultimately left alone with his vision. The larger society also began to withdraw its support as early as 1988–1989, and this registered in polls as well as in growing support for Gorbachev's liberal opposition. Sadly, this did not lead to a major rethinking of the initial strategy, or to attempts to rebuild the coalition of support.

Externally, giving due attention to the political and power context would have meant an effort to achieve a genuine reciprocity from the West in response to the breathtaking Soviet initiatives. One after another, countries in the West politely declined or ignored Gorbachev's initiatives—on nuclear disarmament, abandonment of the principle of deterrence, nonuse of force and nonintervention in the internal affairs of other states, and strengthening the United Nations. Yet the leader of New Thinking kept going with his own agenda of unilateral withdrawals and military concessions. Believing that his efforts would somehow be rewarded and appreciated externally and at home was naïve, all the more so because he was rapidly losing important bargaining chips in promoting his own revolutionary agenda, just as he was losing domestic support for his course. Gorbachev and his team simply did not think in the categories of preserving power and capabilities of the state. This was enormously costly to them because the West was not as naïve in negotiating with New Thinkers in the Kremlin, and the Western leaders did give power factors their due consideration.

It was also very costly to the New Thinkers because over time they lost the ability to sell the course at home. And, if the first lesson to learn from their failure is that a successful foreign policy requires reciprocity, then the second lesson should be that a foreign policy must match domestic needs and have strong roots at home. Trying to revolutionize foreign policy simultaneously with fundamental reforms in the economy, political system, and the area of center-periphery relations is an admirable, but ultimately impossible, task. Priorities should have been chosen, and such priorities should have been domestic, rather than external. Ironically, the harder Gorbachev seemed to push for foreign policy changes, the less control he had left at home. First, in 1988 he lost control over the economy after replacing state orders with nonbinding control figures. Then, he lost control over the political situation after his leading opponent, Boris Yeltsin, was elected president of Russia—first by the parliament and then by popular vote—while Gorbachev remained an essentially nonelected politician. Before 1989, Gorbachev still had a chance to acquire more of a domestic legitimacy and to strengthen the status of the Soviet president through nationwide elections; after that, such opportunity was no longer available. By not dealing with the nationalities crisis in a timely manner, he further worsened his domestic standing, and the public had difficulties with trusting his course. Symptomatically, during 1988–1989 the percentage of those viewing nationalities relations as worsening increased from 38 to 72 percent, and in 1989 30 percent of the respondents thought that a future civil war was likely.[32]

In sum, liberal ideas cannot succeed when they are not backed by power, and they can succeed only to the degree they successfully shape power and use it to achieve their own agenda. Such power can include the support of influential elites, the general public, or developed states abroad, but it must remain a part of the course's support. Liberal ideas should guide a course strategically, but their promoters should also take care to retain sufficient domestic and foreign support of their efforts.

NOTES

1. Mikhail Gorbachev, *On My Country and the World* (New York: Columbia University Press, 2000), 190.

2. For instance, the human rights provisions of the Helsinki Accords, signed by the Soviet Union during détente, emboldened domestic reform-oriented forces and, albeit indirectly, gave rise to a network of committed activists in the Soviet Union and Eastern Europe. For details, see Robert G. Herman, "Identity, Norms, and National Security: The Soviet Foreign Policy Revolution and the End of the Cold War," in *The Culture of National Security*, ed. Peter J. Katzenstein (New York: Columbia University Press, 1996), 292; Robert D. English, *Russia and the Idea of the West: Gorbachev, Intellectuals and the End of the Cold War* (New York: Columbia University Press, 2000), 154–55.

3. Eric Ringman, "The Recognition Game: Soviet Russia against the West," *Cooperation and Conflict* 37, no. 2 (2002).

4. On Gorbachev as a thinker who sought to improve the Soviet Union's world status through an innovative strategy of engaging the West, see Deborah Welch Larson and Alexei Shevchenko, "Shortcut to Greatness: The New Thinking and the Revolution in Soviet Foreign Policy," *International Organization* 57 (Winter 2003).

5. Mikhail Gorbachev, *Perestroika: New Thinking for Our Country and the World* (New York: Harper & Row, 1987), 12.

6. See, for example, Stephen M. Walt, "The Gorbachev Interlude and International Relations Theory," *Diplomatic History* 21, no. 3 (1997); Stephen G. Brooks and William C. Wohlforth, "Power, Globalization, and the End of the Cold War: Reevaluating a Landmark Case for Ideas," *International Security* 25, no. 3 (Winter 2000/01).

7. Gorbachev, *Perestroika*, 152.

8. For example, in his book *On My Country and the World*, Gorbachev discusses at length the October revolution's global significance.

9. Graham Smith, *The Post-Soviet States: Mapping the Politics of Transition* (London: Arnold, 1999), 23. See also Moshe Lewin, *The Gorbachev Phenomenon: A Historical Interpretation* (Berkeley: University of California Press, 1991).

10. As cited in Richard Sakwa, *The Rise and Fall of the Soviet Union, 1917–1991* (London: Routledge, 1999), 188.

11. For a detailed analysis of debates between Old and New Thinkers, see English, *Russia and the Idea of the West*.

12. Stephen Sestanovich, "Invention of Soviet National Interest," *National Interest* 20 (1990).

13. Sestanovich, "Invention of Soviet National Interest," 10.

14. See, for example, Igor' Shafarevich, "Russofobiya," *Nash Sovremennik* 6, no. 11 (1989); Yuri Borodai, "Treti put," *Nash sovremennik* 9 (1991).

15. Sergei Kurginyan et al., *Postperestroika* (Moscow: Politizdat, 1990); Aleksandr Prokhanov and Shamil' Sultanov, "Izmenit'sya, chtoby vyzhit," *Den'* 6 (1991); Aleksandr Dugin, "Anatomiya mondializma," *Den'* 16 (1991).

16. El'giz A. Pozdnyakov, "Formatsionnyi i tsivilizatsionnyi podkhody i mezhdunarodniye otnosheniya," in *SSSR v mirovom soobschestve*, ed. Nodar A. Simoniya (Moscow: Progress, 1990), 143. For a broader context, review the articles published in Russia's academic and literary journals during 1987–1991.

17. Petr Chaadaev, "Apology of a Madman," in *Readings in Russian Civilization*, 2d ed., ed. Thomas Riha (Chicago: University of Chicago Press, 1969), 304.

18. English, *Russia and the Idea of the West*, 201–2.

19. English, *Russia and the Idea of the West*, 203–4.

20. Larson and Shevchenko, "Shortcut to Greatness," 98.

21. Larson and Shevchenko, "Shortcut to Greatness," 99.

22. English, *Russia and the Idea of the West*, 204.

23. David Kotz and Fred Weir, *Revolution from Above: The Demise of the Soviet System* (London: Routeldge, 1997), 76.

24. Yuri Levada, ed., *Est' mneniye! Itogi sotsiologicheskogo oprosa* (Moscow: Progress, 1990), 290.

25. Eduard Shevardnadze, "Vneshnyaya politika i nauka," *Mezhdunarodnaya zhizn'* 2 (February 1990): 17, 18.

26. Levada, *Est' mneniye*, 284.

27. *Sovetskaya Rossiya*, February 6, 1991.

28. Some estimate the defense budget at 20 percent of the GNP and even higher (English, *Russia and the Idea of the West*, 200, 323, n. 31). The official Soviet figures were 8.1 percent for 1975 and 4.6 percent for 1984. See *Finansy i statistika* (Moscow, 1985) as quoted in Janos Kornai, *The Socialist System: The Political Economy of Communism* (Princeton: Princeton University Press, 1992), 137.

29. Mikhail Gorbachev, *Dekabr' 1991: Moya pozitsiya* (Moscow: Novosti, 1992), 175–76.

30. Kotz and Weir, *Revolution from Above*, 147.

31. Michael Ellman and Vladimir Kontorovich, eds., *The Disintegration of the Soviet Economic System* (London: Routledge, 1992); see also Michael Ellman and Vladimir Kontorovich, "The Collapse of the Soviet System and the Memoir Literature," *Europe-Asia Studies* 49, no. 2 (1997); and Vladimir Kontorovich, "Economists, Soviet Growth Slowdown and the Collapse," *Europe-Asia Studies* 53, no. 5 (2001).

32. Levada, *Est' mneniye*, 280, 288.

3

The Post–Cold War Euphoria and Russia's Liberal Westernism

Our country . . . was turned into a hostage of messianic ideas, on behalf of which it sacrificed its national interests.

The United States and other Western democracies are as natural friends and eventual allies of the democratic Russia as they are foes of the totalitarian U.S.S.R.

—Andrei Kozyrev[1]

3.1. THE WORLDVIEW OF RUSSIA'S WESTERNIZERS AFTER THE COLD WAR

The Soviet disintegration ended the previously established sense of national identity in Russia and opened up a space for identity reformulation by the new state. The leaders of post-Soviet Russia developed a pro-Western vision of national identity and foreign policy, which was consistent with their vision of the world. Before we describe this vision in greater detail, let us review the context in which the new foreign policy thinking was to take shape.

The Brave New Liberal World

The most powerful force that shaped the worldview of new Russia's leadership was the economic and political rise of the West. Relative to steadily growing Western economies, Russia's gross domestic product (GDP) showed about a 60 percent cumulative decline from 1985 to 1992.[2] In addition, the West re-

55

emerged as a powerful and cohesive civilization whose political unity contrasted with disarray in the former Soviet Union. Finally, in the late 1980s,
many Western commentators were in a self-congratulatory mood, which also
contributed to the perception of the worldwide ascendancy of Western values
and institutions. By the time conservatives had been in power for a good decade and with the decline of Soviet power, they became convinced of the
West's victory in the Cold War struggle.

For example, Francis Fukuyama's argument about the "end of history" defended the worldwide ascendancy of Western-style liberal capitalism and
captured the vision dominant in American policy circles.[3] In Europe, such
admirers of civil society and "participatory democracy" as Andrew Arato, Ralf
Darendorf, and Timothy Garton Ash expressed similar Western democratic
triumphalism and saw the Soviet decline as a catalyst for a revival of civic
norms of plurality and publicity in Eastern Europe. British journalist Timothy
Garton Ash forcefully stated the mood by maintaining that the European
revolutions "can offer no fundamentally new ideas on the big questions of
politics, economics, law or international relations. The ideas whose time has
come are old, familiar, well-tested ones"—liberal ideas about the rule of law,
parliamentary government, and an independent judiciary.[4]

Although politically the Western leaders were supportive of Gorbachev's
gradual efforts to dismantle the Soviet system, most of them were critical of
his socialist intentions and hoped for the emergence of a Western-like system in place of the Soviet Union. Many increasingly perceived the Soviet
system as "the grand failure,"[5] and as early as 1989 such a perception had
won the support of the mainstream intellectual and political discourse in the
West. The leading policy establishment journal *Foreign Affairs* soon issued
the verdict that "the Soviet system collapsed because of what it was, or more
exactly, because of what it was not. The West 'won' because of what the democracies were—because they were free, prosperous and successful, because
they did justice, or convincingly tried to do so."[6] The vision was finally legitimized on the highest policy level when U.S. president George H. W. Bush
announced the Cold War "victory" of the United States in his 1992 State of
the Union message.

It was this fundamental belief in the superiority of the Western system
that also shaped the minds of the emerged liberal coalition in Russia. Boris
Yeltsin and his liberal foreign minister Andrei Kozyrev believed that history
in a sense had ended and presented no alternatives to the pro-Western development. Before the Soviet disintegration, they used these ideas for dis-
crediting Gorbachev's socialist and therefore "utopian" worldview. Consistently with the Western critics of socialism, they insisted that the Soviet
Union could not be reformed and that Russia needed to adopt a Western

capitalist model of development. After the peaceful end of the Cold War, the arguments of Russia's Westernizers about the "nonconfrontational" nature of the international system and the absence of security threats made their insistence on the rapid modernization and Westernization all the more compelling to the public. Geopolitics seemed irrelevant, while Westernization seemed inevitable and imminent.

The Westernist Vision of Russia's Identity

Loyal to the intellectual tradition of Westernism, the new Russia's leaders saw their country as an organic part of Western civilization, whose "genuine" Western identity had been hijacked by Bolsheviks and the Soviet system. In the Westernist perspective, during the Cold War Russia had acted against its own national identity and interests, and now it finally had an opportunity to become a "normal" Western country. Thus, Kozyrev argued that the Soviet Union was not merely a "normal" or "underdeveloped" country, but a "wrongfully developed" one.[7] This vision was a clear product of a long tradition of Russia's Westernist thinking. Such eminent nineteenth-century historians as Vasili Klyuchevski and Pavel Milyukov saw Russia's national characteristics, but insisted that their country would nevertheless develop in the same direction as the West and go through the same stages of development.

Why such a linear worldview? Because the West was perceived as the only viable and progressive civilization. In this perspective, the world society was increasingly based on democratic values and the respect for human rights as articulated by Western civilization.[8] Main threats to Russia were to come from its economic backwardness and its association with nondemocratic countries, especially with some of the former Soviet allies. Accordingly, the key division in the world, overriding all other divisions, was the one between democratic countries and those in the process of democratic transition, on the one hand, and those that were still practicing authoritarian forms of government, on the other. The West and its supporters had the right to push for their human-rights agenda and even intervene anywhere in the world when gross violations of human rights were taking place. With respect to the agencies that were to enforce a human rights–centered world order, it was best if human rights interventions were sanctioned through the United Nations Security Council.

The new Westernist coalition consisted of idealistic reformers and pragmatic representatives of the former Communist *nomenklatura*. The reformers, such as Gennadi Burbulis, Yegor Gaidar, and Andrei Kozyrev, advocated radical policies that they hoped would bring Russia in line with the politico-economic standards of Western countries within a limited period of time.

Typically, these reformers talked about one or two years of necessary reforms, after which Russians were to considerably improve their living standards. Members of the former party *nomenklatura* realized that the return to the Soviet past was no longer possible. Some of them, especially those originating from the Komsomol (the youth branch of the Communist Party) apparatus and directors of large state enterprises, had entered private business during 1989–1991 and now wanted to obtain control over the state property that had previously been managed under the leadership of the Central Committee. The goals of reformers and the former *nomenklatura* were compatible: reformers wanted pro-Western capitalist reforms, while the party *nomenklatura* was eager to become a class of new capitalists.

United by the popular president Boris Yeltsin, the Westernist coalition found itself in a position to act on its foreign policy beliefs. Gorbachev's reforms had been effectively discredited, and the failed coup of August 1991 eliminated the appeal of the old communist ideas.

The Westernist Concept of National Interest

The defeat of Gorbachev by liberal Westernizers led to assertion of a different concept of national interest. While accepting the general premises of New Thinking, the new Russia's leaders developed these premises in a more sweeping philosophy of Integration with the West and its economic, political, and security institutions. In Kozyrev's words, the country's very system of values was to be changed, as Russia was to accept the priority of the individual and the free market over society and state. As the result, a "natural partnership" with Western countries was to develop, and Russia was to be brought to the front-rank status of such countries as France, Germany, and the United States within ten to twelve years. In the spirit of liberalism, Kozyrev formulated the national interest saying "in transforming Russia into a free, independent state, formalizing democratic institutions, setting up an effective economy, guaranteeing the rights and freedoms of all Russians, making our people's life rich both materially and spiritually."[9] (Table 3.1 summarizes the Westernist view of national interest.)

Table 3.1.   Westernist Course: View of National Interest

What?	"Natural partnership" with the West
How?	Rapid membership in Western organizations Isolationism in the former Soviet region Radical economic reform

It is worth emphasizing three key components of the asserted vision of national interest—radical economic reform, rapid membership in the Western international institutions, and isolationism from the former Soviet states. First, Yeltsin and Kozyrev advocated a strategy of radical economic reform, the so-called shock therapy, so that Russia's transition to a Western-style system would be both fast and irreversible. The argument was made that in the contemporary post–Cold War world, Russia should stop worrying about military power and geopolitics and, instead, invest its resources in the creation of a modern economy and political system. The new leadership linked the idea of radical reform to that of strategic partnership with the West, and the calculation was that the latter would be instrumental in implementing the former. Russian Westernizers hoped that the West had finally recognized them as one of its own and would therefore invest the required resources in Russia's transition. For instance, in addressing a joint session of the United States Congress in June 1992, Yeltsin saw no reason to hide his expectations for massive external assistance in reforming the country's economy. He even chose to be dramatic in linking the success of Russia's reform to U.S. aid and told the joint session that his country had only one chance to survive:

> There will be no second try . . . the reforms must succeed. . . . If we [that is, you Americans] do not take measures now to support Russia, this will not be a collapse of Russia only, it will be a collapse of the United States, because it will mean new trillions of dollars for the arms race.[10]

Joining international organizations was the second critical element in the strategy of Integration with the West. Since the United States and other Western countries were now "natural allies," Russia should gain a full-scale status in such transatlantic economic and security institutions as the European Union, North Atlantic Treaty Organization (NATO), International Monetary Fund (IMF), G-7, and so on. In this brave new world of economic interdependence and Western institutional predominance, Russia would no longer need to pursue its "greatness"; it should instead prepare for a relative decrease of status in a postconfrontational world and try to solve its problems by way of joining the Western "community of civilized nations."[11]

Finally, the new concept of national interest assumed that Russia's Integration with the West would take priority over the relationships with the ex-Soviet republics. The new leadership believed that, just as Russia had suffered from isolation from the West, it had also taken on the excessively heavy Soviet imperial burden. The argument was made that the Soviet Union had been a constant drain on Russian resources, as Russia had had to subsidize other republics. Russia was therefore turned into an "internal colony" of the Soviet Union. The solution was found in the eventual separation of the country from the former republics economically, politically, and culturally. The concept of "little Russia" was introduced to assist the leadership in justifying little, if any, responsibility for the former Soviet region. In the economic realm, Russia's leaders planned to stop subsidies for the ex-republics. In the security area, they wanted to gradually withdraw Russia's military and to rely on the assistance of international organizations, such as the Organization for Security and Co-operation in Europe (OSCE), in solving possible conflicts in the region. Politically, they viewed the newly established organization in place of the Soviet Union—the Commonwealth of Independent States (CIS)—as a mechanism for completing the republics' separation from Russia, rather than for promoting or preserving their integration.

The liberal Westernist concept of national interest shaped the new foreign policy concept prepared in late 1992 and signed into law in April 1993. The concept heavily influenced by the documents and charter of the OSCE favored the promotion of Russia's interests in the first place through participation in different international organizations. The foreign minister's emphasis on Western international institutions in part reflected his own professional experience; for sixteen years (1974–1990), Kozyrev had worked in the Directorate of International Organizations at the Soviet Foreign Ministry. He saw international institutions as the main avenue for resolving conflicts outside the essentially peaceful and prosperous Western Hemisphere, including between the former Soviet republics.

This concept of national interest was in many ways unprecedented—never before had Russia's officials been as supportive of dismantling their imperial institutions, as critical of their own history, and as trusting of Western intentions. In Yeltsin and Kozyrev's design, Russia was not only supposed to cooperate with the West on a broad range of international issues, as Gorbachev had planned; it was to become the West at the expense of its own historically developed identity. Gorbachev wanted the Soviet Union to be more respectful of other nations, but he did not propose to abandon what he saw as his country's socialist values and interests. He argued that security must be mutual, especially in the context of U.S.-Soviet relations, and that it should be broadened to incorporate various aspects of economic and environmental interdependence. But Gorbachev never went as far as to suggest that the West would become the teacher of the rest of the world, whereas Yeltsin and Kozyrev developed their outlook almost exclusively from their infatuation with Western civilization and its accomplishments. This outlook implied that countries outside the West could no longer make a creative contribution to the world's development; at this posthistorical point, all that was left to the non-Western world was to patiently and passively wait to be absorbed by the West-defined modernization. This kind of Westernism would have not been possible without New Thinking, but it became far more extreme and far more critical of the Soviet developments than that of Gorbachev.

Contrary to what realists might assert, the new Russia's leaders did not pursue the strategy of Integration with the West because of a weakness of Soviet material capabilities. The reformers' idealistic worldview could hardly be likened to pragmatic calculations of a weakened superpower. On the contrary, many reformers saw the Soviet collapse as an opportunity to establish a new identity for Russia. Liberal theorists of international relations are closer to the truth when they point to the impact of Western ideas of modernization on Russia's liberals. Yet these theorists could hardly have predicted the intensity of growing opposition to Russia's new Westernist course.

3.2. THE DEBATE ON FOREIGN POLICY WESTERNISM

The Westernist vision of Russia's identity and foreign policy turned out to be deeply contested and soon was challenged by various political classes as well as the larger society (table 3.2 summarizes the spectrum of Russia's post-Soviet foreign policy thinking). The old Civilizationists argued that the West was interested only in global hegemony and weakening Russia. Gorbachev's supporters embraced the government's attempts to engage the world, but condemned the sectarian nature of foreign policy formation and its narrowly procapitalist orientation. But the most formidable challenge to Westernism came from the revived tradition of Statist thinking. The new Statists agreed with the need to cooperate with the West in the interests of rebuilding the economy, but insisted that the guiding principle behind all reforms and foreign policy actions remained the preservation of great power status. As the West began to lose interest in Russia, Statists received an important advantage in asserting their influence. The local conditions that helped them to consolidate their support were the failure of shock therapy, growing instability in the former Soviet region, and institutional channels of a low centralized political system.

Civilizationists

The end of the Soviet Union did not change Civilizationists, who still refused to part with the core principles of the Soviet society. One group—National Communists—was merging some old communist ideas with those of nationalism and was particularly influenced by Joseph Stalin's doctrine of "socialism in one country," which acknowledged the need for Russia to focus on developing military and economic capabilities within the Soviet boundaries. The most active promoter of this group's ideas was Gennadi Zyuganov, the leader of the

Table 3.2.   The Spectrum of Russia's Post-Soviet Foreign Policy Thinking

Principal School of Thought	A Vision of Russia and Its External Threats	Proponent
WESTERNIZERS		
Liberals	Russia is a part of the West and should integrate with Western economic and political institutions; the main threats to Russia come from nondemocratic states	Andrei Kozyrev
Social Democrats	Russia is an independent part of international society; it has its own specific interests, but also shares some common interests with others; the main threats to Russia come from the violation of basic human rights and disrespect for cultural pluralism	Mikhail Gorbachev
STATISTS	Russia is a sovereign state and a great power with its own specific interests in maintaining the stability of the international system; the main threats to Russia come from state-revisionists seeking to change the existing balance of power	Yevgeni Primakov
CIVILIZATIONISTS		
National Communists	Russia is an independent socialist civilization and a great power/ superpower; its interests are incompatible with those of the West and include the restoration of a balance of power between socialism and capitalism and the spread of the influence of Russian civilization; the main threats come from the West and its imperialist intentions	Gennadi Zyuganov
Hard-line Eurasianists	Russia is a land-based geopolitical empire; its interests are mutually exclusive from those of sea-based powers and include the preservation and expansion of Russia's geopolitical sphere of influence; the main threats come from sea-based powers	Vladimir Zhirinovski

Communist Party of the Russian Federation.[12] Another hard-line group referred to itself as Eurasianists, and viewed the world in terms of geopolitical struggle between land-based and sea-based powers. Unlike National Communists who portrayed themselves as adherents to conservative beliefs such as religion and social stability, Eurasianists argued that conservatism was not enough and advocated the notion of a "conservative revolution" and geopolitical expansion.[13] While National Communists had no ambitions beyond restoring the Soviet Union, Eurasianists wanted to build a larger geopolitical axis of allies—such as Germany, Iran, and Japan—in order to resist the American influences. They attracted some support from hard-line military and nationalist political movements, such as Vladimir Zhirinovski's Liberal Democratic Party.

Both groups attacked Kozyrev's course as serving the interests of the West at the expense of Russia. To them, Russia's national interest was, almost by definition, anti-Western. They had no regard for market economy and political democracy and viewed Russia's institutions as diametrically opposed to those of the West. The West's liberalism, they argued, was nothing more than United States–based unipolarity in the making. Russia's adequate response should include rebuilding military capabilities, reforming the economy on the model of China's gradual state-oriented style, and preserving control over Eurasia or the post-Soviet world. In the words of the conservative periodical *Molodaya gvardiya*, "The historical task before Russia and other nations of the world is not to allow for the 21st century to become the American century."[14]

Civilizationist ideas were not principally different from those advanced during the Gorbachev era, and at the time they were not particularly attractive to the elites or the broader society. The mainstream political class typically viewed these ideas as dangerous and too extravagant to be implemented. The general public, too, had little faith in the imperialist policies. National Communists and Eurasianists therefore remained relatively marginalized in the Russian discourse.

Social Democrats

Social Democrats were the former supporters of Gorbachev; they occupied the Westernist part of the foreign policy spectrum during the Soviet era. This group supported the elements of international openness and cooperation present in Kozyrev's thinking, but criticized his excessively pro-Western orientation and isolationism in relations with the ex-Soviet republics. This isolationism and radical Westernism, Social Democrats argued, was a product of sectarian thinking that had underlaid the breakup of the Soviet Union and had no regard for popular opinion or aspirations to preserve the union.[15]

Following the earlier line of Gorbachev's arguments, Social Democrats advanced a vision of the emerging international system that was liberal, and yet very different from Kozyrev's liberalism. They insisted that in constructing Russia's national interest, it was important to identify and creatively follow some preestablished historical values, rather than to passively absorb values and institutions of the West. Social Democrats recommended that Russia actively participate in building a new international order, but they condemned any attempts to shape the world in accordance with a particular culture's standards. In addition, they argued that it was the relations with the whole world, not the West alone, that were of key significance.[16]

Despite the significance of the Social Democrats' critique, their public visibility in debates on Russia's foreign policy was low. Closely associated with Gorbachev, this group was yet to recover from the devastating blow of the Soviet breakup. As Kozyrev's foreign policy began to unravel, the vacuum of ideas emerged and was soon filled by revived Statist thinking.

The Revival of Statist Thinking

As the proposed vision of radical reform and strategic partnership with the West was failing to bring any visible improvements in people's living standards, the population was becoming disillusioned and skeptical. At home, Russians experienced a drastic decline of living standards. Externally, the prospects of NATO expansion toward Russia's borders and military conflicts in the Russian periphery created a sense of insecurity undermining the Westernist foreign policy course. The disintegration of the Soviet Union added to the change in attitude; socialized in the tradition of the Soviet Statist thinking, many Russians felt that economic failures were now exacerbated by the significant loss of territory and world status. The grand strategy of Integration with the West was increasingly perceived as a flawed one. According to one poll, public support for the United States model of society fell from 32 percent in 1990 to 13 percent in 1992, or by more than two-thirds. A similar trend was observed with regard to Russian popular opinion about Japanese and German models of society.[17] The biggest demonstration of declining support for Yeltsin and Kozyrev's policies came during the December 1993 parliamentary elections when liberal parties lost to those of nationalist orientation.

The official Westernist course faced growing resistance, yet Westernizers came across as defensive and unable to offer any new ideas. Many continued to insist on economic and political modernization as the country's only national interest without attempting to address the new fears of insecurity, instability, and poverty. Some lost their faith in liberalism and began to gravitate to nationalist political camps. For example, the executive secretary of the parliamentary constitutional commission, Oleg Rumyantsev, and the prominent writer and athlete Yuri Vlasov—both formerly supportive of the liberal agenda—switched to the ranks of the National Communists. Very few liberals were willing to argue the need for the state to be taking on a stronger role in dealing with instabilities at home and abroad.

Under the new geopolitical and economic situation, a number of members of the political class began to advocate a principally different vision of national interest that included a stronger role for the state and revival of Russia's great power status. Influenced by both Westernizers and Civilizationists, Statists positioned themselves to unite supporters of the old and new Russia. Under the leadership of Yevgeni Primakov, at the time heading the Foreign Intelligence Service, the new coalition united many former Soviet industrialists, state bureaucrats, and members of the military and security services. The members of the new coalition had no faith in the West's willingness or ability to integrate Russia. Instead, they believed in the state's role in preserving security and conducting a less painful economic reform. Statists also had in mind a different model of Russia's relationships with the outside world, and the Westernist vision of the country's identity was soon to be defeated. In late 1995, Kozyrev was removed from office and replaced by Primakov, his prominent critic and the father of Russia's new Statism. The next chapter elaborates on the Statist philosophy and foreign policy record.

Table 3.3 summarizes contending views on the Westernist view of national interest.

Statism's Institutional Advantages

In addition to the West's disengagement and Russia's domestic instabilities, the rise of Statism became possible because of various institutional channels available to the school's advocates. The combination of a historically dominant nationalist political culture and low centralized democratic system provided the new Statists with some institutional advantages. Effective use of institutions, such as parliament, media, and influential nongovernmental organizations, helped Statists to promote their vision and undermine that of Kozyrev.

Parliament, or the Supreme Soviet, played a particularly important role in challenging the Westernist course. One of the earliest critics of Kozyrev's foreign policy was the chairman of the Foreign Affairs Committee of the Supreme Soviet, Yevgeni Ambartsumov. A former supporter of Gorbachev and

Table 3.3.   Westernism (Wsm): Contending Views

Social Democrats: Wsm undermines Russia's social democratic potential		Statists: Wsm undermines Russia's statehood
	VS.	
National Communists: Wsm destroys Russia's socialist system		Eurasianists: Wsm eliminates Russia's geopolitical independence

Yeltsin's team, Ambartsumov had been responsible for formulating the concept of enlightened imperialism in the former Soviet region that was later publicized by his associate Andranik Migranyan. The concept defined the entire territory of the former Soviet Union as the sphere of Russia's vital interests by drawing parallels with the early nineteenth-century policy of American special rights in the Western Hemisphere (the Monroe Doctrine).[18] Another prominent critic of Kozyrev was parliamentarian and future ambassador to the United States Vladimir Lukin, who cautioned against the one-sided pro-Western orientation and expressed his support for a more diversified foreign policy.

An influential agency with direct access to Yeltsin was the Primakov-led Foreign Intelligence Service. Throughout 1992–1994, the agency was arguing the need to reconsider Russia's foreign policy priorities and concentrate on the former Soviet area. In contrast to Kozyrev's emphasis of Russia's "natural partnership" with the West, even at the expense of relationships in the former Soviet Union, Primakov saw his role in pointing to economic and security disintegrations in the post-Soviet area and in proposing remedies. One of these reports, "Russia-CIS: Is the West's Position in Need of Adjustment?" had been a direct response to NATO's expansion initiative, and it eventually influenced Yeltsin's own thinking. In late 1995, Primakov replaced Kozyrev as foreign minister and announced that the former Soviet area would become his first priority.

Other important government channels included the Presidential Administration and Security Council. Presidential adviser Sergei Stankevich took issue with Kozyrev since the latter's first attempt to systematically formulate Russia's national interests at the Foreign Ministry conference "The Transformed Russia in the New World" in February 1992. Stankevich promoted the vision of Russia as a cultural bridge between Europe and Asia and insisted that Russia needed to defend the rights of ethnic Russians in the former Soviet republics.[19] The Russian Security Council was yet another governmental body through which Statists were able to challenge the Westernist course. Already in the summer of 1992, representatives of the Foreign, Defense, and Security Ministries united under the Security Council—at that time headed by Yuri Skokov—to challenge Kozyrev's foreign policy vision and to draw up "Guidelines for the Foreign Policy of the Russian Federation." The eventual document prescribed that Russia take its place as a world power, as a bridge between East and West, with specific interests in the "Near Abroad."

Outside the state, several organizations became prominent in advancing the Statist vision. The Council for Foreign and Defense Policy served as the nongovernmental umbrella think tank expressing views of industrialists, businessmen, intellectuals, and mass opinion leaders. The council has consistently advocated Russia's more "Near Abroad"–oriented policies and pragmatism in relationships with the West.[20] The political movement Civic Union consolidated various voices critical of the Westernist policies. Influential individuals, associated with the Civic Union's philosophy, included Vice President Aleksandr Rutskoi, the chief of the Security Council Yuri Skokov, and the speaker of the Supreme Soviet Ruslan Khasbulatov. In January 1993, the Civic Union adopted its own Concept of Russian Foreign Policy, which advocated Russia's national interests defined in terms of achieving a great power status in Eurasia. Civic Union acted from inside the mainstream, gradually changing the balance of power within the political class. The organization sought to reestablish economic ties with the ex-Soviet republics, and operated throughout the entire post-Soviet space. Intellectually, the Civic Union worked closely with the Council for Foreign and Defense Policy, and the two advocated similar philosophies.

The End of Russia's Westernist Momentum

The Westernist course began to lose its momentum toward the end of 1992. The absence of its practical outcomes was all too visible, and the opposition's criticisms were beginning to bite. Kozyrev had to acknowledge the end of the "honeymoon period" in relations with the West.[21] Yeltsin expressed similar feelings by criticizing the United States for its tendency to "dictate its own terms." Echoing Statist sentiments, he declared that Russia's relations with the West "had to be balanced. After all, we are a Eurasian state."[22] The radical Westernist coalition was falling apart, with some of its members joining the ranks of moderate or even radical opposition. The rhetoric and the agenda of the Statists were gaining currency. Geopolitics was quickly becoming the name of the national discourse, and Westernizers could no longer be taken seriously without framing what they had to say in geopolitical terms.

The calculations of Yeltsin and Kozyrev that the West would recognize Russia as its own and provide all the necessary assistance to integrate it into its midst proved to be flawed. Although the Western governments provided some substantial financial aid to Russia and were willing to cooperate on matters of security and arms control (the next section returns to this point), these measures could not meet the existing highly inflated expectations for Western assistance. Trying to rally domestic support around such expectations was unrealistic. Credits and investment were too negligible to buttress the credibility of the liberal Westernist vision, let alone transform Russia's institutions. In the realm of security, the importance of the Russia-favored OSCE declined visibly, and Russia made no progress in getting closer to NATO. Although Russia gained a nominal standing within an expanded G-8, its formal inclusion did not come about until July 1994. In addition, some influential foreign policy experts in the West spoke of "the premature partnership" with Russia,[23] a statement that came as a cold shower to the Yeltsin-Kozyrev team.

Yeltsin and Kozyrev found themselves in a very difficult position. On the one hand, they had already committed their policies to first-priority relations with Western countries and understood the importance of not alienating the West for both tactical and strategic reasons. On the other hand, the Westernist foreign policy course clearly lost its domestic appeal and had to be modified. Some serious concessions to the Statist opposition had to be made.

In response to this new predicament, Russia's leaders attempted to preserve the strategy of integration, while tempering their expectations and casting the course more in terms of shared interests than of cultural values with the West. Abroad, they continued to insist that strategic partnership with Russia remained the best choice for the West because of "a historic opportunity to facilitate the formation of a democratic, open Russian state and the transformation of an unstable, post-confrontational world into a stable and democratic one."[24] At home, the leadership sought to consolidate support among influential elites. It allowed some of the former economic and party *nomenklatura* to privatize the lucrative energy industry, thereby turning them into the wealthiest businessmen with Western trading preferences. It continued to reward loyal members of the media and banking community with government credits, often interest-free. In early 1993, Yeltsin also attended a Civic Union congress, thereby acknowledging the organization's significance. And in late 1994—partly in his bid for support of the army elite—Yeltsin made a decision about military intervention in Chechnya. Kozyrev supported the decision and demonstratively resigned from the parliament's most pro-Western faction, Russia's Choice.

In addition, both Yeltsin and Kozyrev added the geopolitical dimension to their publicly displayed views of national interest. Yeltsin spoke about moving away from a Western emphasis in Russian diplomacy. Kozyrev acknowledged the importance of preserving economic and cultural relationships with the former Soviet states and became more critical of Western policies toward Russia. In early 1994, writing in the *New York Times*, he warned of "the chauvinistic new banners that flap in the Washington wind."

> I must say, sadly, that in these confused days sometimes we are neither understood nor adequately supported by our natural friends and allies in the West. Even at this critical moment in Moscow, when democracy needs all the help it can get, we hear Western threats to reduce economic cooperation with Russia . . . it appears that some Western politicians, in Washington and elsewhere, envision Russia not as an equal partner but as a junior partner. In this view a "good Russian" is always a follower, never a leader.[25]

All these measures, however, were primarily of a tactical and rhetorical nature. The larger society and much of the political class remained dissatisfied and unaffected by the modification of the course. No less importantly, the general public and elites remained mistrustful of the leaders in charge.

3.3. TOWARD INTEGRATION WITH THE WEST

As brief as Russia's Westernist momentum was, Yeltsin and Kozyrev did try to act on their beliefs. This section reviews their policies toward the outside world that demonstrate the depth of their convictions in Western civilization's primacy in the world. Russia's leaders turned their full attention to the West, while remaining neglectful of relationships with the Asian and Middle Eastern regions.

The West as the Savior

Much like Mikhail Gorbachev, Westernizers predicated their entire course on recognition by the West. The new Russia's leaders hoped that the West would provide all the required material and moral support for reform when it saw how committed Russia was to a liberal transformation. At times the Russians sounded dramatic, even desperate, for massive Western material and moral support because they believed that, short of such support, their reforms were doomed to failure. In the absence of the West's quickly throwing its entire weight behind helping Russia, argued the Kremlin officials, a fascist coup was likely to happen. Much like Gorbachev, Yeltsin and Kozyrev fully acknowledged the groundbreaking nature of their relationships with the West, referring to them as a revolution in cooperation among the states of the civilized world. Unlike Gorbachev, however, they wanted to be fully integrated within Western civilization. Whereas Gorbachev wanted to be recognized as a country with distinct values (socialism), the new Russia's leaders equated recognition with integration and loss of their country's distinct identity. Whereas Gorbachev saw diversity and multiple contributions to world development, the new Westernizers recognized only the triumph of one civilization (the West) over the rest of the world. At the time, Russia's leaders made little distinction between North America and Europe, viewing them as firmly united by common values of market economy and political pluralism.[26] It therefore seemed inevitable to sacrifice Russia's historical identity to that of the West, and the leadership saw no tragedy in it. Indeed, losing such identity seemed necessary only if Russia were to be transformed into a Western nation.

There is no reason to doubt the sincerity of Russia's leaders, and any attempts to present them as cynical calculators of material rewards in exchange for rhetorical loyalty to the West would be highly misleading. Their utopian ideological considerations were the primer in shaping Russia's perception of the world. Rational interests came in a distant second and reemerged as a key foreign policy motivation only at a later stage. It is consistent with Westernist ideological beliefs that Russia's leaders were ready to do everything in their power to gain membership in Western international organizations and support the West's agenda in international security affairs.

Striving to Join Western International Organizations

The leaders of the new Russia had very high expectations about joining Western international organizations. In economic affairs, they did not merely expect loans or assistance in debt restructuring and currency stabilization; they wanted a flow of massive Western investments, and they were correct to measure the success of Russia's integration into the world economy by such investments, rather than high-interest loans. For instance, in July 1992 Yeltsin declared at a G-7 summit that a $24 billion package would not save Russia and that foreign direct investment in the amount of several hundred billion dollars was necessary to do the job. Kozyrev, speaking at a Western forum in September 1992, formulated the idea of a new SDI—Strategic Democratic Initiative (a contrast with the old SDI, the Strategic Defense Initiative)—which was to include attracting Western investments to Russia's economy, supporting small and medium-sized businesses, conducting military conversion, and creating favorable conditions for Russia's exports abroad.[27] Most Russian politicians expected a grand bargain with Russia, something comparable to the Marshall Plan or the "500 Days" plan that had been articulated but never implemented during the Gorbachev era. The latter included $100 billion of support over four years for reforming the Soviet Union, alongside an orthodox IMF program.[28]

Such expectations, of course, assumed an unprecedented level of trust in the new Russia by Western leaders and the world business community—a condition that was hardly in place. The West was neither willing nor able to launch something similar to the massive Marshall Plan for postcommunist Russia. All Western nations could offer was to work through the IMF in trying to reform Russia. Germany embarked on the reunification project that soon proved to be extremely costly. The United States—at the time the key supporter of the new Russia—also was going through an economic downturn and was hardly in a position to put all its eggs in the highly uncertain basket of what was once the largest economy of the communist world.

Gaining the required assistance, not surprisingly, proved to be very difficult, and Russia's overall record was mixed at best. In June 1992, Russia was able to join the International Monetary Fund and the World Bank, which it saw as crucial for creating a market economy. By that time, Yeltsin's chief economic reformer, Yegor Gaidar, had already laid out an ambitious program, which had been predicated on the assistance of the IMF, WB, and European Bank of Reconstruction and Development (EBRD). IMF credits were essential for achieving macroeconomic stabilization and balancing the budget, but they did not (and could not) do much to assist Russia with integration into the world economy. Russia also managed to join the G-7 in July 1992, despite the opposition of both British prime minister John Major and German chancellor Helmut Kohl. Yet the membership did not change much in Russia's economic status. Even psychologically, progress was disappointing—Western leaders saw Russia as an aid recipient, not a donor, and did not treat the newcomer as an equal partner (figures on external aid and investment are shown in table 3.4).

The biggest gains resulted from Russia's emphasis on relationships with the United States. First, in the politically charged atmosphere of Russia's high expectations, Bush, supported by Kohl, announced a $24 billion package in April 1992. At the time, Yeltsin faced a particularly strong opposition to his reform at home, as the Congress of People's Deputies revealed the commitments of many to fight privatization and land reform. U.S. president Bill Clinton was even more supportive of Yeltsin, arguing for a global alliance to support democracy and preventing a world "more dangerous in some respects than the dark years of the Cold War." As a result of the new American president's efforts to mobilize the West to support Russia, the Tokyo G-7 summit declared a $43.4 billion program of assistance for Russia.

Aside from that, the progress with either joining Western organizations or mobilizing them to assist Russia in its integration strategy was hardly satisfactory to the Kremlin leadership. With the assistance of the United States, Russia

Table 3.4.   External Aid and Investment: Russia and Other Recipients, 1990–1995

	World Bank Lending Divided by GDP in 1990 (%)	Direct Investment Divided by GDP in 1990 (%)
Hungary	5.1	32.2
Czech Republic	2.0	12.6
Poland	6.6	11.0
Estonia	1.5	8.6
Turkmenistan	0.4	7.7
Kazakhstan	1.4	1.8
Azerbaijan	0.8	1.1
RUSSIA	0.8	0.6

Source: M. Steven Fish, "The Determinants of Economic Reform in the Post-Communist World," *East European Politics and Societies* 12, no. 1 (1998): 38.

reached an agreement with the Paris Club about restructuring the Soviet debt of $70 million for which it had assumed liability. However, it failed to reach such agreement with the London Club. Russia also did not manage to join those clubs, even as an observer, until much later. The reformers' efforts to gain broader access to the EU market were also unsuccessful. Their attempts to dismantle the Coordinating Committee for Multilateral Export Controls (COCOM) restrictions on trade bore fruit, but only in March 1994. In security affairs, Russia invited the peacekeeping forces of the United Nations and the OSCE in Europe to provide security in the former Soviet Union. Kozyrev wanted to rapidly integrate with European security institutions and even stated Russia's desire to gain membership in NATO. However, in dealing with new security challenges, Russia soon discovered the need to rely on its own army. I return to this point later in the chapter.

Supporting the West's International Security Agenda

Until approximately mid-1993, the new Russia's leaders also loyally supported the West's international security agenda. In Europe, Russia was working toward gaining a full membership in all European security institutions, including NATO. Even when NATO announced its plans to expand east, Russia's new rulers initially raised no objections to the process.

Despite traditionally strong ties with Serbia, Russia's leaders also supported the West's agenda in the Balkans. Initially, they avoided even meeting with the leaders of Yugoslavia and sided with the West in condemning the Serbs for atrocities against the Muslims over the independent Bosnian state. In the spring and the summer of 1992, Russia also supported the United Nations' economic sanctions against Yugoslavia and suspension of the country's membership in the OSCE, although Russia's leaders had initially favored negotiations about the punishment of Yugoslavia. Furthermore, Moscow did not object to the United Nations security resolutions authorizing possible use of force against Yugoslavia, and it did not use its veto power when the UN General Assembly voted to expel the country from the United Nations. Later, Yeltsin also supported the Western plan, devised by U.S. secretary of state Cyrus Vance and British foreign secretary David Owen, for a weak confederation in Bosnia-Herzegovina.

The new Russian leaders also shared—even at the cost of the country's traditional ties—the West's arms control agenda. Yeltsin slashed strategic nuclear arsenals by half and also agreed to eliminate all land-based intercontinental ballistic missiles (ICBMs) armed with multiple warheads, while the United States retained such warheads in submarines. The terms of the new agreement, START II, were agreed upon at the June 1992 summit and signed in January

1993. This was an unprecedented move: for the first time in the history of the nuclear arms race, Russia abandoned the heart of its strategic arsenals, while the United States preserved its own. Even Russia's liberal commentators, such as Aleksei Arbatov, criticized the agreement as unbalanced.[29] Yeltsin acknowledged that Russia was sacrificing strategic parity with the United States, but stated that the parity was "ominous" and did not make any sense now that "the fundamental change in the political and economic relations between the United States of America and Russia"[30] had taken place. Until September 1993, Yeltsin also did not see the need to revise the Conventional Forces in Europe (CFE) treaty, which restricted the internal distribution of forces in Russia and gained strong opposition from the military establishment.

In its efforts to rapidly integrate with the West, Russia forfeited billions of dollars in arms sales by abandoning lucrative markets in the third world and supporting Western sanctions against Libya, Iraq, and Yugoslavia. On Iraq, Kozyrev even supported U.S. bombing, as well as UN sanctions. This policy stance began to change only in 1993 under the pressures of those arguing that Russia could not afford to lose Iraq's $7 billion debt to it. Kozyrev also went along with the United States' attempts to restrict Russia's military ties with China, Iran, and India. In the meantime, while Russia was going out of its way to persuade the West that it had been sincere in its integration drive, the West continued to play power politics and did not seem to care to reciprocate. In the arms markets, as the liberal *Izvestiya* noted, whereas Russia's share from 1991 to 1993 dropped from 38 to 17 percent, the U.S. share increased from 30 to 58 percent.[31]

The Neglect of Asia and the Muslim World

Russia's new Westernism had a clear zero-sum component, which was particularly visible in the attitude toward Asia and the Middle East. More partnership with the West meant less of a relationship with the non-Western regions. In the highly ideological mind-set of Kozyrev's team, the East was associated with "backwardness" and "authoritarianism" rather than the "prosperity" and "democracy" of the Western "civilized nations." Again, the identity argument was made: Russia had been too Asiatic already, and it was now time to move away "from its Asian roots of oriental despotism and toward the Western democratic camp."[32] Many in the Westernist camp believed that the non-Western systems, such as China and the Middle Eastern countries, would soon follow the Soviet and Eastern European example and collapse precisely because these systems were "nondemocratic." China was especially despised because of the Tiananmen massacre of Chinese democrats in 1989 and Beijing's support of the anti-Gorbachev coup in Moscow in August 1991.

Russia's relations with China are a clear example of the new leadership's passivity on the eastern direction. Although Gorbachev laid out preconditions for improving relations with China by signing two important joint communiqués and the border treaty, the progress in the relationship of the two sides was stalled by their growing ideological differences. In February 1992, the border treaty was ratified by Russia's Supreme Soviet, but Yeltsin and Kozyrev remained wary of China as anti-Western and critical of Russia's democratic development. The relationships were on hold until late 1992. Russia's leaders and politicians were avoiding even meeting Chinese officials. In March 1992, Kozyrev traveled to China in an attempt to stimulate economic cooperation between the two. However, the trip lasted only thirty hours, and the two sides disagreed on human rights issues by officially concluding that in Russia-China ties, "elements of considerable agreement coexist with different approaches to some quite significant questions."[33]

A similar pattern could be observed in Russia's relations with the Muslim world. Russia's leaders were initially dismissive of the region's significance. Yeltsin ordered the withdrawal of the CIS troops from Nagorno-Karabakh in the Caucasus and simultaneously asked for the deployment of NATO troops as a peacekeeping force there. Despite the growing instability in Afghanistan and central Asia, he also refrained from any serious involvement in the region, leaving the stage to Iran and Turkey. In April 1992 after the mujahideen takeover of Kabul, Kozyrev visited Afghanistan, but that visit, too, was a goodwill gesture more than an effort to develop the mutual relationship. Despite various complaints from the domestic opposition, Russia's officials had no problems with the increased activism of the United States in the region, evident, for instance, in the February 1992 visit of Secretary of State James Baker to central Asia.

Finally, Russia was slow to recognize the role of India and Korea in its foreign policy. Russia's Westernism meant a reduction of Russia-India trade, particularly in the military area. In the Korean Peninsula, Yeltsin and Kozyrev pursued the one-sided policy of favoring the South over the North. In 1992, both Russian leaders proposed signing a treaty of friendship with South Korea to cement their relationship, despite the assessments of Korea specialists that Russia's interests required balanced relations with the two. The ideological dichotomy between the "civilized" pro-Western South and the "barbaric" Stalinist North severely weakened the link to the North, while the anticipated economic benefits of a Moscow-Seoul relationship were not forthcoming. In June 1993, the North announced its first withdrawal from the Nuclear Non-Proliferation Treaty, and Moscow responded by supporting the United States–sponsored sanctions against North Korea.

The Westernizers insisted that the relationships with the "barbaric" East were to be limited to those of issues of national security. When in March 1992 leading Statist Sergei Stankevich proposed that Russia reactivate its relations with the Muslim world, Kozyrev replied negatively. The foreign minister denied that Russia had any specific interests in Asia aside from those of maintaining security and even those had to be addressed within the Western institutional framework. He singled out the need to put joint pressure on North Korea to relinquish its ambitious nuclear program. Later, when the Statist pressures on Kozyrev to view Russia as a "great power" in Eurasia had increased, he reframed his pro-American argument by linking Eurasia to the United States. Writing in *International Affairs* in early 1993, he asserted that Russia's Eurasian location is part of its status: "Anyone who looks at the map will see that the United States is our next-door neighbor in the East." To stress his point, Kozyrev added: "In the East, not the West."[34]

The Yeltsin-Kozyrev Course Backfires

The Yeltsin-Kozyrev course could not be sustained and began to backfire already in late 1992. The IMF-recommended "shock therapy" was introduced in January 1992 and led to severe economic hardship for ordinary people. Political opposition to reform had emerged and become vocal. The general population was disillusioned with Western aid and disappointed in Yeltsin's overall reform design. Instead of gaining support at home, the reformers' strategy of integrating with the West resulted in public resentment toward the Western Other. A late 1993 poll showed, for example, that two-thirds of Russians were convinced that the West's economic advice represented a deliberate effort to weaken Russia[35]—precisely the message the hard-line opposition to reformers meant to convey to the larger society. In such a context opposition, particularly that of the Statists and conservative Civilizationists, was increasingly successful in challenging the Westernist foreign policies.

The first wake-up call came when Yeltsin had to cancel his trip to Japan to settle the old territorial dispute over the Kuril Islands. To Russia's leaders, Japan was a part of the West and therefore deserved the appropriate attention. The initial strategy was to embrace the 1956 Soviet-Japanese agreement as the basis for regulating the issue and return two of the four northern islands, seized by Stalin at the close of World War II, to Japan. Yeltsin's visit was planned for September, yet—in a stunning reversal—he canceled the trip scheduled to begin four days later. The argument about returning the islands provoked immediate negative reaction from Russia's parliament and the military-security lobby. The Supreme Soviet held a special hearing, and the Ministry of Defense openly insisted that the geostrategic interests dictated against any military withdrawals from the Kurils. This was a serious blow to Russia's course that revealed that it had major limitations.

Yeltsin-Kozyrev's Balkan policy also came under heavy attack. The former Supreme Soviet emerged as especially active in criticizing the official policy toward the Balkans and even engaged in its own shuttle diplomacy with Belgrade. In December 1992, the Supreme Soviet passed a resolution calling for sanctions on all the warring sides and demanding that Russia use its veto in case of UN consideration of military intervention in the region. As a result of those pressures, Russia first abstained from a UN vote on additional sanctions against Yugoslavia and then refused to send its blue helmet troops from Croatia into Sarajevo to help police a UN-brokered military agreement. The opposition's pressures on Russia's foreign policy in the Balkans further intensified in 1994 when NATO launched air strikes against the Bosnian Serbs.

In this increasingly politicized context, NATO made a decision to expand eastward by incorporating members of the former Soviet bloc in Eastern Europe. The decision provided domestic nationalist opposition with additional arguments and resources to mobilize against the Westernist course. If the West wanted to expand its military alliance without planning to include Russia in it, this could have been and was interpreted by the opposition as a threat. Military and security services were especially active in arguing this position. Yevgeni Primakov, then director of Russia's Foreign Intelligence Service, issued a sharp criticism of the expansion, referring to the historical memory of Cold War hostilities and warning that it would result in a new isolation of Russia. The military responded by adopting in November 1993 a new doctrine, which now proclaimed Russia's immediate periphery the area of its geopolitical interests and most vital concerns. Russia's military, military industrialists, and security services also opposed concessions to the West in arms reductions and sales.

In mid-1993, largely in response to growing domestic criticism, the attitude of Russia's leaders began to change. The devastating December elections made it painfully clear that the sought-after Integration with the West was not meant to happen and that Westernizers needed to adjust to new realities. The elections brought many anti-Western forces into the parliament, partly the result of the state's uncompromisingly pro-Western policies. The victory of Vladimir Zhirinovski's extreme nationalist party reflected in part state neglect of the army and its needs. In response, Kozyrev spoke of a serious correction of his course. Immediately after the December elections, he announced changes in Russia's foreign policy according to the voters' preferences. Kozyrev proclaimed that these changes would include declaring the former Soviet region the sphere of Russia's vital interests, and the continuation of a military presence in regions where Russia had traditionally been dominant. Russia's leaders also refused to cooperate with NATO. Furthermore, faced with hardline opposition at home, they had to reject the offer to join the Partnership for

Peace program, which was designed to preserve cooperative military ties with the alliance.

The proclaimed change hardly meant the strategic reappraisal of the foreign policy course. Rather, it should be understood as a series of tactical concessions that reflected the changing balance of domestic power. Statists, such as presidential adviser Sergei Stankevich and Russia's ambassador to Washington, Vladimir Lukin, had formulated a "Eurasian" alternative to Kozyrev's "Atlanticist" foreign policy, and the overall pressures on the official course were considerable. The opposition pressed for more active policies toward Asia and the Middle East. By that time, Yeltsin had visited China in December 1992 and recovered some of the lost trade between the two countries. Kozyrev, too, had explicitly acknowledged the need for Russia to boost its foreign policy activities in China, India, and the East in general. None of these corrections, however, proceeded from principal reevaluation of the strategic beliefs that had underlain the Westernist course.

3.4. ISOLATIONISM IN THE FORMER SOVIET REGION

Yeltsin-Kozyrev's isolationism toward the former Soviet republics was an extension of their radical Westernist beliefs. Eager to integrate with the West, the new leaders had no time to wait for the republics to pursue similar policies. Nor did they feel responsible for assisting their neigbors in their transformation. Russia had to go West alone and, in order to overcome potential resistance from the ex-leaders of the republics, it had to erect nationalist economic, political, and security barriers against the former Soviet nations.

The Isolationist Thinking

Westernizers justified the isolationist course on economic, political, and cultural grounds. Economically, they argued, Russia had been turned into an "internal colony" of the Soviet Union and, as a result, suffered from being a core of the Soviet empire even more than all other republics. As the largest and the wealthiest nation in the region, Russia had to subsidize the republics, instead of selling its raw materials, such as oil and natural gas, at the world market's prices. Were Russia to continue to serve as an economic locomotive, the argument went, it would have become the first victim of such generosity. The roots of this argument can be traced to Gorbachev's era when Yeltsin's umbrella organization, Democratic Russia, presented itself as an anti-imperial movement by emphasizing the autonomy of Russia and other republics and even openly calling for the dissolution of the Soviet Union. The Soviet Union was presented as an "empire" that was to be dismantled for the sake of Russian prosperity. Throughout the political campaigns of 1990 and 1991, Yeltsin had advanced the "Russia-victim" argument, and it was his advisers who eventually wrote a scenario for dissolving the union. Ironically, the argument was borrowed from Russian anti-Western nationalists, who often complained about the Russian burden of providing for the rest of the union (although they never wanted to break up the union).

Furthermore, the post-Soviet Westernizers believed that during the Soviet era Russia also suffered politically and culturally, and it should now rebuild its identity in nonimperial or "civic" terms. Valeri Tishkov, the director of the Institute of Ethnology and Anthropology and the minister for nationalities in 1992, had provided the intellectual justification and first put forward the concept of a civic nation publicly in 1989. The central thrust of viewing Russia as a civic nation was its deethnification, or the removal of the categories of ethnicity and religion from the identity-building project. Tishkov argued that Russia should form a civic Russian (*rossiyskaya*) nation, or a community of all citizens of the Russian Federation regardless of their cultural and religious differences, rather than any form of ethnic Russian (*russkaya*) nation. Domestically, the new vision categorized Russia within its current post-Soviet borders as a political nation, and one of "co-citizenship."[36] Externally, it meant to relieve the new Russia of responsibility for the Soviet policies and their historical legacies in the region. In particular, Russia was not to be responsible for the well-being of twenty-five to thirty million ethnic Russians—about 30 percent of the homeland Russians—who resided in the former Soviet republics outside Russia.

The liberal foreign policy community supported the isolationist component in the country's national interest. For instance, one prominent report of the Foreign Ministry's Institute of International Relations warned against Russia's assuming the role of a new core in the Commonwealth of Independent States. It insisted that Russia's key interest was in entering the G-7 as a full-fledged participant, thereby moving from the periphery of the world economy to its core. The ambition of becoming the CIS's center would make it impossible to meet that key interest and therefore Russia had to be prepared to "give up the CIS in favor of orientation toward Europe."[37]

Political and Security Isolationism

Politically, Russia's isolationism aimed at separating from the ex-Soviet republics institutionally. Yeltsin and Kozyrev concentrated on strengthening sovereignty and independence from the former Soviet region and its transnational institutional umbrella, the CIS. The organization emerged to do away with the

Soviet Union and initially—before it included all ex-republics except the Baltic ones—had had only Russia, Ukraine, and Belarus as members. Yeltsin, who had proposed the CIS mainly in order to defeat his political opponent Gorbachev, never meant for the organization to facilitate cooperation and interdependence in the region. Rather, he wanted it to complete the ex-Soviet republics' political and economic separation, and that vision permeated the organization's founding agreements and subsequent seminal documents, such as the CIS charter. In its practical policy, Russia preferred to deal with its neighbors on a bilateral, rather than multilateral, basis. It was also far from active in relations with the states of the region. Despite Kozyrev's rhetoric about the priority of the CIS in Russia's foreign policy, his first trips were to Western Europe, North America, and other regions of the world. Apart from a quick visit to Estonia, he first traveled to the former Soviet region only in April 1992. By July of the same year, Russia opened only one embassy in the region, in Kiev. Moscow assumed that, even if some of the former states were to eventually gravitate toward Russia, this would happen much later and on a market basis. That attitude began to change in 1993 when Russia initiated the CIS Economic Union agreement, which was supposed to develop a multilateral economic cooperation.

In security matters, Russia's isolationist policies reflected the desire to reduce to a minimum responsibility for maintaining order in the former Soviet region. The Russian analyst Alexander Pikayev captured four specific goals that the Kremlin sought to accomplish: the fastest possible withdrawal of Russian troops from outside Russia; tacit support of the control introduced by governments in the former Soviet republics on the former Soviet troops; ignoring separatist tendencies within individual CIS states and maintaining relations with the central governments; and inviting foreign participation in settling conflicts in the post-Soviet region.[38]

Russia's officials tried to accomplish those goals until approximately mid-1992. Yeltsin ordered the withdrawal of troops from Nagorno-Karabakh, while simultaneously asking for the deployment of NATO troops as a peacekeeping force there. When Chechnya proclaimed independence in November 1991, he ruled out military intervention as a policy option. Yeltsin also did not initially oppose Ukraine's, the largest CIS state outside Russia, taking control over the former Soviet troops located on the republic's territory. Furthermore, by establishing Russia's Ministry of Defense in April 1992, Yeltsin indicated his unwillingness to maintain the collective status of the former Soviet Armed Forces, which had been favored by the central Asian leaders. A signatory of the CIS collective security treaty (May 1992), Russia did little to activate the treaty, and over the year, it continued to seriously discuss the possibility of deploying the UN or NATO peacekeeping troops in the areas of ethnic conflict. Nor did it show serious concern over the status of ethnic Russians in the former Soviet states.

The leadership's position showed signs of change only when military conflicts in various parts of the former Soviet Union had threatened to spill over to Russia. The first challenge came from Moldova in the spring of 1992. The intention of Moldova's leadership to reunite with Romania had provoked violent secessionism in the Transdniester area, which gravitated to Russia economically and culturally. Moldova's efforts to involve the OSCE had failed to produce any results in a timely manner, and Russia intervened to stop widespread fighting. It put the fourteenth former Soviet division under its control, negotiated a cease-fire, and took on the task of maintaining peace in the region. Kozyrev at first condemned the army involvement and rejected the opportunity to establish ties with the separatist Transdniester leaders. By late June, however, even he favored an intervention and deployment of Russia's military forces. This proved critical for preventing a further spread of violence and civil war in Moldova. It also established the precedent for further interventions in Tajikistan, Georgia, and elsewhere.

Economic Isolationism

In economic matters, Russia planned no coordination with the former republics. In the aftermath of the failed coup of August 1991, Yeltsin first formulated the idea of Russia's going it alone as a matter of economic strategy. In his speech to the Russian Congress of People's Deputies, he committed himself to the strategy of shock therapy—or freeing up all prices by the end of the year, rapid privatization of both industry and land, large reductions in state spending, and a tough monetary policy. He argued that Russia must go first and that, by so doing, it would provide an example for other republics.[39] Yeltsin shared the widely held liberal convictions that the republics were nothing but a "burden (*girya*) on the Russian legs," and that Russia had little choice but to "break away" (*uiti v otryv*) from the former Soviet Union.

Acting on those convictions, Russia reformed its currency by unilaterally withdrawing from the ruble zone. In July 1993, it stopped money supplies to the ex-republics and withdrew old Soviet/Russian ruble notes from circulation on its territory. Russia had earlier pledged to consult with the republics in matters of economic policy, which had been written in the CIS founding principles in the Minsk agreement of December 1991. Yet, despite those obligations, it chose to proceed with the currency reform, as well as price deregulation, which immediately created a crisis for the republics relying on the ruble in their transactions. In addition, Russia began erecting trade barriers as soon as the Soviet Union fell apart, and maintained them at a relatively high level even after most-favored-nation and free-trade agreements with the republics were concluded. In part, those policies responded to relative trade disadvantages for Russia, since it had continued to export goods to the republics at prices considerably below those of the world market. Such policies also reflected Russian dissatisfaction with the state of payments by a number of republics in the aftermath of the Soviet disintegration. Both considerations further reinforced the leadership's belief that economic isolationism from the cash-stripped republics and extensive ties with the West would serve Russia's national interest best.

Cultural Isolationism

Finally, Russia acted on some of its cultural isolationist beliefs. Until 1993, the government subscribed to the civic identity policies, as outlined by Minister of Nationalities Tishkov. Tishkov argued for understanding nationality as citizenship; for abolishing the principle of ethnic autonomies; and for giving priority to individual, rather than collective, rights. In November 1991, the government confirmed its commitment to the civic identity project by adopting the citizenship law. The law recognized all those living on the territory of the Russian Federation as citizens, regardless of their ethnic characteristics, and called a citizen of the Russian Federation *rossiyanin* (defined in civic terms), not *russki* (ethnic Russian). In foreign relations the government denied any responsibility for ethnic Russians outside territorial Russia. Although Yeltsin had made some statements about the need to defend "our compatriots abroad," Kozyrev argued until the autumn of 1992 that ethnic Russians outside Russia did not constitute a special problem for the Russian government.

Many of Tishkov's principles were never implemented, however. The citizenship law was not fully consistent with the new vision of civic identity, as it allowed all citizens of the Soviet Union outside Russia to obtain Russian citizenship by a simple process of registration. The government never issued new nonethnic passports to all citizens of Russia. Nor did it ever redivide the country's regions along nonethnic principles or try to legally ban Russia's ethnically based parties.

The Opposition Challenges the Isolationist Course

The isolationist course found a formidable opposition. Partly as a result of new institutional channels that had become available under the new political system, Statists and conservative Civilizationists grew stronger over time. With the collapse of the communist authority structure, various agencies could more readily assert themselves.

Former Soviet managers and military industrialists with strong regional ties were the prime force opposing the government's economic isolationist policies. United by the Civic Union, they linked the isolationist course to disastrous outcomes, arguing for joint solutions and integration within the former Soviet region. Civic Union and its Russian heir, the Union of Industrialists and Entrepreneurs, consolidated ties with trade unions and established branches throughout the entire post-Soviet space. It was impossible to ignore these groups' arguments because of collapsing economies in all the successor states. In the two years after 1991, all of these states experienced negative economic growth rates and a breakdown of their trade, production, labor, and energy ties. The non-Russian republics were hit particularly hard. Their trade structure was developed exclusively out of demands of the former Soviet "single economic complex," and they were forced to trade primarily with Russia and one another, rather than with countries outside the Soviet borders. The share of interrepublic trade comprised up to 85–90 percent of the republics' total trade. Furthermore, their industrial structure did not favor the establishment of full-fledged economies: some were primary-resource suppliers, while others specialized in manufacturing. Many were asymmetrically dependent on Russia's market, fuel, and supplies, and this dependence further complicated the task of creating independent economies. A number of the republics—such as Armenia, Belarus, Kazakhstan, Kyrgyzstan, and Tajikistan—were especially critical of Russia's isolationism. Russia, too, was hit hard, and its economy contracted severely (see table 3.5).

The army grew especially prominent in opposing the Kremlin's security policies. Responding to growing pressures of instability in the post-Soviet area, some military branches openly challenged civilian authorities. Moldova is a case in point. When in May 1992 Yeltsin publicly announced the upcoming withdrawal of the Fourteenth Army, the defense minister, General Pavel Grachev, immediately corrected him, saying that the division could leave only after the conflict in the area had been defused. When in June of the same year Yeltsin had appointed General Lebed to command the Fourteenth Army as a neutral peacekeeping force, Lebed did not hide that he saw his mandate differently. He likened Moldova's officials to "fascists" and defended ethnic Russians in the area. Within the political class, the position of defending Russians in the entire former Soviet region was strongly reinforced in both parliament and the executive branch. Parliament's International Affairs Committee, chaired by Yevgeni Ambartsumov and Vice President Aleksandr Rutskoi, was particularly vocal.

The larger population, too, opposed the isolationist policies. Ethnic autonomies resisted the civic nation project out of fear of losing their own identities. Many Russians also could not accept Russia's new national identity and continued to favor the preservation of strong cultural ties across the former Soviet

Table 3.5.   Post-Soviet Economic Decline: Russia Relative to Other Ex-Republics

	GNP Growth Over Previous Year				
	1990	1991	1992	1993	1994
Armenia	−7	−11	−52	−15	5
Azerbaijan	−12	−1	−23	−23	−22
Belarus	−3	−1	−10	−12	−22
Estonia	−8	−11	−14	−7	6
Georgia	−12	−14	−40	−39	−35
Latvia	3	−8	−35	−15	2
Lithuania	−5	−13	−38	−24	2
Moldova	−2	−12	−29	−9	2
Kazakhstan	0	−13	−13	−12	−25
Kyrgyzstan	3	−5	−25	−16	−27
RUSSIA	−4	−13	−19	−12	−15
Tajikistan	−2	−7	−29	−11	−21
Turkmenistan	2	−5	−5	−10	−20
Ukraine	−3	−12	−17	−17	−23
Uzbekistan	2	−1	−11	−2	−3

Source: Bert Van Selm, *The Economics of the Soviet Break-up* (London: Routledge, 1997), 25.

region. Polls indicated that most Russians supported voluntary reunification of the ex–Soviet republics with Russia.[40] A powerful identification of many Russians outside Russia with their homeland, and vice versa, emboldened conservative Civilizationist thinking and organizations, such as the Congress of Russian Communities, to speak on the Civilizationists' behalf. Kozyrev attempted to protest against the growing influence of the military and nationalists on foreign policy, but without much effect. Yeltsin and Kozyrev therefore saw their agenda being taken away by the military, the Ministry of Defense, and conservative members of the political class.

Table 3.6 summarizes various dependencies and interdependencies between Russia and other former republics.

The Leadership Signals Change

All these developments made Yeltsin and Kozyrev depart from their initial isolationism and proclaim, at least rhetorically, their understanding of the priority relations with the ex-Soviet republics. The new emphasis was also explicitly acknowledged in the official Foreign Policy Concept of the Russian Federation, which was adopted in 1993. In response to pressures from the Statists, the officials spoke about Russia's "special responsibility" in the former

Table 3.6. Russia and the Ex-Republics: Economic, Military, and Cultural Dependencies

	Share of Russia in a Republic's Trade in 1987	Russian Interrepublican Trade (% of Foreign Trade in 1990)	Ethnic Military Bases and Troops, 1993	Fluency in Russian by Titular	
				Russians (% of Population in 1989)	Nationality (% of Population in 1989)
Armenia	49.7	90	5,000	1.6	44.3
Azerbaijan	52.7	88		5.6	31.7
Belarus	62.6	87	30,000	13.2	60.4
Estonia	58.3	92	5,000	30.3	33.6
Georgia	55.5	86	20,000	6.3	31.8
Latvia	53.5	89	18,000	33.9	65.7
Lithuania	64.9	90		9.4	37.4
Moldova	50.0	88	8,000	12.9	53.3
Kazakhstan	64.4	89		37.8	62.9
Kyrgyzstan	48.2	86		21.5	36.9
RUSSIA	—	61			
Tajikistan	45.0	87	23,000	7.6	30.0
Turkmenistan	45.2	93		9.5	27.6
Ukraine	72.9	82		22.1	59.5
Uzbekistan	51.4	89		8.4	22.2

Sources: Michael Bradshaw, *The Economic Effects of Soviet Dissolution* (London: Royal Institute of International Affairs, 1993), 27; Constantine Michalopoulos and David Tarr, *Trade and Payments Arrangements for States of the Former USSR* (Washington, DC: World Bank, 1992); *New York Times*, November 30, 1993, A12; Graham Smith, *Post-Soviet States* (London: Arnold, 1999), 36.

Soviet Union. In June 1993, Yeltsin told a group of military officers that Russia must maintain and formalize its military presence in Moldova, Georgia, Armenia, and central Asia. Kozyrev echoed these sentiments by emphasizing the former Soviet region as a "zone of special responsibility and special interest."[41] The concept of involving international institutions, such as the OSCE or NATO, in solving conflicts in the region was also receding into the past. Convinced that Russia's troops would be most effective in maintaining security, Moscow also asked the UN to grant Russia special peacekeeping power in the region. In addition, Moscow no longer seemed to be as eager to predicate its policies upon the West's recognition. This was the case even once the champion of Westernist thinking, Kozyrev, complained about Western claims of Russian neoimperialism in the former Soviet region and insisted that Russia would not listen to the West's "lectures."[42]

The reevaluation of rhetorical policy had been completed in early 1994, when the foreign minister announced the need to follow the preferences of the voters after the nationalist victory in the December elections. The emphasis on the civic nation identity stance had changed, with Tishkov's resigning and the government's proclaiming its commitment to promoting dual citizenship in the former Soviet region. It looked as if the leadership indeed learned its lessons from the Statist coalition. Some of the former opponents, such as the parliamentarian Ambartsumov, even conceded that Kozyrev's approach had changed sufficiently to make him retract his call for the minister's resignation.[43]

3.5. ASSESSMENT

The new foreign policy project of Integration with the West proved to be a flawed one and was soon defeated by the opposing Statist coalition. The Statists acknowledged the need to cooperate with the West in creating a market economy and viable democratic institutions, but insisted that those goals should be subjected to the objective of strengthening Russia's great power status. Several developments assisted the Statists in defeating the Westernizers. First, the West itself did not satisfy Yeltsin's and Kozyrev's expectations when it treated Russia more as a dependent client than as a full participant in a coalition of Western nations. By not extending to Russia's leadership the sought-after recognition, the West contributed to the already growing feelings of public alienation from the new Westernist course. Second, the Russian domestic context greatly favored the revival of Statist thinking. The political culture was supportive of independent state and great power status, and new threats both inside (Chechnya, growing crime, and sharp decline of living standards) and outside the country (military conflicts in the periphery) created the environment permissive to the rise of Statist opposition. In challenging the Westernizers, the Statists also successfully exploited some cultural affinities of ethnic Russians, as well as institutional channels available in the new political system.

The departure during the second half of 1993 of Russia's leaders from their initially pro-Western foreign policy should not be understood as if their entire course was a calculation of strategic benefits. Nor does it mean, as some Western observers argue, that Russia had in mind to use the West in order to restore its weakened power capabilities and to rebuild its empire.[44] To argue this is to confuse the post-1993 tactical concessions and politically driven opportunism of Russia's leaders with their strategic beliefs. It is also to ascribe one's own realist viewpoint to policymakers, who made sense of the world in liberal categories of cooperation and integration. Russia's genuine beliefs had been revealed in these leaders' pre-1993 actions, and these beliefs unmistakably betray radical Westernism and liberal institutionalism. After 1993, these beliefs were modified in response to opposition pressures, but this modification must not be equated with full acceptance of Statist or Civilizationist beliefs.

This section provides a more detailed analysis of the Westernizers' foreign policy record and summarizes lessons of their defeat.

The Record

The policy of Integration with the West was supposed to finally achieve Western recognition, by which Russia's new leaders meant full moral, political, and material support for their country as a new pro-Western democracy that broke away from anti-Western totalitarianism. Their highly inflated expectations were born in the political struggle with Gorbachev, who they believed was much too conservative to achieve the "true" recognition of the West. Since the West was skeptical of Gorbachev's socialist reform design, Russian Westernizers assumed it to be on their side and in full accord with their pro-Western policy course. Once arriving in power, they went as far as possible in proclaiming the convergence of Russia's interests and identity with those of the West. Their new concept of national interest, which emphasized rapid economic and political modernization, was designed to attract Western assistance and to prove that Russia was indeed a part of the West. The concept and the policy based on it proved to be a failure if we are to judge them by the earlier-specified criteria of security, welfare, autonomy, and identity. Too many eggs were put in one basket. Too many important national priorities were sacrificed in order to acquire the recognition of Western leaders, who were interested mainly in preventing a re-emergence of Russia as a security threat.

Table 3.7 summarizes the record of Westernism.

Russia's Westernizers could hardly take credit for removing the external threat of the West as a result of their pro-Western foreign policy. By the time they as-

Table 3.7.   The Record of Westernist Course

Security	New threats in Moldova, Central Asia, and Caucasus
Welfare	Macroeconomic stabilization
	New poverty and collapsed social services
	Industrial stagnation
Autonomy	Dependence on Western lending agenies
	Dependence on Western security policies
Identity	Hurt Russian pride

sumed power, such a threat had already been eliminated thanks to Gorbachev's efforts. However, new security threats reemerged in the former Soviet region in the form of military conflicts in Moldova, central Asia (Tajikistan), and the Caucasus (Georgia and Chechnya), and Russia's leaders did little to preempt those threats or to react to them in a timely fashion. They acted under pressures of opposition, which had little trust in the West as the ultimate peacemaker in the region or as the central object of Russia's foreign policy.

Nor could Westernizers convincingly defend their foreign policy record in social and economic welfare. Their hopes that a proclaimed commitment to Western values and shock therapy, as the strategy of marketization, would bring sufficient private investments and assistance to quickly revive the economy, did not materialize. The heavy reliance on IMF and World Bank loans only allowed Russia to stabilize the economy in macroeconomic terms. However, the old economic structure remained in place, and the state did little to conduct an institutional reform or to assist former Soviet managers and workers in their difficult transition to a capitalist type of economy. High interest rates for repaying the borrowed money, collapsed social services, skyrocketed poverty, and stagnation in most economic sectors were the price of the shock therapy the Westernizers used as a method of bringing Russia into the family of rich Western nations. In the meantime, Western investments remained scarce. The radical policies alienated a considerable portion of the elites and the general public, and many Russians developed resentment toward Western nations, particularly the United States. For instance, during 1993–1995, the number of those viewing the United States as a threat increased from 26 to 44 percent among the general public and from 27 to 53 percent among elites.[45]

In addition, Russia developed a considerable dependency on Western lending agencies, with negative implications for its policy autonomy. The opposition charged that Russia's foreign policies were being made in Washington, and the public was increasingly believing that Russia was indeed ceding its autonomy to the West in economic and other affairs. In 1995, 44 percent of the elites and 75 percent of the population believed that the economy was essentially in foreign hands.[46] Additionally, the number of those viewing the West as seeking to weaken Russia also increased. The increased dependency on the West in economic affairs went hand in hand with a loss of autonomy in security affairs, as Washington was often dictating Moscow's foreign policy in such critical areas as the Balkans and Iraq. In the meantime, Russia was losing its traditional allies in Asia and the Middle East.

All these developments further exacerbated the sense of Russian hurt pride and identity. The pro-Western foreign policy course did little to address those feelings. Accompanied by failures to protect the nation's security, welfare, and policy autonomy, this course in fact deepened the sense of cultural loneliness among Russians. Confronted with a considerable loss of territory after the Soviet disintegration and NATO's decision to expand east, Russia was bound to seriously rethink the assumptions of its pro-Western foreign policy.

Lessons of the Failed Course

Much like Gorbachev's New Thinking, Yeltsin and Kozyrev's Integration with the West failed as a foreign policy course. Yet the lessons one can learn from its failure are somewhat different from those of the New Thinking failure.

First, much like Gorbachev's New Thinking course, the post-Soviet Westernism divorced itself from domestic and international power considerations and could not be successful in the face of the growing opposition from both Statists and conservative Civilizationists. However, Westernizers went much further in neglecting potential opposition to their course. Unlike Gorbachev, who had first emerged as a consensus builder with some support secured among military and party officials, Yeltsin and Kozyrev did little to reform the country "from the middle." Instead, their strategy was to seize the moment and impose their vision on the rest of the society, while it was not yet mobilized to respond.

Second, unlike Gorbachev, who had offered his country a culturally distinct perspective and an opportunity to reformulate its sense of national pride, the new Russia's leaders were astonishingly unimaginative in their vision of national identity. Ultimately, what were the odds that a country with centuries-old distinct economic, political, and cultural experiences would be satisfied merely with a status of a "part of the West"? The kind of Western recognition Russia's Westernizers sought was impossible to obtain, and it was naïve to predicate a foreign policy course on such recognition, often at the expense of national history and traditions. At the time when Russian society was desperately searching for self-defintion after the end of the Soviet system, Westernizers gave little consideration to the country's past experience and, by offering it the "solution" of becoming a part of the West, they denied it the very legitimacy of a search for its own post-Soviet identity.

Not surprisingly, the course that was both politically and culturally insensitive could only lead to the strengthening of Russian nationalists, who were at most sanguine about the West. Russia's core perceptions of the West changed from those of a friend or a strategic partner to those of a potential threat. Hard-line opposition did not come to power, as Yeltsin and Kozyrev had feared. But the economic and political system that emerged was hardly reminiscent of those of the West and was far from the one the Westernizers had hoped for. In the economic realm, Russia built not a free-market model of capitalism, but rather what scholars call oligarchical capitalism. Under oligarchical capitalism, the economy is largely controlled by and divided among those with business interests in the West. In this environment, the Western assistance enriched the elites and provided support for the new regime that was evolving away from democracy. Oligarchs began to play the role of the new post-Soviet *nomenklatura* and influenced many key decisions of the state. In both Russia and the West, observers raised questions of the aid donors' responsibility for such developments.[47] In the realm of political and legal institutions, Russia developed a superpresidential system with few effective checks and balances. Under the 1993 constitution, the president gained enormous power and could exercise it to prevent a strongly integrated opposition from emerging.

Such was the irony of the radically pro-Western course that it could produce only non-Western, at times even anti-Western, economic and political outcomes.

NOTES

1. Andrei Kozyrev, "Rossiya v novom mire," *Mezhdunarodnaya zhizn'* 3–4, (1992): 92; Kozyrev, "The Lagging Partnership," *Foreign Affairs* 73, no. 3 (1994): 59.

2. Leonid Gordon and Leonid Fridman, "Rossiya—velikaya derzhava vtorogo ranga," *Nezavisimaya gazeta*, April 4, 1995.

3. Francis Fukuyama, "The End of History?" *National Interest* 16 (Summer), 1989.

4. Garton Ash, *The Magic Lantern: The Revolution of '89 as Witnessed in Warsaw, Budapest, Berlin and Prague* (London: Vintage, 1989), 154.

5. The expression is that of U.S. president Jimmy Carter's former national security adviser Zbigniew Brzezinski. See his book, *The Grand Failure: The Birth and Death of Communism in the Twentieth Century* (New York: Charles Scribner's Sons, 1989).

6. William Pfaff, "Redefining World Power," *Foreign Affairs* 70, no. 1 (1991): 48.

7. Andrei Kozyrev, *Preobrazheniye* (Moscow: Mezhdunarodnye otnosheniya, 1995), 16.

8. Kozyrev, "Rossiya v novom mire," 93; Kozyrev, "Russia and Human Rights," *Slavic Review* 51, no. 2 (1992).

9. Kozyrev, "Rossiya v novom mire," 93.

10. As cited in George Breslauer, *Gorbachev and Yeltsin as Leaders* (Cambridge: Cambridge University Press, 2002), 157.

11. The terminology is that of Kozyrev. "Russia: A Chance for Survival," *Foreign Affairs* 71, no. 2 (1992): 9–10.

12. See, especially, Gennadi Zyuganov, *Drama vlasti* (Moscow: Paleya, 1993); *Rossiya i sovremennyi mir* (Moscow: "Obozrevatel," 1995); and *Geografiya pobedy* (Moscow, 1998).

13. Aleksandr Dugin, *Konservativnaya revolyutsiya* (Moscow: Arktogeya, 1994) and *Osnovy geopolitiki* (Moscow: Arktogeya, 1997).

14. Nikolai Fon Kreitor, "Stoletiye novogo mira," *Molodaya gvardiya* 6 (1998). See also Natalya Narochnitskaya, "Natsional'nyi interes Rossiyi," *Mezhdunarodnaya zhizn'* 3-4 (1992); Aleksandr Khatsankov, "Gorchakov—koshmar Kozyreva," *Den'*, August 8-14, 1992; El'giz Pozdnyakov, "Geopoliticheski kollaps i Rossiya," *Mezhdunarodnaya zhizn'* 8-9, 1992.

15. See, for example, Dmitri Furman, "Rossiiskiye demokraty i raspad soyuza," *Vek XX i mir* 1 (1992).

16. Boris Kapustin, "Rossiya i Zapad na puti k miru mirov," *Kentavr* 1, no. 2 (1993); Yuri Krasin, "O rossiyskikh natsional'nykh interesakh," *Svobodnaya mysl'* 3 (1996).

17. Vladimir Sogrin, "Zapadnyi liberalizm i rossiyskiye reformy," *Svobodnaya mysl'* 1 (1996): 32.

18. Andranik Migranyan, "Podlinnye i mnimye orientiry vo vneshnei politike," *Rossiyskaya gazeta*, August 2, 1992.

19. See "Rossiya v novom mire," *Mezhdunarodnaya zhizn'* 3-4 (1992).

20. See, especially, "Strategiya dlya Rossiyi," *Nezavisimaya gazeta*, August 1992, and "Strategiya—2," *Nezavisimaya gazeta*, May 27, 1994. The term "Near Abroad," coined for referring to Russia's former Soviet periphery, was introduced in one of the first statements of the organization.

21. Andrei Kozyrev, "Partnership with the West: A Test of Strength," *Moscow News*, October 25, 1992.

22. Cited in Richter, "Russian Foreign Policy and the Politics of National Identity," in *The Sources of Russian Foreign Policy after the Cold War*, ed. Celeste A. Wallander (Boulder, CO: Westview Press, 1996), 86. After the December 1993 elections, even leaders of Gaidar's radically pro-Western Russia's Choice Party, among them Sergei Blagovolin and Boris Fedorov, acknowledged in private that it was a mistake on their part not to present themselves as a patriotic/nationalist group concerned about Russia's great power status. Astrid Tuminez, "Russian Nationalism and the National Interest in Russian Foreign Policy," in *The Sources of Russian Foreign Policy*, 65.

23. Zbigniew Brzezinski, "The Premature Partnership," *Foreign Affairs* 73, no. 1 (1994).

24. Andrei Kozyrev, "The Lagging Partnership," *Foreign Affairs* 73, no. 3 (1994): 59.

25. Andrei Kozyrev, "Don't Threaten Us," *New York Times*, March 18, 1994, A28. In his book, Kozyrev writes about the evolution in his thinking toward Statism, acknowledging that by 1994, he "definitively had turned into a democrat-'Statist'" and "became convinced that Russia was doomed to remain a great power." Kozyrev, *Preobrazheniye* (38-39).

26. This attitude was well reflected in the documents of Russian-U.S. summits in 1992 and 1993. In June 1992, for example, Yeltsin and Bush signed a Charter of Russian-American Partnership and Friendship, affirming "the indivisibility of the security of North America and Europe" that would "rest on lasting common values" and a common commitment to "democracy, the supremacy of law . . . and support for human rights." Leszek Buszynski, *Russian Foreign Policy after the Cold War* (New York: Praeger, 1996), 54.

27. Andrei Kozyrev, "Osnovnaya opasnost'—v nomenklaturnom revanshe," *Nezavisimaya gazeta*, October 8, 1992.

28. The figure of $100 billion was calculated as the equivalent per capita value of aid to Eastern Europe from 1989 to 1991. Nigel Gould-Davies and Ngaire Woods, "Russia and the IMF," *International Affairs* 75, no. 1 (1999): 5.

29. Buszynski, *Russian Foreign Policy*, 57.

30. Robert H. Donaldson and Joseph L. Nogee, *The Foreign Policy of Russia: Changing Systems, Enduring Interests* (Armonk, NY: M. E. Sharpe, 2002), 193.

31. Peter Shearman, "Russian Policy toward the United States," in *Russian Foreign Policy since 1990*, ed. Peter Shearman (Boulder, CO: Westview Press, 1995), 121.

32. Yevgeni Bazhanov, "Russian Policy toward China," in *Russian Foreign Policy* (Boulder, CO: Westview Press, 1995), 161.

33. Bazhanov, "Russian Policy toward China," 170.

34. Shearman, "Russian Policy toward the United States," 129.

35. Donaldson and Nogee, *The Foreign Policy of Russia*, 198.

36. Vera Tolz, *Russia: Inventing the Nation* (Oxford: Arnold, 2001), 250.

37. Andrei V. Zagorski et al., *Posle raspada SSSR: Rossiya v novom mire* (Moscow: MGIMO, 1992), 6–11, 15, 17.

38. Alexander A. Pikayev, "The Russian Domestic Debate on Policy towards the 'Near Abroad,'" in *Peacekeeping and the Role of Russia in Eurasia*, ed. Lena Jonson and Clive Archer (Boulder, CO: Westview Press, 1996), 52.

39. David Kotz and Fred Weir, *Revolution from Above: The Demise of the Soviet System* (London: Routledge, 1997), 167.

40. In 1994, the rate of approval among Russians outside Russia ranged from 84 percent in Ukraine and Belarus, the two Slavic states, to about 50 percent in four central Asian states, with Kazakhstan falling in between these two poles (United States Information Agency, September 1994, 1).

41. Astrid Tuminez, "Russian Nationalism and the National Interest," in *The Sources of Russian Foreign Policy*, 59.

42. Wynne Russell, "Russian Relations with the 'Near Abroad,'" in *Russian Foreign Policy* (Boulder, CO: Westview Press, 1995), 65.

43. Russell, "Russian Relations with the 'Near Abroad,'" 65.

44. The earliest case of such an interpretation of Russia's early post-Soviet foreign policy was made by Brzezinski, "The Premature Partnership." See also Allen C. Lynch, "The Realism of Russia's Foreign Policy," *Europe-Asia Studies* 53, no. 1 (2001): 140.

45. William Zimmerman, *The Russian People and Foreign Policy* (Princeton: Princeton University Press, 2002), 91.

46. Zimmerman, *The Russian People*, 92.

47. For Western scholarship, see especially Peter Rutland, "Mission Impossible? The IMF and the Failure of the Market Transition in Russia," *Review of International Studies* 25, no. 5 (1999); Janine Wedel, *Collision and Collusion: The Strange Case of Western Aid to Eastern Europe, 1990–1997* (London: Palgrave, 1998); Peter Reddaway and Dmitri Glinski, *The Tragedy of Russia's Reforms: Market Bolshevism against Democracy* (Washington, DC: United States Institute of Peace, 2001).

4

The New Security Challenges and Great Power Balancing

> Russia has been and remains a great power, and its policy toward the outside world should correspond to that status.
> Russia is both Europe and Asia, and this geopolitical location continues to play a tremendous role in formulation of its foreign policy. . . . Geopolitical values are constants that cannot be abolished by historical developments.
>
> —Yevgeni Primakov[1]

The appointment of Primakov as Russia's foreign minister officially completed Yeltsin and Kozyrev's early Westernist course. The new appointment signaled a revival of Russia's most influential foreign policy thinking, which put the key emphasis on statehood and great power status.

4.1. RUSSIA AS A GREAT POWER IN A MULTIPOLAR WORLD

The Grave New World and the Rise of Security Challenges

The revival of Statism as Russia's official foreign policy philosophy would have been impossible without gathering security threats both inside and outside the country. At home, Russia was confronted with the growing challenge of secessionism and instability in one of its key southern regions, Chechnya. Yeltsin's failure to respond to Chechnya's announcement of independence in 1991, as well as the largely political nature of his decision to intervene in late 1994, contributed to a long and bloody confrontation. For Yeltsin, the decision was an attempt to shift the public attention away from

his own promises to improve or, at least, sustain the living standards of ordinary Russians. In the meantime, the actual income of ordinary Russians,
most of whom were wage earners and pensioners, fell drastically and the
economy shrank considerably (see table 3.5 in the previous chapter). Partly
as a reaction to Yeltsin's opportunism, the public remained largely skeptical
of his military intervention. With little support at home, the army was unable to solve the conflict by force, as disorder and terrorism were increasingly spreading throughout Chechnya and outside.

Outside Russia, threats emerged from instabilities and ethnic conflicts in
Moldova, central Asia, and the Caucasus. No less importantly, the West extended little recognition to Russia as one of its own, instead treating it increasingly as a potential threat. The Western decision to expand the North Atlantic
Treaty Organization (NATO), despite Russia's opposition, greatly contributed
to the return of Statist thinking to the country. Statism assumes that respect
and recognition can come only from strength, and weakness is not worthy of
respect. The decision to expand NATO by excluding Russia from the process
strengthened the Russian perception of the West as playing power games and
attempting to take advantage of Russia's temporary weakness. Nationalists felt
vindicated, whereas liberals were confused and at a loss for arguments. Many
politicians and intellectuals, including those of a liberal orientation, saw
NATO's expansion as a dangerous and threatening development.

As important as the decision to expand NATO was, it reflected the broader
change in the West's perception of the world. From the rhetoric of victory in
the Cold War and the "end of history," the Western political community
moved to a feeling of anxiety over its growing inability to preserve peace and
stability throughout the globe. The new ethnic conflicts in Europe and the
former Soviet Union, the perceived threat from the undefeated regime of the
Iraqi leader Saddam Hussein, and environmental and demographic pressures
from Asia and Africa seemed to pose great risks. Various intellectual projects
emerged to reflect the rising pessimism among U.S. policymakers about the
future of the world order and to reject the early rosy perceptions of the world.
With the growing awareness of new dangers came fear and suspicion of the
non-Western world, which was best summarized by Samuel Huntington's
thesis of the "clash of civilizations." Just as Fukuyama once expressed the
West's optimism, even euphoria, about the future world order, Huntington
expressed the growing feelings of anxiety and frustration. He insisted that
instead of expanding globally, the West should go on the defensive and prepare to fight for its cultural values in coming clashes with non-Western
"civilizations."[2] In this new intellectual context, Russia, with its authoritarian
past and politically unstable present, was often viewed as a source of threat
rather than a "strategic partner." The once newly born liberal ally was now

increasingly perceived to be driven by traditional imperial aspirations or a failing state·unable to govern itself.

The Statist Vision of Russia's Identity

In this context of growing security threats, the Statist insistence on viewing Russia as first and foremost a great power resonated with the elites and the broader public. Primakov and his supporters did not see the forces of international cooperation as shaping the nature of world politics. They appealed to the historical notion of Russia as a *Derzhava*, which can be loosely translated as a holder of international equilibrium of power. A *Derzhava* is capable of defending itself by relying on its own individual strength, and its main goal should be the preservation of that status. Although many Statists were former Westernizers, they no longer agreed that Russia was becoming a part of the West, and they argued that the country had its own interests to defend. Without implying the confrontation with the West, Statists sought to defend the image of Russia as a power holder striving to preserve its own geopolitical interests and areas of influence in the world. Geopolitical categories often used by Civilizationists—such as "national idea," "great power," and "Eurasia"— became intrinsic to Statist vocabulary.

To many Statists, the notion of Eurasia became symbolic in describing Russia's special geopolitical location and multiethnic nature. Taking issue with Westernizers, Statists pointed to the need to maintain a multicultural balance inside Russia. They also warned against Russia's unequivocally siding with Europe or the United States at the expense of relationships with key participants from the Eurasian continent, such as China, India, and the Islamic world. Committed to an essentialist vision of geography, Statists insisted that, by its geopolitical location, Russia was destined to act as a political bridge between Western and non-Western civilizations.

Unlike Civilizationists, however, Statists were more pragmatic and were prepared to cooperate with anyone defending the existing balance of international power and Russia's role in it. While viewing the world primarily in terms of disparities and competition among great powers, Statists were not anti-Western and did not see Russia as inherently hostile to the West. The school maintained that, although Russia's interests and values differed from those of the West, it had historically interacted with the West, and this limited interaction had not threatened Russian sovereignty. Although the school understood security as resulting more from the state's individual strength than from collective efforts, it saw the value of tactical coalitions and alliances. Statists were also different from conservative Civilizationists in their evaluation of Soviet foreign policy. Rather than putting all the blame on the West (as com-

munists and Eurasianists did), Statists proceeded from the thesis of mutual
and equal responsibility for the Cold War. Several Statists, including Primakov, were originally supportive of Gorbachev's New Thinking as it was emerging in 1986–1987.

The Statist worldview then was a familiar realist picture of power competition
between sovereign states reminiscent of nineteenth-century European politics;
that is, the world is not inherently hostile, but it does consist of selfish power-
seeking state actors whose interests must be balanced in order to maximize
peace and stability. Statists thought about the international system in terms of
power poles and favored the United Nations as the key institution for maintaining a multipolar balance of power, particularly among great powers.[3]

The Statist coalition combined the military industries, army, and security
services that saw the largely ignored potential to generate revenue through the
development of new technologies and exportation of conventional weapons.
In one of its documents, the Council for Foreign and Defense Policy, an influential nongovernmental organization, expressed the attitude typical of Statist
circles when it described the military-industrial complex as "a key, possibly,
the key factor of Russia's struggle for a dignified place in the twenty-first
century."[4] Over time, the Russian large "security class" gained strength and
was able to challenge the emerging and still nascent "commercial class" that
promoted the Westernist image of Russia's identity. The Statist coalition
greatly benefited from the 1993 and 1995 elections, in which nationalists and
communists did well, compelling Yeltsin to modify the liberal agenda. Primakov's appointment was symbolic in this respect. As the *Financial Times* edito-
rialized, of all the possible successors to Kozyrev, Primakov was "probably the
least welcome in Washington. By selecting him, President Boris Yeltsin has
signaled that he cares more about assuaging nationalism at home than sooth-
ing U.S. fears."[5] Primakov served as foreign minister from January 1996
through September 1998, and as prime minister he remained a guiding influence on foreign policy until May 1999. It was now up to the Statists to define
and defend the country's national interests.

The Statist View of National Interest

Primakov and his team proposed two central elements for recovering Russia's
status as a great power in a multipolar world: balancing the United States'
unipolar ambitions in a coalition with other states and integrating the former
Soviet region under a tighter control from Moscow. Primakov understood
that Russia was weak and had limited resources for foreign policy grandeur.
Yet his thinking was, counterintuitively, that the country had to pursue "active" foreign policy (*aktivnaya vneshnyaya politika*)[6] in order to compensate

Table 4.1.   Great Power Balancing: View of National Interest

What?	A great power in a multipolar world
How?	Flexible alliances Reintegration of the former Soviet region Economic reform

for currently limited resources in reforming the economy and preserving territorial integrity. He believed that Russia was in a geopolitically dangerous environment and simply could not afford to concentrate on purely domestic issues (table 4.1 summarizes the Statist view of national interest).

In relationships with the West, Primakov insisted that Russia be motivated primarily by its own interests, and he proclaimed the vision of a multipolar world. According to this perspective, Russia had a tendency to become dependent on the strongest and, to preserve its significant global geopolitical role, it had to pursue the goal of becoming an independent power pole. The Statist logic was simple: the power dictates its rules, and under the conditions of a unipolar world Russia would have no independent voice in international politics. The unipolar world was not going to be liberal or democratic, despite the American promises, and Russia should not succumb to the rhetoric of the strongest. Instead, it must use a combination of both cooperation and balancing policies for the purpose of undermining the unipolarity. Confrontation with the West was unnecessary; unlike the conservative Civilizationists, Primakov believed that a limited and pragmatic cooperation with either the "strongest" or the West was both feasible and important. Unlike the Westernizers, however, Primakov and his supporters insisted that the principle of absolute power equality must be honored in each instance of cooperation.

In addition to cooperating with the West, Statists believed that Russia also had to engage in balancing tactics against the strongest power, the United States. Because of Russia's presumed responsibility for maintaining world equilibrium and the balance of power, its cooperation with the West and the United States could not be as deep and far reaching as Westernizers saw it. In a multipolar world, which Russia wanted to see built, Russia had to be able to prevent the formation of an opposing coalition by using balancing tactics in relating to all its foreign partners—Western, Eastern, and Southern. When necessary, it had to capitalize on the potential conflicts that already existed in world politics, for example, those between the Western and Muslim or Asian countries or those within the West itself. Russia's policy orientation in the world then should have been multilateral, or "multivector," aiming to develop balanced relations with Western and non-Western countries. In Yevgeni Primakov's words,

Russia is both Europe and Asia, and this geopolitical location continues to play a tremendous role in formulation of its foreign policy. Its [geopolitical interests] include China, India, and Japan, and not just the United States or Europe. They also include the Middle East and the "Third World." Without such geopolitical scope, Russia cannot continue to be a great power and to play the positive role it has been destined to play. In building relationships with all these countries, one must remember that geopolitical values are constant and cannot be abolished by historical developments.[7]

Primakov made it explicit that his strategy was reminiscent of State Chancellor Alexander Gorchakov's "concentration" course after Russia's defeat in the Crimean War. After the March 1856 Paris peace treaty, which legitimized Russia's defeat, Gorchakov recommended to Czar Alexander II that, facing the new conditions, Russia "will have to focus persistently on the realization of [its] internal development and the entire foreign policy will have to be subordinated to this main task."[8] Such policy would be only temporary and, after rebuilding the domestic base, Russia would again be in a position to press for changes appropriate for its great power status. In combination with flexible alliance making, Russia at least partially achieved the goal: in 1870 it felt strong enough to act unilaterally and partially renounce the conditions of the Paris peace treaty. Primakov, too, was hoping that, after rebuilding the economy, Russia would "return" to world politics.

In the former Soviet Union, Statists defended the notion of a tightly integrated region with Russia's informal control over policies of the former republics. Primakov argued that Russian geopolitical needs stretched well beyond Russia, and it was only pragmatic to act on those needs. For him, the task of maintaining the world geopolitical equilibrium required that Russia remain a sovereign state with capabilities to organize and secure the post-Soviet space to resist hegemonic ambitions anywhere in the world. Unlike neocommunists or Eurasianists, the new foreign minister wanted no formal responsibility for the "postimperial space" and preferred to refer to Russia's relations with its post-Soviet neighbors as "multilateral integration."

Such thinking about Russia's national interests was adequately reflected in official documents. The country's National Security Concept of 1997 described "the new geopolitical and international situation" followed by "negative processes in the national economy" as key threats to Russia. It identified Russia as an "influential European and Asian power," and it invariably termed the country's relationships with "other great powers" as an "equal partnership." Furthermore, it recommended that Russia maintain equal distancing in relations to the "global European and Asian economic and political actors" and presented a positive program for the integration of the efforts of the Commonwealth of Independent States (CIS) in the security area. The government's official Foreign Policy Concept of 2000 referred to the Russian Federation as "a great power . . . [with a] responsibility for maintaining security in the world both on a global and on a regional level" and warned of a new threat of "a unipolar structure of the world under the economic and military domination of the United States."[9]

Although Primakov's perspective was definitely the closest to realist thinking, it is difficult to apply realism as an international relations theory for explaining Russia's turn to Great Power Balancing. Realists expect that policy change follows evolution in state material capabilities. Yet Russia's capabilities did not improve. As table 3.5 in the previous chapter indicates, the country's economic decline continued, and there was hardly a material basis for developing a more assertive foreign policy. What changed, however, was the behavior of the West toward Russia and its local conditions; this contributed to an altered domestic perception and brought to power the identity coalition of Statists.

4.2. THE NATIONAL RECEPTION OF GREAT POWER BALANCING

The new foreign policy vision found broad support in Russian society and, especially, among the political elites. After Kozyrev's departure, Yeltsin embraced the rhetoric of great power and multipolarity and pronounced the discussion of Russia's foreign policy priorities to be "completed" and the new foreign policy conception to be supported by a "consensus of various social and political forces."[10] Statists and many Social Democrats welcomed the new foreign policy course. Civilizationists, too, accepted some of Primakov's arguments while at the same time pushing him to adopt a more confrontational line in relations with the West. Finally, Westernizers got their act together and found some new arguments against aspirations for a great power and multipolar world order.

The Initial Support of Statists and Social Democrats

An overwhelming majority of Russia's political class welcomed the change in policy, defending Primakov's concept of national interests on political, historical, and geopolitical grounds. Politically, the argument went, the new policy reflected a broad agreement of various social and political forces in Russia. Foreign policy was ceasing to be an exclusive domain of the president and had more chances to be corrected in a timely fashion. Historical parallels between the new course and the notion of Gorchakov's "concentration" were, too, widely accepted in scholarly and political circles. Since 1998, an annual

Gorchakov conference for scholars and practitioners has been held at the Moscow Institute of International Relations for debating various issues of current foreign policy. And in 2001, Primakov was awarded the State Gorchakov Commemorative Medal for "outstanding service in strengthening peace and promoting international cooperation." Finally, the new course's pragmatic nature found a great deal of support. Although virtually all Statists wanted Russia to become one of the five great powers in the world—along with Germany, France, Japan, and China—most warned against attempts to organize foreign policy around resistance to the global influence of the United States. In fact, some questioned the notion of a multipolar world as the guiding vision of the international system.[11] Outside the Statist camp, some Social Democrats praised the new foreign policy for its proclaimed pragmatism, restraint, and sense of priorities.[12]

Conditional Criticism of Civilizationists

Many neocommunists and Eurasianists had long attacked Kozyrev for "betraying" Russia as a holder of the global balance of power, and they welcomed the new course and the concept of a multipolar world. Yet they challenged Primakov to go much further in resisting Western influences and to adopt a more radical notion of multipolarity. The new minister planned to pursue a moderate course and consolidate Russia's position by cooperating with the West, where possible, and by avoiding confrontation, where such cooperation was not an option. Aware of the scarcity of available resources, he saw a multipolar world as a desired objective, rather than a fact of life. To conservative Civilizationists, on the other hand, the notion of great power implied the restoration of the Soviet Union, and multipolarity meant isolation from and competition with the West.[13]

Fear of the West and its global aspirations were the dominant obsessions of Civilizationist writers, such as the leader of Russian communists Gennadi Zyuganov. For Zyuganov, Russia was a unique civilization that must be isolated from the West to survive and preserve its uniqueness. What Statists saw as Russia's special geographical and ethnic features, Zyuganov developed into the principal line of cultural confrontation with the West. The leader of the Russian communists never made his peace with the dissolution of the Soviet empire and insisted that the Soviet Union was a "natural" geopolitical form of "historic" Russia, whereas the current political boundaries of the country are "artificial" and imposed by the West through covert actions. To "return" to world politics and build a genuinely multipolar world, Russia must accomplish politicoeconomic autarchy (*samodostatochnost'*) and enter a strategic alliance with China.[14] Other writers, too, presented the choice of Russia's survival as the one between an independent Eurasian power and a virtual colony of the West, and they complained about the lack of radicalism in Primakov's vision.[15]

Opposition from Westernizers

Westernizers stood out from the rest of the political class in their most irreconcilable critique of the course of Great Power Balancing. They repeated the old Kozyrev argument that Russia's national interest is in building a competitive market economy and a vibrant democratic system, not in balancing against the West or integrating the former Soviet Union. In supporting this line of reasoning, Westernizers drew attention to the fact that ordinary Russians were concerned primarily with the state of the Russian economy and internal security, and not the issues of military capabilities and great power status. Insisting, as before, on Russia's politicoeconomic integration with European institutions, they saw as fundamentally misplaced Primakov's priorities of reviving the CIS as a vehicle of the post-Soviet integration, resisting the eastern expansion of NATO, developing military cooperation with Iran, and trying to build the Russia-China-India security axis. Furthermore, they challenged the relevance of Gorchakov's "concentration" on contemporary foreign policy. In their view, Gorchakov's flexible alliances had deprived Russia of a chance to side firmly with democratic France and—ultimately—contributed to the rise of Germany and Russia's own revolution. They charged that, by not siding firmly with the West and trying to play Europe or China against the United States, Primakov's policy, too, was likely to result in failure.[16]

While echoing many of the old Westernist arguments, the new Westernizers became more pragmatic and less ideological in their reasoning. Increasingly, they were concentrating on various material benefits of Russia's pro-Western orientation. Some spoke of the need in "pragmatic liberalism" for successfully opposing Primakov's "pragmatic nationalism," whereas others acknowledged that the road to Europe would not be an easy or straightforward one.[17] Westernizers therefore learned the key lesson: ideology alone was a recipe for failure when not supported by interests and pragmatic reasoning.

(Table 4.2 summarizes contending views on the Statist view of national interest.)

Table 4.2.   Great Power Balancing (GPB): Contending Views

Civilizationists:		Westernizers:
GPB must more decisively confront the West	VS.	GPB leads to confrontation with the West

4.3. CONTAINING WESTERN INFLUENCES

Thinking about the West and East

Primakov's strategy for dealing with the West included two central elements—upholding the power of the United Nations as the key agency for defining and enforcing rules of international conduct and developing close ties with influential states outside the Western Hemisphere, such as China and India. This emphasis on both power and institutions brought Russian thinking about international politics closer to the British International Society school, rather than to American-style neorealism that does not see institutions as having particular significance in shaping the world order. Primakov was careful not to isolate Russia from mainstream international politics centered on the United Nations Security Council. As a permanent member of the Security Council, Russia planned to exercise its voting power as it saw fit, while at the same time contributing to world peace and stability as a member of the world "concert of great powers." The minister and his supporters saw these elements as critical in establishing a multipolar world order and containing the power of the West, particularly the United States. In practical terms, the new foreign policy strove to resist American hegemony by using the legitimate tools of diplomacy and power balancing, while avoiding confrontation with the United States. It sought to mobilize Russia's power resources to pursue that goal (for a summary of these resources relative to other nations, see table 4.3).

The East had a special role in this dual-track strategy. Unlike Westernizers, Primakov was a firm believer in special relations with Asian and Middle Eastern countries. This belief firmed up during his long career as a Middle East specialist and policymaker. For many years, the future minister worked in

Table 4.3. Russia's Power Resources Relative to Other Powerful States (%)*

	U.S.	Japan	Germany	France	RUSSIA	China
Population (1995)	4.7	2.2	1.4	1.0	2.6	21.2
Territory (1994)	7.1	0.3	0.3	0.4	13.2	7.3
GNP (1995)	25.2	18.7	8.7	5.5	1.2	3.0
Manufacturing (1995)	22.6	25.4	11.7	5.9	3.1	5.3
Merchandise Exports (1995)	12.1	9.2	10.8	5.9	1.7	3.1
Nuclear Weapons (1996)	46.8	—	—	2.9	46.1	2.5
Military Expenditures (1993)	41.0	5.9	5.4	5.3	4.3	4.1
Military Personnel (1996)	6.7	1.4	1.6	1.8	5.7	13.2

*Share as a percentage of the world's total.
Source: Robert A. Pastor, ed., *A Century's Journey: How the Great Powers Shape the World* (New York: Basic Books, 2001), 19.

several Middle Eastern countries as a correspondent for the leading communist newspaper *Pravda*. Primakov subsequently moved to academia to serve as director of the Institute of Oriental Studies and, later, of the prestigious Institute of World Economy and International Relations. He then began to work for Gorbachev. However, while advocating strong ties with Asia and the Muslim world, he differentiated sharply between the Islamic states and the Taliban's form of Islam, which he described as "Islamic extremism." Primakov wanted to engage the former for the sake of balancing against growing Western influences and to isolate the latter.

Opposing NATO Expansion

The key focus of Primakov's policy was undoubtedly NATO's eastward expansion and Russia's adaptation to this new reality. The decision to expand the alliance was made in January 1994 in response to several security crises in the Balkans and pressures from the former Eastern European states. By the time Primakov had assumed his responsibilities, it became clear that NATO, rather than the Russia-desired Organization for Security and Co-operation in Europe (OSCE), was turning into the cornerstone of European security. It was also clear that, despite Russia's original hopes, it was not about to be considered for membership in the organization.

Many in Russia saw the expansion as the most serious foreign policy challenge and made their opposition to the process explicit.[18] The expansion was incomprehensible in light of Russia's historical commitments, its new relationships with the Western countries, and the West's own promises not to expand the alliance. Many Russians felt deceived, as the expansion followed Gorbachev's military withdrawals from Eastern Europe, Kozyrev's restriction of some profitable arms sales in order to comply with Western rules, and Russia's general commitment to develop a strategic partnership with the West. Overwhelmingly, the Russian foreign policy community perceived the expansion as a violation of the norm of reciprocity and the very spirit of the post–Cold War transformation. Eventually, even radical Westernizers, such as Kozyrev, had announced their disappointment with the decision. The general public, too, expressed concerns, and those concerns only increased over time. As former U.S. defense secretary William Perry put it, Russian reaction to NATO expansion "ranged from being unhappy to being very unhappy. . . . This is a very widely and very deeply held view in Russia."[19]

Under these conditions, Primakov saw his task as limiting potential damage of the expansion. His very appointment, in fact, served the purpose of ameliorating the anti-NATO backlash further because of his already-established reputation as a tough defender of Russia's national interests. Primakov soon recognized that the expansion of the alliance became inevitable and that Russia had to shift from the mode of resistance to that of adaptation. Although he was highly critical of the Western decision, he recognized the reality for what it was—"the expansion of NATO is not a military problem; it is a psychological one."[20] To narrow the gap of perception, Russia had little choice but to work on establishing closer diplomatic and political ties with the alliance. The result was the negotiated document signed by the two sides in May 1997 and entitled the "Founding Act on Mutual Relations, Cooperation and Security between Russia and NATO." Russia saw this as a quasi institutionalization of its relationship with NATO, and it also received the opportunity to join NATO in establishing a special body, the Permanent Joint Council, to consult about and—when appropriate—even join in decision making and joint action. In December 1997, in his speech to the State Duma, Primakov referred to the Founding Act as a major accomplishment and evidence of Russia's diplomacy in obtaining its own objectives.

Admittedly, the Founding Act did not give Russia the veto power it sought, and the subsequent intervention in the Balkans demonstrated this situation all too painfully. Domestic critics, such as the leader of the communists, Zyuganov, went as far as to compare the charter to a new Yalta, in which Russia was a defeated party signing its act of capitulation. Even some of Primakov's supporters felt he went too far in acquiescing to the West. Yet his strategy worked in terms of shifting Russia's focus to adaptation to the new reality and attempting to influence outcomes through diplomacy and bargaining from within. Despite the Kosovo crisis (described below), Russia was brought closer to NATO, and the question of the alliance's expansion was largely defused in domestic politics, depriving hard-line critics of the ability to pressure the government. Russia now had a mechanism for permanent consultations with the alliance. In addition, NATO reaffirmed in writing its commitment not to deploy nuclear weapons or substantial new forces on the territory of new member states. Russian diplomats extracted what they could given Russia's weak bargaining position.

Working to Improve Economic and Military Independence

A Statist, Primakov made an effort to improve Russia's economic and military capabilities, without which his strategy of containing Western influences could hardly have been sufficient. In economic affairs, rather than continuing with Kozyrev's policy of joining Western international organizations, he worked to restore a measure of Russia's independence. He argued against a West-dependent economic recovery and entering the world economy as a supplier of raw materials, and he insisted on separating the economic issues from those related to politics and security. This attitude generally corresponded with how hard-line opposition felt about Russia's receiving financial assistance from the West's leading lending agencies. At the time, many of the government's critics charged that the assistance served to further corrupt the circles of the ruling elite and to entice them to "sell" Russia to the West.

Despite Primakov's efforts, there was little he could do to restore the country's economic independence. By the time of his arrival in office, Russia's foreign debt and domestic budget deficit figured prominently. The heaviest debt approached in 1999 when Russia had to pay $17.5 billion, at a time when its domestic budget was around $20 billion.[21] The budget deficit—which resulted mainly from the government's inability to collect taxes—was consistently sizable since the beginning of Yeltsin's economic reform (see table 4.4). The government was desperate to find noninflationary ways to reduce the deficit and to restructure and reschedule the growing debt. The room for political maneuvering was severely limited, and the government continued the practice of borrowing from the International Monetary Fund (IMF). In its turn, the IMF required a tight conditionality and secured a more politically compliant Russia. For all its talk about depoliticized relations with recipient countries, the political side of the IMF-Russia relationship was always visible. The 1995–1996 lending, for example, was conducted in the context of the approaching presidential elections, in which Yeltsin's victory was the number one priority for the West. The Western intervention in Yugoslavia—against which Russia objected vehemently—took place as the Russian government was in the process of negotiating the restructuring of the approaching $17.5 billion payment.[22]

After assuming the responsibilities of prime minister, Primakov realized ever more painfully the difficulties of maintaining the independence posture; even with what was considered to be a "leftist government," he had to submit to the State Duma a tight budget and to fully comply with the IMF conditions.

In military affairs and arms control, the foreign minister turned prime minister sought to reduce the heavy economic burden of maintaining the largest nuclear arsenal in the world. Primakov believed in the political power of nuclear weapons, but advocated a relatively small arsenal. Against the hard-line opposition and even some of his supporters, he argued for ratification of

Table 4.4.   Russia's Government Revenue and Expenditure, 1992–1998 (% of GDP)

	1992	1993	1994	1995	1996	1997	1998
Revenue	15.6	13.7	11.8	12.2	13.0	11.9	10.2
Expenditure	26	20.2	23.2	17.6	22.0	18.9	16.1

Source: Nigel Gould-Davies and Ngaire Woods, "Russia and the IMF," *International Affairs* 75, no. 1 (1999): 15.

START II, which had been signed in January 1993. Yet his efforts, accompanied by support from the Ministry of Defense, failed because of the United States' bombing of Iraq and, subsequently, NATO's military intervention in Yugoslavia. The events strengthened conservative Civilizationists and other hard-liners in the Duma, who feared U.S. intentions to develop a missile defense system and consequently blocked the ratification. START II, which promised to reduce the number of nuclear missiles to the new 3,000–3,500 threshold, remained formally dead until the arrival of Putin.

Resisting Military Solutions in Iraq

Primakov's principal opposition to what he viewed as imperialistic and hegemonic tendencies in world politics placed limits on his flexibility and pragmatism in dealing with the United States. However dependent Russia was on Western creditors, the minister could not support the United States–sanctioned military interventions, as did his predecessor. Intervention in Iraq emerged as one of the two key issues—the other being Yugoslavia—on which Primakov felt compelled to forcefully disagree with the American position. In his view, there were at least three major reasons why Russia could no longer limit its policy to supporting the U.S. bombings and opposing lifting the United Nations' sanctions in Iraq. First, because of his opposition to "unipolarity," he wanted to contribute to opposition to the United States–promoted military methods of dealing with Saddam Hussein. The second reason was a sizable debt—around $7 billion—of Iraq to Russia, which could not be repaid without lifting sanctions. Third, Russia's growing energy companies, such as Lukoil, were eager to acquire contracts in Iraq and the Arab markets in general.

It was this perception of Russia's interests that shaped Primakov's handling of two main crises in late 1997 and early 1998. In the first crisis, Primakov responded to the U.S. threat to attack Iraq following the latter's unwillingness to comply with the UN inspections and the inspectors' subsequent departure. In alliance with France, he negotiated a deal whereby all the inspectors were allowed to return in exchange for a vague promise to work for the lifting of sanctions. The deal did not last long, however, as sanctions were never lifted and Saddam Hussein made it difficult for inspectors to access "presidential sites," some of which were suspected of activities related to weapons of mass destruction. This time, Russia seemed to have failed to produce a mutually acceptable agreement, and the UN secretary-general assumed the diplomatic initiative. Primakov, at least, felt satisfied that the issue was left to the United Nations, and not solved unilaterally by the United States. In the meantime, Saddam Hussein was playing his own game trying to pressure Moscow to be more aggressive on the issue of lifting sanctions.[23] During 1999, Russia—in part dissatisfied with Baghdad's uncooperative behavior, in part as a trade-off for the United States' not raising at the UN Security Council the issue of Russia's ruinous war in Chechnya, and in part having an insufficient number of options in the face of the U.S. military pressures—was less willing to work with Iraq. Much to Iraq's dismay, Russia eventually chose not to exercise its veto on Security Council Resolution 1284 (it abstained), which demanded Baghdad's compliance with the inspectors' ruling and promised lifting the sanctions on the importation of civilian goods to Iraq.

Primakov's approach appeared to have accomplished little. Sanctions remained in place, negotiations did not produce any visible results, and therefore Russia's economic interests were left unsatisfied. Yet, in one important respect Russia held its ground—the key political decisions with regard to Iraq remained the United Nations' prerogative, and those decisions were different from those favored by the United States. This remained so until the March 2003 decision of President George W. Bush to attack Iraq.

Confronting NATO's Intervention in Yugoslavia

Until the Western military intervention in the Balkans, Primakov followed the policy of pragmatic cooperation with NATO members. When he took over, the Dayton Accords of November 1995 had been signed with minimal input from Russia, and the hard-line opposition insisted on realignment with Serbia. The new foreign minister indeed moved to reevaluate the role of Belgrade in European security, but he did not go nearly as far as hard-liners wanted him to. While advocating pragmatism over Kozyrev's ideological commitment to the West, Primakov actively worked through the Contact Group—the framework for diplomatic coordination among Russia, the United States, France, Britain, and Germany created in response to Yeltsin's call in February 1994. Although Russia opposed NATO's command of peacekeeping and in some cases objected to specific acts of force against the Bosnian Serbs, in general it did not interfere with UN-sanctioned Western actions in Bosnia.[24]

NATO's decision to begin air strikes against Belgrade in March 1999 changed this framework of relationships. Despite a number of important disagreements between Russia and the West, the military intervention came as a shock to Russia's foreign policy community. This was illustrated by Prime Minister Yevgeni Primakov's decision to cancel the upcoming negotiations with the United States and the IMF in Washington on March 24, 1999. Although his airplane had already been approaching the United States, he ordered it to return home. Russia's official reaction was harsh and included issuing a statement of NATO's aggression in its violation of the United Nations' jurisdiction and the Helsinki Act on the preservation of sovereignty, suspension of participation in the Founding Act agreement, withdrawal of the military mission from Brussels, and ordering NATO representatives to leave Russia.

Such reaction reflected the largely negative attitudes toward NATO within Russian society and its foreign policy community. The overwhelming majority believed that the Western actions were driven by power and hegemonic ambitions, rather than by concerns over Yugoslavian leader Slobodan Milošević's actions against Kosovo Albanians. Among the general public, about 90 percent opposed NATO's bombing of Belgrade and felt threatened by the alliance's actions.[25] It was the expansion of NATO, rather than the ethnic war in the Balkans, that shaped Russia's perception of the intervention in Yugoslavia. By that time, the Western alliance had already invited the Czech Republic, Poland, and Hungary to apply for membership. In the Madrid summit in the summer of 1997, the United States secretary of state Madeleine Albright specifically promised to extend the invitation to the Baltic states, which had been a part of the Soviet Union before 1991. Primakov's foreign ministry insisted again on the unacceptability of the alliance expansion. Despite the Founding Act agreement of May 1997, the post-Madrid atmosphere of Russia-West relationships was tense. The clash over Kosovo manifested the depth of the Russian fears. It brought in some elements of political escalation and, at times, came close to military confrontation. Russia's Duma, for instance, fell short by two or three votes of passing a resolution on accepting Yugoslavia into the Russia-Belarus Union, which would have made Russia a participant in the war.

Primakov had no plans to throw his support behind Serbia, as some conservative Civilizationists called on him to. Instead, he got involved in mediating the conflict. Using the West's interest in Russia's involvement, he formulated tough conditions for ending the war, which included guarantees for Yugoslavia's preserved sovereignty, a broad autonomy for Kosovo, and the UN's assuming leadership in the postwar settlement. Yet the peace was reached more on the West's than on Russia's terms. Out of fear of further Russia-West political escalation, Yeltsin dismissed Primakov as the key negotiator and replaced him with former prime minister Viktor Chernomyrdin, who was much too pro-Western and inexperienced in foreign affairs to negotiate the peace that Primakov had in mind. In early June, under pressure from Chernomyrdin, Serbia finally accepted the conditions for peace, but Russia's initial conditions had not been honored. As one Russian observer described the outcomes of the war, "Russia took part in Yugoslavia's acceptance of the same NATO conditions that it had previously called unacceptable."[26]

Statist Lessons from Engagement with the West

Primakov and the larger Statist community drew some tough lessons from Russia's engagement with the West. This engagement widened the gap between the two sides in perception and reinforced the sense of Russia's identity as distinct from that of the West. Russia's inability to stop NATO's expansion and Western military strikes on Iraq and Yugoslavia, as well as heavy economic dependence on Western lending organizations, reinforced the already-existing sense of isolation, at times even desperation, among the political class. Despite dubious outcomes of the strategy to contain Western influences, many believed that Russia had no other choice but to develop capabilities for external balancing. Some saw the nation as already in the process of disintegration (Chechnya), and they insisted that breaking with the West was the only alternative to Russia's slavery or disintegration.[27] As one political scientist wrote, "The bombing of Yugoslavia became a turning point in the development of Russia's consciousness. Both authorities and common people begin to realize that . . . without Russia, the world can be turned into one big McDonald's, the road to which will be paved with missiles."[28]

To reduce what Statists saw as the country's external insecurity, they recommended a series of steps. First, the main external threat was perceived to be from NATO, even though previously many analysts had seen China as equally threatening. After the war in Yugoslavia, many now viewed Kosovo as a template of NATO's future strategy. This found its reflection in proposals to increase the defense budget, as well as in official documents. The new draft military doctrine emphasized that the threat of direct aggression against Russia and its allies could only be "deterred by conducting active foreign policy and maintaining high readiness of conventional and nuclear forces." The Security Council further proposed extending and updating strategic and tactical nuclear weapons, among other measures.[29] In this context, many argued against the ratification of START II. Second, Russian elites insisted on strengthening the UN Security Council in its decision-making and peacekeeping capacity at the expense of NATO. Third, many called for tightening the defense space in the former Soviet Union. Last but not least—and this had been an essential element of Primakov's strategy—Statists no longer saw as much of a threat coming from China and argued for stepping up strategic ties with countries and regions outside the West. Indeed, while Yeltsin was trying to broker peace in Yugoslavia, Primakov was proposing that Russia enter into a tripartite partnership with China and India (which had long been an agenda of neocommunists and Eurasianists). I now turn to Russia's efforts to increase its ties with non-Western nations.

Capitalizing on Relations Outside the West

The active foreign policy defended by Primakov meant the development of geostrategic and economic ties outside the West. Both objectives were designed to improve Russia's relative power position in the world at the expense of Western nations, particularly the United States. An Arabist by training, Primakov was notably more active in the Middle East than his predecessor. In addition to expressing interest in playing a more active role in the peace process, Primakov considerably increased Russian arms sales in the region. Outside the Middle East, Russia was especially interested in the Asia-Pacific region, often describing the Association of Southeast Asian Nations (ASEAN) as an influential center of the developing multipolar world. Everywhere he traveled the new minister spread his message about the necessity of building a multipolar world order. However, three states played an especially important role in his vision—China, Iran, and India.

China's significance for Russia is difficult to overestimate. China shared a 4,300-kilometer-long border with Russia and demonstrated a very high rate of economic development. China was also the main buyer of Russian weapons; it purchased almost all of its arms and military equipment from its northwestern neighbor. Politically, the two shared concerns about the United States' global dominance and perceived as threatening developments NATO's expansion, the United States' plans to build a national missile defense system, and interventions in Iraq and Kosovo. Finally, both countries faced similar threats to internal security, with the separatist activities of the Chechens in Russia and the Muslim Uighur minority in China's province of Xinjiang.

All of these factors brought the two countries closer together. In April 1996, the sides affirmed that they were entering into a new stage of partnership, and a year later the countries' leaders signed the "Joint Declaration on a Multipolar World and the Formation of a New International Order," which reflected Primakov's vision of multipolarity as a work in progress. The late 1998–1999 developments, such as U.S. military strikes against Iraq, plans for the creation of a U.S.-Japanese theater of missile defense, NATO expansion, and bombing of Yugoslavia again brought the two together to actively coordinate their responses to what they saw as threatening developments in world affairs. Economic relations between Russia and China did not progress as fast as the countries had desired, but they did improve in areas of border trade and arms sales.

Yet despite a pronounced progress, the Russia-China relationship did not go as far as Primakov would have wanted. His efforts met opposition across the political spectrum. China was leading Russia in GDP terms by a factor of five, and that worried both Westernizers and conservative Civilizationists, who sensed the danger of a Chinese encroachment in the Far East. Western-

Table 4.5.   Russia and China: Demographic and Economic Disparities in the Far East, 1997

	Russian Far East (Southern Regions)	Northeast China
Population (millions)	5.0	104
Population Density (sq km)	3.8	132
Population Growth	−40	1,000
Regional GDP Growth (%)	−8	13
Industrial/Agricultural Growth	−12/−15	14/8

Source: Dmitri Trenin, *The End of Eurasia: Russia on the Border between Geopolitics and Globalization* (Washington, DC: Carnegie Endowment for International Peace, 2002), 209.

izers were particularly critical of Chinese authoritarianism, arguing that, sooner or later, it would translate into foreign policy expansionism. One prominent Westernizer provided the following chart to summarize the alarming picture of disparity in the two's economic and demographic indicators (see table 4.5). The strong Chinese gravitation to the global economic markets also complicated Primakov's geostrategic calculations. The full-fledged strategic partnership of Russia and China, therefore, remained only a possibility.

Another potentially strategic partner in Primakov's calculus was Iran. Politically, he saw the country as a regional ally in containing the influence of the Taliban regime in Afghanistan and Turkey, particularly on the states of central Asia and Azerbaijan. Globally, Iran was yet another potential ally in resisting the U.S.-controlled unipolarity. Economically, Russia was building nuclear reactors, supplying industrial equipment, and planning on forming a common policy in developing energy pipelines in the Caspian region. As with China, Primakov's record on Russia's cooperation with Iran was mixed. The two sides cooperated on economic matters and in arranging a cease-fire in Tajikistan and resisting the Taliban in Afghanistan. Despite objections from Washington that Iran was building a nuclear weapon in violation of the existing nonproliferation regime, Russia continued to cooperate with Iran while denying all the allegations.

Over time, however, Russian-Iranian relations demonstrated their limits. Politically, Russia did not want to see Iran emerging as a possible military threat in the region, and some officials publicly spoke against such a development. The issue subsequently became even more pronounced as Iran became the head of the Islamic Conference and emerged more supportive of the Chechen rebels and Kosovo Muslims. Furthermore, while acting in concert with Russia in trying to block the Baku-Ceyhan and Trans-Caspian pipelines, Iran developed an interest in serving as an alternative export route for central

Asian oil and gas. Finally, neither Yeltsin nor Primakov was willing to go too far with testing the United States' patience. The end result was what one scholar labeled a "minimax" policy, in which Russia tried to minimize the damage to U.S.-Russian relations, while at the same time maintaining the maximum amount of influence in Iran.[30]

Finally, Primakov's diplomacy sought to engage India as a partner of strategic importance. The foreign minister was capitalizing on the old Soviet ties in trying to revive Russia as India's key rearmament agent. In 1997, the Indian prime minister announced that his country had purchased $3 billion in arms from Russia in the previous two years, and that the two sides had discussed potential contracts worth another $7 billion—a level that would move India ahead of China in the ranks of Moscow's arms customers.[31] Politically, Primakov was interested in building closer relations with Russia, India, and China to balance the power of the United States, which was a marked shift from the previous policy of balancing China though an alliance with India. In December 1998, Primakov spoke of the desirability of the three's alliance as a "new pole in world politics." This, however, remained wishful thinking, as neither India nor China had a similar interest.

On balance, Primakov's efforts to engage non-Western countries into strategic partnership with Russia for the purpose of balancing against the West hardly worked. Potential for developing bilateral ties with China, Iran, and India was there and likely to be more fully realized in the future. However, in the world of global economic interdependence, none of these countries was eager to enter into the Russia-sought balancing coalition. In addition, Russia's regional political interests proved to be too complex for it to fully commit to building such a coalition with explicitly articulated geostrategic objectives.

4.4. INTEGRATING THE FORMER SOVIET AREA

The Concept of Integration

Integration of the former Soviet area was another key pillar of Primakov's strategy of balancing Western power and resisting NATO expansion. The new foreign policymakers defined Russia's interests in terms of accumulating national power and sought to accomplish the three objectives. First, being pressured by the new conflicts in the former Soviet Union, they wanted to maintain Russia's military presence in the area. Second, they wanted to protect the status of ethnic Russians living outside Russia. Furthermore, Moscow was interested in obtaining valuable economic assets and facilities in the post-Soviet world.

Using a strong bargaining power in relations with the former republics, Russia was planning to obtain more informal control over their economic and security policies, without being overly responsible for the costs of such control. The country did possess considerable power to take a more assertive approach in the former Soviet Union. It had the most sophisticated weaponry, as well as the largest and the most experienced army in the region. Russia was also economically powerful due to the large size of its domestic market, rich endowment with natural resources, and more diversified commercial ties with countries beyond the former Soviet region. Politically, it was the only state in the region with the recognized reputation of a United Nations Security Council member, and it had also obtained membership in the prestigious G-8. Furthermore, it had a diversified linguistic diaspora of twenty-five million people, many of whom identified with their "homeland" and, therefore, could assist Russia in projecting its influence abroad. Some indicators of Russia's relative power in the post-Soviet region are summarized in tables 3.6 and 4.6.

The concept of integration was first clearly articulated on September 14, 1995, when Yeltsin issued a wide-ranging decree entitled "The Establishment of the Strategic Course of the Russian Federation with Member States of the CIS." The eight-page document had been developed out of one of the Primakov-led Foreign Intelligence Service reports, and it was transformed into the CIS Concept of Economic Integrational Development adopted in March 1997. For the first time since the Soviet breakup, the Kremlin acknowledged the priority significance of the CIS for Russia's national interests and defined Russia as the leading power in the formation of a new system of interstate political

Table 4.6. Russia's Power Capabilities Relative to Former Soviet States

Country	Population, 1989 (millions)	GNP, 1993 ($billions)	Military Personnel
Armenia	3.4	1.9	60,000
Azerbaijan	7.5	4.4	86,700
Belarus	10.5	16	98,400
Estonia	1.6	1.7	3,500
Georgia	5.7	2.3	?
Latvia	2.6	1.6	6,950
Lithuania	3.8	2.9	8,900
Moldova	4.5	4.1	11,850
Kazakhstan	17.4	18.2	40,000
Kyrgyzstan	4.7	2.9	7,000
RUSSIA	148.9	1,160	1,520,000
Tajikistan	5.9	2.5	2–3,000
Turkmenistan	3.9	3.8	11,000
Ukraine	51.9	54.2	542,000
Uzbekistan	22.3	14	25,000

Source: Neil MacFarlane, "Realism and Russian Strategy after the Collapse of the USSR," in *Unipolar Politics,* ed. Ethan B. Kapstein and Michael Mastanduno (New York: Columbia University Press, 1999), 225–26.

and economic relations in the region. The proclaimed goal was to create "an economically and politically integrated alliance of states capable of achieving a worthy place in world society," which was similar to Primakov's own definition of integration as a Russia-led "policy aimed at bringing together the states formed on the territory of the former Soviet Union."[32]

In addition to the Primakov-led Foreign Intelligence Service, originators of the concept of integration included conservative Civilizationist and moderate Statist influences. Conservative Civilizationists defended the territorial unity of Russia and the former Soviet region on culturally essentialist grounds. Eurasianists advocated a cultural unity of Slavs and Muslims, whereas Russian ethnonationalists promoted the primacy of the Russian language and religion in the region. The Congress of Russian Communities, for example, proclaimed Russia responsible for Russian speakers in the former Soviet republics; this was the view Yeltsin himself later adopted. The Council for Foreign and Defense Policy (Sovet po Vneshnei i Oboronnoi Politike)—an influential nongovernmental organization that united industrialists, businessmen, intellectuals, and public opinion leaders—contributed greatly to the notion of integration by consistently challenging Gaidar's and Kozyrev's economic policies and advocating Russia's more region-sensitive actions. The notion was therefore a hybrid of hard-line and moderate influences. It sought to revive the social, economic, and political coherence of the former Soviet region, without reviving the empire.

The strategy of integration had a good portion of pragmatism in responding to the new challenges Russia was facing both in the region and outside. While a major departure from Kozyrev's early isolationism, integration could not be likened to a restoration of the empire or a revival of aggressive imperial nationalism. Certainly, Primakov's supporters did not see it that way. For instance, the influential Council for Foreign and Defense Policy, which was also close to Primakov, issued a report entitled "Will the Union Be Revived?" in which it referred to the idea of the Soviet restoration as a "reactionary utopia."[33] At the same time, the report argued that a reasonable alternative to post-Soviet integration was not available and that Russia should assume the role of leader of such an integration.

For Primakov, the security context, particularly NATO's expansion, prompted the strategy's necessity. For the politically driven Yeltsin, however, the strategy was a way to neutralize his opposition and to restore the state-diminished capacity to conduct foreign policy. Yeltsin's opposition included members of the military, industrialists, and some hard-line nationalists who had ties with Russians outside Russia. In security affairs, the Primakov-recommended strategy helped to seize the initiative that the military had increasingly been taking away from civilian authorities. Under Primakov, the

Ministry of Foreign Affairs took considerable power away from the Ministry of Defense. For instance, it led the resolution of the Tajik civil war and the Moldovan conflict, and in both cases it produced peace treaties. In economic and cultural affairs, integrationism meant promoting Russian state interests by taking the initiative away from nongovernmental organizations that sought to restore the Soviet Union. In response, in his February 1995 state of the nation address, Yeltsin unfavorably referred to some "forces abroad" who wanted to downgrade Russia's international role, arguing for a new integration of the CIS.[34] By late 1995, Russia had already undertaken a series of activities to intensify its relations with Belarus, Kazakhstan, and Ukraine, and, in 1996, in attempting to further neutralize opposition to his policies, Yeltsin made a series of other new appointments. Among them was the appointment of Aman Tuleyev—a communist supporter and a defender of the CIS integration—as minister for cooperation with CIS states.

The new assertive course also had considerable social support at home. The general public was strongly supportive of Russia's closer economic, political, and cultural relations with the ex-Soviet states, although it did not favor the empire's restoration. For instance, in December 1997, 61 percent of Russian citizens were sorry that the Soviet Union had collapsed—up from 33 percent in December 1992. At the same time, most respondents did not approve of military interventionism to integrate the former Soviet region. Even more telling, in 1996 about 65 percent were convinced that the only way to regain the former great power status was through the successful development of the Russian economy.[35] Political elites, too, were supportive of the notion of integration. Even some observers of liberal orientation were now arguing the "inevitability" of integration within the former Soviet Union.

Political and Security Aspects

Integration of the post-Soviet area concerned first and foremost the political and security aspects. It was the new conflicts in the region that pushed the leadership to revise its originally isolationist stance with regard to the former Soviet Union. As early as the spring of 1992, Russia had to deal with ethnically based domestic and international military conflicts, particularly in the Caucasus, Moldova, and Tajikistan. Increasingly, Russia also faced threats of instability and terrorism in the south. It also had to confront the instability of borders with countries outside the former Soviet region and the emerged issues of illegal immigration and narcotics trafficking, especially on the Sino-Russian and Tajik-Afghan borders. It was in response to these threats that Moscow applied to the United Nations for special peacekeeping power in the region and began to see the region as an area of "special responsibility and special interest." It also began to advocate the CIS collective security forces and joint activities. Taking as a point of departure the 1992 Treaty on Collective Security, the Russia-led CIS members developed a fairly ambitious vision of military and defense coordination, which the CIS summit adopted in February 1995 as the Collective Security Concept. The concept, among other things, assumed the right to set up CIS peacekeeping forces.

Russia's leadership therefore effectively legitimized its security efforts, taking considerable power away from the military authorities. It saw its task in the region as twofold—first, to bring order and stability, and second, to preserve Russia's traditional powerful influences. In order to accomplish this, Yeltsin declared his intention to set up some thirty Russian military bases in the CIS states, and he envisioned the emergence of a common economic, political, and defense union in the area.[36] The new vision was based on the Foreign Intelligence Service's view of the security threat, which indicated a determination to prevent outsiders from filling a possible "power vacuum" in the region. The perceived security threats included especially the activities of Muslim states, such as Iran and Pakistan, in central Asia and the Caucasus. These threats resulted partly from Yeltsin's neglect of the area. The definition of the security threats also prominently included those from the United States and NATO's expansion.

Consistent with such a perception of threats, Russia sought to maintain its military presence in central Asia and the Caucasus. To keep away influences of Iran, China, and Afghanistan, it contributed greatly to guarding the borders of Turkmenistan, Kyrgyzstan, and Tajikistan. In the case of the last, Russia's presence was so extensive that Afghan border guards negotiated directly with Russian military commanders. Primakov's appointment led to the reestablishment of a balance between political and military tools of policy and helped to facilitate the end of the Tajik civil war and a peace treaty that was signed in June 1997 in Moscow. When it came to the Caucasus, however, Russia's stabilizing efforts were far less successful. Despite Primakov's more firmly established control of peacekeeping forces, he failed to stabilize the situation in Georgia. The earlier support of Russia's military of the Ab-khaz separatist movement backfired and contributed to Moscow's inability to mediate the conflict. It also resulted in Georgia's declining to support the CIS's collective security efforts. Finally, Russia intervened in Chechnya in order to respond to the republic's secessionism and to maintain a presence in the Caucasus. In addition to territorial integrity, Russia sought to defend the important Baku-Novorossiysk pipeline that runs through Chechnya. However, after the first Chechen war (1994–1996) and the May 1997 Chechen presidential elections, Moscow developed no specific policy in the republic, and Chechnya continued its slide into anarchy.

Russia's integration efforts on the western front differed from those in central Asia and the Caucasus. In the west, Moscow was especially eager to respond to the "threat" of NATO's expansion by normalizing and developing military ties with Belarus and Ukraine. Belarus, given its vital geostrategic location and pro-Russian orientation, emerged as particularly important. Ever since the two sides had signed the Treaty on the Formation of the Russia-Belarus Union State in April 1996, they committed themselves to a far-reaching integration in political and military areas. They developed a common perception of security threats and a close coordination of foreign policies, and they pledged the establishment of a defense alliance. Under Primakov, Russia also activated political ties with Ukraine, which the new foreign minister saw as his first priority. The key issue here was the status of the Black Sea fleet, which Russia sought to preserve without jeopardizing its relations with Ukraine. Ukraine, on the other hand, was interested in legalizing the Russia-Ukraine post-Soviet borders by signing an appropriate treaty and therefore politically normalizing the two countries' relationship. As a result of Primakov's efforts, the two sides signed in May 1997 the so-called Big Treaty, which settled the fleet issue and legalized the borders. The treaty provoked some criticism on both sides, but Primakov's support was instrumental in its ratification in February 1999. Despite the hard-line domestic criticism, both Primakov and his successor Igor' Ivanov saw the political normalization with Ukraine as a step toward improving the two's relations, rather than as a concession to Ukrainian aspirations to join NATO. This attitude found broad social support at home, as 70 percent of Russians supported the "Big Treaty."[37] As for the policy toward the most pro-Western Baltic states, Russia sought to minimize the negative consequences of NATO's expansion by offering those states security guarantees, and by making explicit its position that Baltic membership in NATO would endanger Russia's good relations with NATO.

Economic Integration

Economic integration was another important aspect of Primakov's strategy. During the Soviet era, Russia and the former republics were tightly integrated economies (see table 3.6) and could not successfully break the multiple bonds of their mutual dependency. The initial opposition to Yeltsin's early policy of isolationism came from the former Soviet managers, who lobbied their views through the Civic Union. The appointment of Viktor Chernomyrdin as prime minister helped to further this group's agenda and signaled the change from the "West first" to the more region-sensitive approach. A former economic manager and the president of the largest gas company, Gazprom, Chernomyrdin lent Russia's regional policies more sensitivity with regard to its interdependence, rather than irreconcilable differences, with the former republics. His vision of relations in the former Soviet Union included a manipulation of energy supplies for the purpose of making the energy-deficient former republics invest in Gazprom, as well as other large energy-related companies, such as Lukoil, Yukos, and Sidanko. Yeltsin endorsed this approach in his Decree No. 472, which was issued on May 7, 1995, and approved a new long-term energy strategy for Russia until 2010.

Primakov's own approach was different and more state oriented. Like Chernomyrdin, Primakov understood that what the Civic Union industrialists referred to as the "broken politicoeconomic ties" could not be easily repaired, and he, too, wanted to promote the interests of Russian businesses in the region. At the same time, the foreign minister wanted to actively practice "economic diplomacy"—the Kremlin's label for both negative and positive sanctions—for strengthening Russia's political interests in the region. He had in mind to capitalize on Russia's relative economic power (see table 4.4) for facilitating Russian-favored bilateral and multilateral political ties with the post-Soviet states. In the Statist spirit, Primakov reasoned that the state interests were superior to those of the private sector, and therefore one had to be prepared to invest in projects with the potential to facilitate the reintegration of the former republics.

This vision implied that integration of the former Soviet space would weigh heavily on the Russian state, rather than on the private sector—yet another indicator that the identity coalition behind the new vision in the region was at its core of a security nature. At the time such a vision had Yeltsin's support. The aforementioned presidential decree on the establishment of Russia's strategic course with the CIS members promised to draw the current members of the Economic Union into the Russia-dominant Customs Union based on "their deeply integrated economy and strategic political partnership."[38] It also proposed "the acceleration of practical steps toward the formation of a Payment Union," common foreign currency regulations, and, eventually, use of the Russian ruble as a reserve currency. Finally, the decree envisioned the creation of common "industrial, scientific-technical, and related structures," as well as "common interstate investment programs." While the decree mentioned the Interparliamentary Assembly of the CIS states as the preferred forum to develop the normative aspects of economic integration, the document also warned that a former republic's failure to adhere to "the model proposed by Russia" could have consequences in terms of "the scale of economic, political, and military support from Russia."

Yet the outlined strategy of multilateral integration remained largely unrealized partly because of Russia's own economic difficulties and partly because some republics were eager to diversify their ties away from the former imperial core. These republics perceived the CIS economic integration projects as Russia's thinly veiled imperialism and therefore resisted even some commonsensical measures to coordinate economic policies. For instance, the Payment Union, as well as interstate investment cooperation, never materialized. Other economic agreements were not working effectively. The only major exception was the Customs Union, which was signed by Russia, Belarus, Kazakhstan, Kyrgyzstan, and Tajikistan in March 1995 and continued to function during Primakov's tenure. Russia made more progress in developing bilateral than multilateral relations in the region. In some cases, it successfully applied its economic power to achieve important political goals. In central Asia, for example, Russia used Turkmenistan's and Kazakhstan's dependence on Russia's energy pipelines to negotiate a more favorable treatment of ethnic Russians residing in these states. It also further consolidated its economic and political relations with Belarus.

With regard to Ukraine, Russia initiated and signed in February 1998 the ambitious Program of Economic Cooperation, which helped to revive the trade between the two countries and dealt with all major aspects of their economic relations from trade barriers to cooperation in various industries. The signing of the program became a part of the Russia-Ukraine treaty on economic cooperation for 1998–2007 and it followed the previously signed "Big Treaty" between the two. It helped to promote political normalization with the largest and most important of the post-Soviet states and therefore could be viewed as an achievement of the Kremlin's flexible economic diplomacy. Although it hardly promoted the integration originally envisioned by the Kremlin, it did defy the hard-line nationalist arguments on both sides and encouraged international cooperation in the region.

Cultural Aspects

The vision of post-Soviet integration also had a cultural component to it. Primakov felt that Russia had an obligation to respond to the political and cultural feelings of twenty-five million Russians who had found themselves outside their "homeland" and continued to identify with it. As early as in his sponsored 1994 Foreign Intelligence Report, Primakov directly linked the fate of the Russians in the former Soviet Union to the survival and prosperity of Russia. In addition to ethnic Russians, there were many who grew up speaking Russian as either their native or preferred language (see table 3.6). Combined, the Russian language–influenced community totaled about 30 percent of the entire population of the non-Russian post-Soviet states, which makes Russia, as one scholar acknowledged, "not simply a marginal national European state, but a potential center of a revived, distinct civilization."[39] The issue was closely related to preserving cultural balance inside Russia, which included by far the largest number of ethnic groups (some 140) with only five of its twenty-one ethnic republics having a clear majority of the titular nation (Chechnya, Chu-vashia, Ingushetia, Tuva, and North Ossetia).

The challenge, as Primakov and Yeltsin saw it, was to find a way to revive the identity of the transnational community in the former Soviet area without giving ground to the hard-line Civilizationist opposition. Primakov's support-ers cautioned against pushing the Russians-first vision too far and argued that such a vision could jeopardize Russia's own fragile multicultural balance. Al-though the leadership did not share the Civilizationist agenda and did not want to be led by it in its regional policies, it could no longer ignore close cultural ties in the region. The public opinion inside Russia seemed support-ive of the government's efforts to find a middle ground between the earlier cultural isolationism and the hard-line ideas of imperial revival. Although most people consistently regretted the Soviet breakup, many did not see the Russian ethnicity or Orthodox religion as the key characteristics of the new "Russianness." Instead, 87 percent identified the obligatory features of a Rus-sian as love for the country and perception of it as the motherland. In addi-tion, most disagreed with the idea of Russia's political unification with adja-cent territories populated mostly by Russians.[40] The solution, Primakov's supporters argued, was to embrace and to cautiously promote the idea of Eur-asia as a multicultural, multiethnic, and multireligious community in place of the former Soviet Union.[41]

Russia's leadership seemed responsive to the idea. To promote it, the gov-ernment first developed and began to promote the idea of dual citizenship in the former Soviet states, viewing it as an alternative to the direct support for Russians abroad advocated by the hard-line opposition. The government also hoped to curb the uncontrolled flow of migrants to Russia by providing them with some security and peace of mind. Russia aggressively promoted dual citizenship, but by 1995 all the post-Soviet states, with the exception of Turk-menistan and Tajikistan, rejected the idea. In response, the Russian govern-ment began to advocate CIS citizenship. Both ideas meant to revive the iden-tity of transnational community in the former Soviet area and would have given Russia the upper hand in shaping such a community. Yet none of these ideas was able to take strong root in the region.

The leadership was more successful in responding to the challenge of do-mestic multiculturalism. Rather than giving ethnic Russians "a leading role," it promoted what some political commentators interpreted as "hybrid, an eclectic mixture of values," while others viewed it as a Eurasian vision of multicultural federalism.[42] Most important in this respect was Presidential Decree No. 909, which was issued in June 1996 to approve the concept of the state nationalities policy of the Russian Federation. It stated the goal of a multiethnic Russia to ensure "the cultural self-preservation and further development of national traditions and cooperation of Slavic, Turkic, Caucasian, Finno-Ugric, Mongolian and other peoples of Russia within the framework of Eurasian national-cultural space." The decree came close to Spain's model of offering autonomy to all interested constituent units by encouraging them to enter into power-sharing agreements with the center, rather than pursuing a path of complete independence. By March 1999, about fifty of Russia's eighty-nine constituent units had successfully negotiated various degrees of privileged status, with "work in progress" on a dozen or more. Although Chechnya was a notorious example of a violent deviation from the model of multicultural federalism, other Muslim republics, such as Dagestan, Ossetia, Tatarstan, and Bashkortostan, indicated their support for the project of Eurasian federalism.

To sum up, the foreign policy aspect of cultural integration did not materialize the way Yeltsin and Primakov had hoped. The issue of successfully bridging various ethnicities outside Russia remained largely unresolved partly because of Russia's low credibility in the former Soviet region, and partly because the cultural aspect of integration remained poorly defined. The leadership itself was far from clear as to what should replace the earlier ideas of civic nation and cultural isolationism.

4.5. EVALUATING GREAT POWER BALANCING

The arrival of Primakov as the second foreign minister brought with it major changes in how the government perceived Russia's national interest and conducted international policies. The course of Great Power Balancing that had been advocated by the identity coalition of Statists did not mean to replicate the Soviet isolationist policies toward the West. The timing of Primakov's course, as well as domestic and international conditions, was fundamentally different. Yet the course that contained attempts to balance Western influences did bear some similarities to Soviet policies of containing the West, and to the extent that it did, it failed in accomplishing central foreign policy objectives. Trying to achieve the West's recognition through restoring a great power status had a limited effect under the conditions of Russia's increased economic and political dependence on Western nations. Russia had changed since the Soviet rule, and the course of Great Power Balancing proved to have a mixed record in improving the country's international conditions.

The Record

Primakov's foreign policy had a number of successes, particularly in the realm of security. His attention to the former Soviet area and intense diplomatic involvement made a difference in negotiating peace in Moldova and Tajikistan (although not in Georgia). He also negotiated and pushed through ratification of the "Big Treaty" with Ukraine that put the two countries' relations on a new security footing. The minister could also be credited for making progress in Russia's negotiations with NATO. Despite a number of setbacks in the two's relationship, Russia had developed a mechanism of permanent consultations with the alliance and obtained its written commitment not to deploy nuclear weapons or substantial new forces on the territory of new member states. In addition, the new minister worked hard to improve ties with the countries of Asia and the Asia-Pacific region.

Through his course, Primakov also restored some attributes of foreign policy autonomy. Although Russia continued to be highly dependent on the West in economic affairs, it made Washington more attentive to its national interests in the area of security issues. On such issues as arms sales and security in Yugoslavia, Primakov took a much tougher line than his predecessor, who, in the words of one journalist, "had corrupted Americans" by his willingness to follow in Washington's footsteps.[43] Both the elites and the general public expressed their strong support for the new course, welcoming its greater independence and concentration on solving security issues in the former Soviet Union. For example, on the issue of sending troops to the former Soviet republics, provided that Russia was asked to do so, the general public support grew from 35 to 56 percent during the 1993–1999 period. The elite's support on the same issue over the same period increased from 56 to 72 percent.[44]

Table 4.7 summarizes the foreign policy record of Great Power Balancing.

As analysts have acknowledged, Primakov accomplished these positive changes despite Russia's continuous decline in 1992–1997 and lack of balancing options. In the former Soviet region, one scholar noted, "Despite the sharp decline of its power, Russia has been far more successful and far less reticent in asserting its interests in the southern Near Abroad than is generally acknowledged."[45] Another realist scholar was surprised to note that the weak-

Table 4.7.   The Record of Great Power Balancing

Security	Peace agreements in the former Soviet region
	Mechanism of permanent consultations with NATO
	Improved ties with Asian world
Welfare	Failed economic union in the CIS
	Continued industrial stagnation at home
Autonomy	Less dependent decision making
Identity	Continued identity crisis

ened Russia showed "a capacity to extract concessions"[46] in relations with the West. This policy activism from the position of weakness suggests yet again the limitations of realism as an international relations theory for understanding Primakov's foreign policy. Rather than being driven by material power alone, that policy was a response to a particular combination of international and domestic factors of a political and cultural nature.

However, the Great Power Balancing had some major flaws as well. Primakov's failures to assert his vision in Iraq and Kosovo—as well as his uninspiring attempts to establish a strategic triangle of Russia, China, and India to contain the United States' global hegemony—are cases in point. Even more obvious were his failures to improve Russia's welfare—the issue for which dealing with the strategy of balancing Western influences had not been designed in the first place. Yet every foreign policy—especially that of a country during an economic depression—must have the welfare dimension as its central guiding criterion. The project of integrating the former Soviet region was especially misguided in this respect. Integration partly meant to respond to the imperative of improving life throughout the region, but it proved to be excessively geopolitically driven and not as founded on economic grounds. Most multilateral CIS-based economic agreements were not working properly, and the former Soviet states continued to drift separately. Most of them also rejected Russia's citizenship initiatives. Several regional initiatives emerged, including those without Russia as a participant. Faced with Primakov's state grandeur in the former Soviet region, the Russian private sector was not willing to invest in the relationships in the former Soviet Union. The energy companies, for example, grew strong by the time of the integration strategy, but often did not feel compelled to back up the state with their resources. While interested in expanding to the former Soviet space and maintaining stability there, the energy entrepreneurs did not want to subsidize the former republics or supply them at lower energy prices in exchange for their political loyalty to the Russian state. Despite some serious efforts on Russia's part to make integration work, its results left much to be desired. As far as the Russian economy was concerned, the post-Soviet integration did not provide the economy with new opportunities for growth. Nor did it bring any foreign investments or relieve the burden of foreign debt.

Nor did the new foreign policy strategy make serious progress in improving Russia's cultural well-being. The fact that Russia was going through an identity crisis was obvious to policymakers and observers alike. Symptomatic of the identity search was, for example, the discussion about Russia's new "national idea" that Yeltsin initiated immediately following his 1996 reelection as president. Primakov addressed the crisis by proposing a Eurasianist foreign policy orientation in building strategic relations with China, Iraq, and India. His cooperation with the West was merely pragmatic, as opposed to strategic, and NATO's intervention in Yugoslavia pushed Russia further away from the West. Yet the Westernist component of Russia's cultural identity had been confirmed by Russia's post-Soviet developments, and many Russians continued to identify with the West. The strategy of Eurasia-oriented Great Power Balancing was not successful in addressing this part of the Russian national psyche.

Lessons

What lessons can one learn from the foreign policy of Great Power Balancing? Undoubtedly, Primakov's diplomacy had important accomplishments, such as the already-discussed more democratic policymaking process, greater attention to the former Soviet region, generally pragmatic nature of relationships with Western nations, and aggressive search for new opportunities outside the West. Yet the central thrust of this diplomacy rooted in Primakov's view of Russia's national interest, as that of a contributor to balancing U.S. unipolar ambitions in the world, was a misguided one. If Russia would ever have to be preoccupied with the role assigned to it by its second foreign minister, it would have to take place in a different era and under different circumstances. Devoting valuable material and political resources to the task of building a multipolar world was hardly a worthy central task. Such preoccupation was hardly pragmatic and, despite Primakov's own convictions, bore only a superficial resemblance to Alexander Gorchakov's strategy of "concentration." Rather than "concentrating" on domestic economic and social revival, as that strategy had prescribed, Primakov's Russia occupied itself with balancing the West and integrating the periphery (also in the context of balancing the West). Two more specific lessons can be formulated.

First, during this difficult era of economic and geopolitical decline, Russia would have accomplished more by attempting to engage the West in cooperative projects than by trying to assemble a coalition of those unhappy with Western policies. Persistent thinking about the West as a "power pole" prevented Russia's foreign policymakers from probing and pursuing economic and security opportunities that might have been mutually beneficial.

Certainly, a great deal of blame for missing such opportunities lies with the Western side, which preferred to develop relationships with the narrow and corrupt ruling elite while simultaneously pursuing policies of containing Russia on security issues. Flawed Western financial assistance is an illustration of the overall narrow and self-serving strategy of working with Russia. Instead of encouraging social safety nets and rule of law in the process of fundamental structural transformation, Western assistance served merely to encourage a destruction of the previous economic system. The newly emerging system was far from socially or legally responsible. The fact that the West-sponsored re-form strategy did not help to facilitate the transformation was reflected, among other things, in the figures of the overall capital flight during 1992–1999, which exceeded the amount of financial assistance. According to Russia's official statistics, the overall capital flight during that period was \$182 billion, whereas the amount of foreign assistance constituted \$174 billion.[47] The so-called reformers in Russia were well aware of the state of affairs and yet were unable to say "no" to Western "assistance."

While providing financial assistance, Western nations pursued policies that kept Russia safely at arm's length on security matters. First, there was the ex-pansion of NATO, which even the liberal-minded Kozyrev saw as a "continu-ation, though by inertia, of a policy aimed at containment of Russia."[48] Many in Russia perceived the decision largely as an attempt to fill the existing secu-rity vacuum by taking advantage of Russia's weakness. In addition to NATO's expansion, Russia took a lot of heat for its "imperialist intentions" in the for-mer Soviet region and "human rights violations" in Chechnya; other countries often ignored Russia's legitimate considerations of security and territorial in-tegrity. Many in the West continued to mistrust the former "red menace," viewing it as threatening and barbaric. The United States, as the strongest Western power, bears prime responsibility for the inadequate policies toward Russia. European leaders, too, contributed to Russia's security isolation. Con-cerned with the country's lack of democracy and the conduct of the Chechen war, they suspended Russia's moves toward integration into Western Euro-pean institutions. As a result, the Russian-sought "Common Strategy of the EU on Russia"—an elaborate document that formulated principles of relations with Russia and made its integration dependent on progress in building democratic and market institutions—was adopted only in June 1999.

Still, the West's flawed strategy was no excuse for giving up engagement in favor of limited cooperation. The lesson to draw is that, without sacrificing its interests, Russia should stay actively engaged with policies of Europe and the United States. This does not mean approval of every Western action (or ac-ceptance of every criticism from the West), but it does mean that for the time being, resistance and condemnation should be restricted to political rhetoric. If anything, Russia's more than modest economic capabilities, relative to those of Western nations (see table 4.3), should be a sober reminder to ambitious politicians. If one has no special tools to make an elephant move, trying to do it anyway is not a smart strategy.

The second lesson is that the state must look for economic opportunities more aggressively and work with the private sector to advance national inter-est. The Statist identity coalition of nonliberal origins proved sufficiently strong to challenge the initially isolationist policies in the former Soviet region, but it failed to rally sufficient support for economic integration. Neither the Russian state nor former republics had resources sufficient for reviving the economic ties in the region. A number of Primakov-outlined initiatives remained on paper only, and his efforts made many former republics wary of Russia's power intentions. The latter prompted them to create security groups of their own. Most prominently, in October 1997 a coalition of key states that had never signed the Russia-initiated Collective Security Concept—Georgia, Ukraine, Azerbaijan, and Moldova—established a regional group, GUAM, with an explicit purpose of containing Russia. If anything, this action was an indicator of a failure of multilateral integration. Multilateral arrangements cannot be forced and are not always superior to those concluded on a bilateral basis.[49] Working with the private sector and facilitating mutually beneficial bilateral agreements is a better means to accomplish economic integration.

NOTES

1. Yevgeni Primakov as quoted at his first official press conference as foreign minister (Robert H. Donaldson and Joseph L. Nogee, *The Foreign Policy of Russia: Changing Systems, Enduring Interests* [Armonk, NY: M. E. Sharpe, 1998], 119) and at the conference "Preobrazhennaya Rossiya" held at Moscow Institute of International Relations in 1992 ("Preobrazhennaya Rossiya," *Mezhdunarodnaya zhizn'* 3–4 [1992]: 104).

2. Samuel Huntington, "The Clash of Civilizations?" *Foreign Affairs* 4, no. 72 (1993).

3. For elaboration, see especially Yevgeni Primakov, "Mezhdunarodniye otnosheniya nakanune XXI veka: Problemy, perspektivy," *Mezhdunarodnaya zhizn'* 10 (1996); and Yevgeni Primakov, "Rossiya v mirovoi politike," *Mezhdunarodnaya zhizn'* 5 (1998).

4. "Strategiya Rossiyi v XXI veke," *Nezavisimaya gazeta*, June 18, 1998.

5. "The Need for a New Ostpolitik," *Financial Times*, January 16, 1996.

6. Yevgeni Primakov, *Gody v bol'shoi politike* (Moscow: Sovershenno sekretno, 1999), 213, 217–21.

7. Primakov, presentation at the conference "Preobrazhennaya Rossiya," 104.

8. As cited in Primakov, "Rossiya v mirovoi politike." For a more extended analysis, see Flemming Splidsboel-Hansen, "Past and Future Meet: Aleksandr Gorchakov and Russian Foreign Policy," *Europe-Asia Studies* 54, no. 3 (2002).

9. National security concepts and foreign policy concepts are available in *Vneshnyaya politika i bezopasnost' sovremennoi Rossiyi*, ed. Tatyana Shakleyina (Moscow: ROSSPEN, 2002), 4: 51–90, 110–11. For analysis, see Alla Kassianova, "Russia: Still Open to the West?" *Europe-Asia Studies* 6, no. 53 (2001).

10. Boris Yeltsin, "Mesto i rol' Rossiyi v period formiruyuschegosya mnogopolyarnogo mira," *Mezhdunarodnaya zhizn'* 6 (1998): 3.

11. For instance, Aleksei Bogaturov proposed viewing the post–Cold War international system as "pluralistic unipolarity," in which the unipolar center is a group of

responsible states, rather than one state (the United States). Bogaturov saw Russia as a member of the group and argued for consolidation of its position within the global center, as well as for discouraging the formation of one-state unipolarity in the world. Aleksei Bogaturov, "Pluralisticheskaya odnopolyarnost' i interesy Rossiyi," *Svobodnaya mysl'* 2 (1996); "Amerika i Rossiya: Ot izbiratel'nogo partnerstva k izbiratel'nomu soprotivleniyu," *Mezhdunarodnaya zhizn'* 6 (1998).

12. For instance, Gorbachev's key foreign policy adviser, Georgi Shakhnazarov, prepared an analytical report on Russia's foreign priorities, in many respects sympathetic to Primakov's vision ("Vneshnepoiliticheskiye prioritety Rossiyi," *Politicheskaya mysl'* 1, 1998).

13. For instance, the Ministry of Defense officials, such as General Leonid Ivashev, for quite some time dreamed of restoring Russia's superpower status ("Rossiya mozhet snova stat' sverkhderzhavoi," *Nezavisimaya gazeta*, March 7, 1995).

14. Gennadi Zyuganov, *Geografiya pobedy* (Moscow, 1998).

15. Aleksandr Dugin, "Yevraziyski proyekt," *Zavtra*, August 1996.

16. Yuri Fedorov, "Krizis vneshnei politiki Rossiyi," *Pro et Contra* 6, no. 1–2 (2001).

17. Irina Kobrinskaya, "Pragmaticheski liberalizm vo vneshnei politike," *Otkrytaya politika* 7–8 (1997); Viktor Sheinis, "Rossiya i Yevropa: Interesy protiv mifov," *Nezavisimaya gazeta*, December 20, 2000.

18. For analysis of the decision to expand NATO and Russia's reaction to it, see James Goldgeier, *Not Whether, but When: The US Decision to Enlarge NATO* (Washington, DC: Brookings Institution Press, 1999); and J. L. Black, *Russia Faces NATO Expansion: Bearing Gifts or Bearing Arms?* (Lanham, MD: Rowman & Littlefield, 2000), respectively.

19. As cited in Neil MacFarlane, "Realism and Russian Strategy after the Collapse of the USSR," in *Unipolar Politics*, eds. Ethan B. Kapstein and Michael Mastanduno (New York: Columbia University Press, 1999), 242.

20. As cited in Leonid Mlechin, *Ministry inostrannykh del: Romantiki i tsiniki* (Moscow: Tsentrpoligraf, 2001), 620.

21. Richard Sakwa, *Russian Politics and Society*, 3d ed. (London: Routledge, 2002), 294.

22. Some Statists linked the two events directly. See, for example, Aleksei Pushkov, "Otrezvlyayuschaya yasnost," *Nezavisimaya gazeta*, March 1999.

23. I draw here on Robert O. Freedman, *Russian Policy toward the Middle East since the Collapse of the Soviet Union* (Seattle: The Henry M. Jackson School of International Studies, University of Washington, 2001), 34–40; and Donaldson and Nogee, *The Foreign Policy of Russia*, 301–5.

24. Allen Lynch, "Realism of Russian Foreign Policy," *Europe-Asia Studies* 53 (2001): 15, 28.

25. Oksana Antonenko, "Russia, NATO and European Security after Kosovo," *Survival* 41, no. 4 (1999/2000): 143.

26. Aleksei Pushkov, "Sindrom Chernomyrdina," *Nezavisimaya gazeta*, June 11, 1999.

27. Aleksandr Belenski, "Mudrost' sily," *Sovetskaya Rossiya*, April 27, 1999; Gennadi Zyuganov, "Yugoslavski rubezh," *Sovetskaya Rossiya*, April 6, 1999.

28. Aleksandr Lukin, "Den' pobedy pod bombami," *Nezavisimaya gazeta*, May 27, 1999.

29. Antonenko, "Russia, NATO and European Security," 134–36.

30. Freedman, *Russian Policy toward the Middle East*, 23.

31. Donaldson and Nogee, *The Foreign Policy of Russia*, 316.

32. *Rossiyskaya gazeta*, September 23, 1995; Primakov, "Rossiya v mirovoi politike," *Mezhdunarodnaya zhizn'* 5 (1998): 11.

33. "Vozroditsya li soyuz? Buduscheye postsovetskogo prostranstva," *NG-Stsenariyi*, May 23, 1996.

34. *Rossiyskaya gazeta*, February 17, 1995, p. 5. Yeltsin's change of perception toward a more hegemonic role of Russia can be traced to an early-1994 television interview, in which he called Russia "the first among equals" in the post-Soviet region.

35. The poll data are from: Dimitri K. Simes, *After the Collapse* (New York: Simon & Schuster, 1999), 220; and Susan Birgerson, *After the Breakup of a Multi-Ethnic Empire* (New York: Praeger, 2002), 88.

36. Mark Webber, *CIS Integration Trends: Russia and the Former Soviet South* (London: Royal Institute of International Affairs, 1997), 13–14.

37. Georgi Shakhnazarov et al., "Vneshnepoliticheskiye prioritety Rossiyi."

38. *Rossiyskaya gazeta*, September 23, 1995.

39. Igor Zevelev, *Russia and Its New Diaspora* (Washington, DC: United States Institute of Peace, 2001), 175.

40. The poll data are from: Zevelev, *Russia and Its New Diaspora*, 61; Vera Tolz, *Russia: Inventing the Nation* (London: Arnold, 2001), 263.

41. Graham Smith, *Post-Soviet States* (London: Arnold, 1999), chap. 6; Tolz, *Russia: Inventing the Nation*, chap. 8.

42. Smith, *Post-Soviet States*, 143.

43. Izvestiya correspondent Stanislav Kondrashev, as quoted in Leonid Mlechin, *Ministry inostrannykh del*, 607.

44. William Zimmerman, *The Russian People and Foreign Policy* (Princeton: Princeton University Press, 2002), 91.

45. Rajan Menon, "After Empire: Russia and the Southern 'Near Abroad,'" in *The New Russian Foreign Policy*, ed. Michael Mandelbaum (New York: Council on Foreign Relations, 1998), 148.

46. MacFarlane, "Realism and Russian Strategy," 244.

47. Ivan Korolev, "Integratsiya Rossiyi v mirovuyu ekonomiku," *Pro et Contra* 6, no. 1–2 (2001): 76.

48. Andrei Kozyrev, "Partnership or Cold Peace?" *Foreign Policy* 99 (Summer 1995): 13.

49. Primakov had a tendency to view bilateral ties in the former Soviet region as a "negative process" relative to those of a multilateral nature (see, for example, his *Gody v bol'shoi politike*, 387).

5

The World after September 11 and Great Power Pragmatism

> Such a country as Russia can survive and develop within the existing borders only if it stays as a great power. During all of its times of weakness . . . Russia was invariably confronted with the threat of disintegration.
> We are a part of the Western European culture. No matter where our people live, in the Far East on in the south, we are Europeans.
>
> —Vladimir Putin[1]

With the arrival of Vladimir Putin and especially after the terrorist attacks on the United States in September 2001, Russia's foreign policy took yet another turn. This turn, while surprising, was not entirely unexpected. The new course of Great Power Pragmatism was both a continuation of and a departure from the previous Great Power Balancing. Changed international and internal conditions brought to prominence a new identity coalition, which helped to articulate a new vision of Russia's national interest.

5.1. RUSSIA'S NEW PRAGMATISM

The Changed World Context

Two global developments were particularly important in leading to the reformulation of Russia's foreign policy. The first was encouraging and of an economic nature. It had to do with the relative recovery of the Russian economy after the August 1998 financial crisis and new opportunities that the recovery was promising for the country. The growth had been steady, and other indicators, too, had been encouraging (see table 5.1). Commercially, Russia, too, was in a relatively advantageous position. Its foreign trade had been enjoying a structural surplus, and the economy was wide open for commercial operations. The share of foreign trade had been around 50 percent in the gross domestic product (GDP), making Russia's economy, on that measure, about as open as Germany's. The stock of foreign direct investment accumulated since 1989 remained low: about ten times less than in China and five times less than in Brazil.[2] Yet the rising world oil prices further provided Russia with new opportunities to explore.

The second development was negative and had to do with an intensification of terrorist activities in the Caucasus and worldwide. In Russia, the Kremlin's inaction in the aftermath of the 1996 peace agreement with Chechen rebels led to the further spread of anarchy inside the republic, not to political stabilization. The newly elected leader of Chechnya, Aslan Maskhadov, failed to maintain order, and mass kidnapping and extortion by local warlords continued. In August 1999, Chechen rebels led by Shamil Basayev and the Arab fighter Khattab had occupied parts of the neighboring republic Dagestan, in response to which the Kremlin resumed military operations in the region. Also in August, two bombs exploded in apartment buildings in Moscow, killing hundreds of civilians. The sheer magnitude of violence was unprecedented. Russians united behind Putin, who was running for president on the platform of "eradicating extremism" in Chechnya and reestablishing a "strong state" throughout the entire Russian territory. Initially, the popularity of then prime minister Putin was at the level of only 2 percent, but in two months it jumped to 26 percent, and as the war in Chechnya progressed, it reached the unprecedented 58 percent mark in January 2000.[3]

It was at this point that the domestic sense of insecurity was reinforced by the September 11, 2001, terrorist attacks on the United States. The horrific acts created a principally different social and political atmosphere inside Russia. President George W. Bush proclaimed terrorism to be "pure evil" directed at freedom-loving people throughout the world and argued the necessity to

Table 5.1. Russia's Economic Recovery, 1998–2001 (1998 = 100%)

	GDP	Consumption	Investment	Government Spending	Capital Flight
1998	100	100	100	100	100
1999	105.4	87.2	104.6	105.4	94
2000	114.1	96.2	122.7	131.4	123.6
2001	120	101.3	131.1	133.7	73.6

Source: Philip Hanson, "The Russian Economic Recovery: Do Four Years of Growth Tell Us That the Fundamentals Have Changed?" *Europe-Asia Studies* 55, no. 3 (2003): 386.

launch the strategy of preemption. Several leading intellectuals called to capture or kill Osama bin Laden and linked the violent attacks to Islam and the Middle Eastern region. In Russia, these developments provided Putin with a formidable opportunity to bolster his domestic and international posture and to vindicate his conception of security threats. Russia's new president wasted no time in taking advantage of September 11 for reshaping Russia's relations with the United States and redefining the threats to Russia as being characterized by global terrorism.

New Identity Coalition

In response to these global developments, Putin put forward the ideology of pragmatism and self-concentration. The ideology articulated the vision of a new identity coalition, which combined both Westernist and Statist influences. With Westernizers, Putin came out critical of past practices of overextending foreign policy resources—a possible reference to both the Soviet and Primakov periods. However, he also committed himself to traditional values typically emphasized by Statists and Civilizationists. For instance, in his programmatic article "Russia at the Turn of the Millennium," which he addressed to his electorate, the future president emphasized patriotism, a strong state, and social solidarity as his country's key values. Unlike Gorbachev or Kozyrev, Putin was not eager to replicate Western social democratic or liberal values on Russian soil, and he made it clear that Russia would never become the "second edition of . . . the U.S. or Britain."[4] Rather, he saw his country as a modern great power capable of adapting to a changing world under state leadership. In the tradition of Statism, the priority is given to governability and the state's ability to exercise its power, whereas democracy comes second.

> Our state and its institutions have always played an exceptionally important role in the life of the country and its people. For Russians a strong state is not an anomaly that should be gotten rid of. Quite the contrary, they see it as a source and guarantor of order and the initiator and main driving force of any change.[5]

Also in Primakov's Statist spirit, Putin spoke of the Eurasianist dimension of Russia's identity, and in late 1999–early 2000, he visited the key states of central Asia, China, India, Mongolia, North Korea, and Brunei. Furthermore, he was determined to continue the war in Chechnya as he saw fit, despite criticism of his Westernist opponents inside and outside the country. The Statist thinking therefore proved to be resilient in post-Primakov Russia.

Yet, unlike Primakov, who tended to view the world primarily in terms of new threats to Russia's security, Putin pointed to both threats and opportunities. In particular, he was keen on emphasizing the economic nature of the

contemporary world and the need for Russia to be successful in its geoeconomic, rather than military, struggle. In the president's own words, "The
norm of the international community and the modern world is a tough
competition—for markets, investments, political, and economic influence . . .
nobody is eager to help us. We have to fight for our place under the economic
sun."[6] As far as security threats to the modern system of international relations
were concerned, Putin saw them coming from terrorist activities, rather than
state-organized military capabilities. In this, his Statism was also distinct from
that of Primakov. Putin's "no one is going to war with us" was a reference to
states, yet he was convinced that terrorism had interests in attacking Russia.
His support for the Western countries and the United States' efforts in fighting
international terrorism after September 11 was therefore not tactical, but
came from his principal belief system.

This new vision was hardly an exclusive product of Putin's own imagination. Rather, it represented interests of the new mixed social coalition. Because commercial elites often defended Russia's Westernist identity, whereas
military and security elites promoted Statism, the new coalition was sometimes referred to as the alliance of oligarchs and *siloviks*, or chekists (from the
Russian Cheka, the original name of the Bolshevik security service). Liberal
and commercially oriented Westernizers strongly supported Putin's election.
Especially important were Russia's oligarchs, the group of superwealthy businessmen that had emerged as a powerful force in 1996. At that time they had
managed to overcome their differences and pull together enough financial
resources to reelect Boris Yeltsin, who was unpopular then. At the same time,
many Statists and Civilizationists felt compelled to embrace Putin. Statists and
various members of Russia's military elite supported him because of his background in the security service and his stated beliefs in strengthening the state
and social order. Initially, even Aleksandr Prokhanov, the editor of the hard-
line newspaper *Zavtra*, had written favorably about him, although a year later
he returned to his typical "irreconcilable" opposition to the Kremlin. Although the members of the new coalition were committed to principally different worldviews, at this time they agreed on Putin as the preferred leader of
the state. The new identity coalition rose to prominence in the post–1998 new
domestic and external context. The relative recovery of the Russian economy
improved the oligarchs' position, and the intensification of terrorist activities
in the Caucasus and worldwide strengthened the *siloviks*' position. In the new
world context of both threats and opportunities, the oligarchs and *siloviks*
each hoped to increase their influence on the president.

In his turn, Putin was planning to take advantage of the unstable coalition's
resources, while exercising his authority as he saw fit. He did not hide his
preference for the state-dominant model of economic development and made

known his lack of respect for how oligarchs emerged and enriched themselves. But he also expressed his readiness to honor the already-underway privatization and market reforms. In one of his private meetings with businessmen, Putin summed up his philosophy by telling businessmen that "they could keep what they had already stolen, but now they had to play clean, pay taxes, make investments and stay out of politics."[7] The president was being ruthless to those oligarchs, such as Boris Berezovski, Vladimir Gusinski, and Mikhail Khodorkovski, who he perceived as violating his new deal. The first two had to emigrate, and the third, the heir of the oil giant Yukos, was arrested on charges of multiple fraud and tax evasion. The president had more respect for security elites, especially the army, which had been much humiliated under Yeltsin. The first war in Chechnya taught the military, among other things, that it could not count on the civilian leadership for adequate financial assistance. Putin moved to change that by proposing a considerable reduction in the army's personnel—from 1.2 million in 2001 to between 800,000 and 850,000 by 2005[8]—along with modernization and a considerable increase in the military budget (see table 5.2 for details of the budget increase).

The New Vision of National Interest—Pragmatic Westernism

Consistent with the new vision of Russia's identity, a new conceptualization of national interest was adopted. In the earlier period of his presidency, Putin had indicated that he was wary of U.S. policies and intentions, and he acted in ways that coincided with Primakov's Statist philosophy of multipolarity and Great Power Balancing. Yet Putin soon revealed his principal differences from his predecessors. For him, the most important national interest lay in Russia's modernization and economic growth, not balancing American influences in the world. Such perspective assumed that in today's world, geoeconomics gained the upper hand over geopolitics, and thus Russia had to learn to defend its national interests by economic means. It also implied that Russia had to economize its resources and not overstretch itself in world political affairs. Balancing, therefore, needed to yield to pragmatism. Finally, it meant that any integration in the former Soviet area had to be open to and compatible with domestic private interests and the task of Russia's gradual integration with the world economy.

Table 5.2.   Russia's Increased Military Budget, 1999–2002

Year	1999	2000	2001	2002
Billions of Rubles	109.0	111.0	218.9	284.1

Source: Dale R. Herspring, "Putin and the Armed Forces," in *Putin's Russia: Past Imperfect, Future Uncertain*, ed. Dale R. Herspring (Lanham, MD: Rowman & Littlefield, 2003), 170.

To substantiate his vision, Putin warned of the danger of turning into a third world country. Ridiculing overly noisy great power rhetoric—"let us not recollect our national interests on those occasions when we have to make some loud statements"—Russia's new leader compared Russia to Portugal, the EU's poorest member. He then drew the uncomforting conclusion, "It would take us fifteen years and an eight percent annual growth of our GDP to reach the per capita GDP level of present-day Portugal."[9] The reality was that, despite Russia's economic recovery after the 1998 financial crisis, the size of its economy and purchasing power was less than one-fourth of the economies of China and Japan, and less than one-tenth of the economies of the United States and the European Union.[10] Putin's support for the concept of multipolarity was also muter, and the key emphasis of the new National Security Concept was on economic decline, organized crime, corruption, terrorism, and separatism. After September 11, his support for multipolarity continued to decline, and the focus was on pragmatism and self-concentration in foreign policy. Despite some common anti-Western sentiments among the members of Russia's political class, the president became far more active in promoting Russia's relationships with the United States and Europe, and more passive on the Eastern and Asian fronts.

Yet it would be a mistake to cast Putin as a pro-Western liberal. It is true that he saw the first task in improving the state of the Russian economy by capitalizing on domestic oil reserves and increasing the ability to export to the West (provided that the West would invest more actively in the Russian petroleum industry). But at the same time, such economic improvement was seen as a way to confirm Russia's great power status and to preserve the required space to maneuver to defend Russia's political interests in world politics. Without antagonizing the West, and given the West's need to have Russia as an ally, Putin planned to promote its interests in relations with Chechnya, Iran, and Iraq as he saw fit. This vision of Russia as a defensive and pragmatically pro-Western power was different from the earlier described visions of integration with the West or balancing the West's global influences. So long as the new Russian leader was attempting to synthesize across Russia's political spectrum by incorporating both nationalist and Westernist perspectives, the new vision of national interest was culturally sustainable (table 5.3 summarizes Putin's view of national interest).

Table 5.3.   Defensive Pragmatism: View of National Interest

What?	A great power in the West-centered world
How?	Counterterrorist cooperation with Europe and the U.S.
	Limited integration in the world economy
	Market-based principles in the former Soviet region

5.2. RESHAPING THE DEBATE ON NATIONAL INTEREST

Putin's decision to support the United States in the post-September 11 struggle against terrorism and his redefinition of national interest led to an important change in the Russian discourse. Although many representatives of Russian foreign policy elites supported his move, others offered their reservations and even hard-line criticisms. Many politicians and intellectuals were worried that U.S. policies may undermine, rather than strengthen, peace and stability in the world. They were therefore reminding the president that an unqualified support for the United States had the potential to damage Russia's relations with Europe, China, and Muslim countries.

Tentative Support of Liberal Westernizers and Social Democrats

Despite their criticism of Putin's early foreign policy, liberal Westernizers threw their support behind his post-September 11 vision. Yet they urged him to go beyond a tactical alliance with the West and toward forging a development of common identity and cultural values. A leader of the liberal Yabloko Party, Grigori Yavlinski, in an article entitled "A Temporary Friendship or an Eternal Alliance?", insisted that Putin's vision of national interest had to be viewed as a "choice in favor of a long-term unity with Western or European civilization, of which Russia is an organic part." In Russian, the word "alliance" (*soyuz*) is the same as the word "union," and this fact made the proposed rapprochement with the West sound similar to Kozyrev's strategy of integration. Without such a long-term strategic union with the West, argued Yavlinski, Russia was doomed to remain in what he saw as "oligarchic capitalism" without sufficient respect for human rights and freedoms of expression.[11]

Ideologists of another liberal party, the Union of Right-Wing Forces, went even further. Not unlike some Western politicians and commentators, they viewed the events of September 11 as a clash between "civilization" and "barbarians," who had yet to learn the "universal" rules of "civilization."[12] In a similar way, President George W. Bush and his defense secretary, Donald Rumsfeld, viewed the problem of terrorism in terms of pure evil against "freedom-loving people" throughout the world. Thomas Friedman, writing in the *New York Times*, specified the evil as not just Osama bin Laden, but "angry people" from "failing states in the Muslim and third world." For Friedman, the real war was between those with a modern and progressive outlook and those with a medieval one.[13] This group of Russian Westernizers also came out critical of the pragmatic element in Putin's vision of national interest and insisted that Russia make a decisive choice in favor of "civilized nations." In addition to supporting the United States after September 11, many Westernizers also supported its military intervention in Iraq and argued that Russia had to side with the United States.

The attitude of the Social Democrats was a more complex and cautious one. Because Social Democrats viewed the world as culturally pluralist, rather than centered on the West, they were more inclined to search for solutions to September 11 by developing a global intercultural dialogue. This group, with supporters in the broader political center, was also supportive of Putin's new vision and generally sympathetic toward the West. At the same time, the group cautioned that, among other issues, the cause of the spread of terrorism was the United States' unilateral use of power and the narrowly chosen pro-American model of globalization. The quest for future policy choices for Russia, as the leader of Russia's Democratic Socialist movement Aleksandr Buzgalin put it, "needs to be pursued in the context of looking for alternatives to the current model of globalization."[14]

The Social Democratic group also did not view the West as a culturally essentialist entity shaped by an American liberal capitalist outlook, as did the Russian Westernizers. Instead, Social Democrats perceived the West as an arena of competition between liberal capitalist and social democratic values, often represented by the American and European models, respectively. Accordingly, the choice for Russia was broader than merely joining the West versus remaining marginalized. As the group was less inclined to view the United States and Europe as culturally similar, some Social Democrats recommended that Putin explicitly side with Europe in the post-September 11 world. They urged Russia's president to choose in favor of the "social democratic" Europe of Tony Blair and Gerhard Schroeder, and not the American "neoconservatism" of George W. Bush. In their view, the former had a broad domestic appeal and would improve Russia's international standing, whereas the latter had the potential to isolate Russia from Europe and turn it into a raw material appendage of the American economy. Social Democrats also cautioned against Russia's pro-American choice, which they feared would strengthen (and not weaken, as Yavlinski has argued) Russian nondemocratic tendencies.[15] Many other scholars in Russia and elsewhere called for the formation of a broad coalition of countries and cultures, including China and India, to respond to the global terrorist threat.[16]

In several respects, the views of this school of thought corresponded with those of President Putin. First, Putin also downplayed military interventions as a long-term solution to the problem of terrorism (which at the time contrasted with his choice of solutions in Chechnya). He did not commit Russian troops to the effort, and instead emphasized the relevance of international law and the United Nations. He was also careful to not cast his actions in a pro-American or an anti-Islamic light, and immediately after the terrorist attack, warned against framing the policy response as a war of civilizations. The latter is important given the aforementioned tendency of some of Russia's liberal Westernizers to characterize 9/11 as a clash of Western "civilization" with a cultural "barbarianism." Second, and somewhat consistent with the Social Democrats' philosophy, Putin seemed to have differentiated between Europe and America, and indicated his interest in developing strategic relationships with European countries. In his April 2002 state of the nation address, Putin strongly emphasized Russia's European priority, stating, "We have to firmly proclaim our priorities on the European direction." He went on to define Russia's policy priorities in relations with Europe and the United States as those of "integration" and "maintenance of constant dialogue," respectively.[17] He also sided with France and Germany against military intervention in Iraq.

Criticism of Statists and Civilizationists

While Westernizers were critical of the new vision's pragmatism, Statists and Civilizationists were worried about its pro-Western component. The range of their reactions varied from moderate support to the idea of pragmatic cooperation against the "common enemy" of terrorism to an outright rejection of any association with the West.

Statists who were former supporters of Primakov's foreign policy course aimed to preserve Russia's independence and great power status in world politics. This school continued to view as Russia's main national priority the preservation of such status and the development of a multipolar world. Primakov himself felt uneasy about Putin's post-9/11 strategy, referring to it as "justified, yet a big risk" and worrying about the American military presence in the Caucasus and central Asia.[18] Other Statists emphasized the "harmful" aspects of American military hegemony and political unilateralism as one of the reasons for the attacks of September 11. One influential commentator argued:

> Under the slogan of the struggle with terrorism, the United States achieved an important geopolitical victory, especially in central Asia and the Caucasus—regions that Russia viewed in the area of its vital interests. . . . As the result of the antiterrorist operation, Russia has lost important mechanisms of international influence related to the CIS Collective Security treaty and the "Shanghai Six"—these mechanisms have never been mobilized and are now falling apart.[19]

Many Statists saw the benefits of cooperation with the United States in some areas, including in central Asia, but insisted on the tactical, rather than strategic, nature of the cooperation. Strategically, Russia's pro-American and, more broadly, pro-Western choice had the effect of worsening the country's relations with the Muslim and Asian regions and irreparably damaging its moral, economic, and political standing. A broad coalition of great powers, including Russia, China, and India, was something that most Statists favored as the most appropriate response to the threat of global terrorism.

Table 5.4 summarizes contending views on the new vision of national interest.

The National Communists and Eurasianists went much further in criticizing Putin's vision and the response of the West to the events of September 11. Although this group also placed blame for the tragedy on Western shoulders, its representatives conceptualized the role of the West differently. The problem, in the minds of the Communist/Eurasianist group, was not merely the American strategy and hegemonic ambitions; such strategy and ambitions themselves should be viewed as inevitable products of Western culture and its creature—modern civilization. For this group, the politics of the West were inseparable from its culture and economics. The tragedy of September 11 was seen as reflecting the spiritual program of modern history and the West (first and foremost, the United States). The forces responsible for September 11 were of a transnational economic and military nature, and had little to do with developments in the third world.[20]

For this group, September 11 was nothing less than part of an epic struggle for liberation from the unipolar/unicultural Western world, a world in which Russia had a duty to side overtly with anti-Western and especially anti-American forces. Much like President Bush, the hard-line Civilizationists viewed the post–September 11 world in terms of a struggle between "good" and "evil," except they found themselves on the other side of the barricade. To win in this struggle, they recommended building a broad coalition of anti-American cultures and civilizations. Among these cultures and civilizations, some saw an alliance of Russia and Muslim countries as having the strongest potential to successfully resist Western modernity and hegemonic policies. Others added to the alliance China and even, potentially, Germany.

Russian foreign policy perceptions are summarized in table 5.5.

The Wariness of the Broader Public

The political class's cautious reaction, described above, was broadly representative of the feelings within Russia's general public, which remained wary of

Table 5.4.   Defensive Pragmatism (DP): Contending Views

Civilizationists/Statists:		Westernizers:
DP is not sufficiently respectful of cultural and political independence	VS.	DP is not sufficiently pro-Western

Table 5.5. Russia's Foreign Policy Discourse after September 11

	Liberal Westernizers	Social Democrats	Statists; Civilizationists
Causes of September 11	Non-West: "Barbarism"	Both West and non-West	West: unilateralism and modernity
The necessary response	Spread Western values	Develop intercultural dialogue	Avert Western hegemony
Implications for Russia	Side with the West	Support the UN; integrate with Europe	Balance against the West

Adapted from: Andrei P. Tsygankov, *Whose World Order? Russia's Perception of American Ideas after the Cold War* (Notre Dame: University of Notre Dame Press, 2004), 124.

Western intentions. The country's most traumatic postcommunist experience and the failure of Gorbachev's and Yeltsin's early attempts to develop a strategic partnership with the West made the Russian political class, military, media, and general public skeptical of the new efforts at rapprochement. At least three major issues drew public attention. First, many politicians and military officers pointed to the United States' unilateral decision to develop a national missile defense system and abandon the antiballistic missile (ABM) treaty, which the Russians continued to view as a cornerstone of strategic stability. Second, there was still the issue of NATO's expansion, often perceived as an essentially anti-Russian process that continued to follow the old maxim "Keep America in, Germany down, and Russia out." In addition, there was a concern over U.S. and NATO troops' presence in the central Asian states, which are in immediate geographic proximity to Russia.

Because all these issues were in the spotlight, few factions in the Russian Duma initially supported Putin's decision to side with the United States after 9/11. Russia's Muslim leaders reacted critically to the American military campaigns in Afghanistan and Iraq. Of special importance was a series of published "open letters" signed by retired generals, including one of Yeltsin's former defense ministers, accusing Putin of "selling out" the country and "betraying" the nation's vital interests. Federal Border Guard Service head Konstantin Totski issued a characteristic statement maintaining that, if U.S. forces remained in central Asia after the counterterrorist operation in Afghanistan, "we are unlikely to remain friends."[21] Even the mainstream media described what they perceived as a sense of Russian "encirclement" by U.S. and NATO troops. For example, *Rossiyskaya gazeta*, the newspaper of the Russian government, rang the alarm with this statement: "One way or another Russia, the entire former USSR, remains encircled by a dense ring of military and intelligence-gathering installations belonging to the North Atlantic alliance." The American presence in the region, argued another source, resembled post–World War II events, when the Americans quickly turned from allies into enemies.[22] The Russian general public, although supportive of Putin's leadership, also showed signs of increased concern over American actions in the world. According to data from the Russian Center for the Study of Public Opinion, 63 percent of all Russians felt that the terrorist attack on the United States was a form of "retribution for American foreign policy."[23]

5.3. REENGAGING THE WORLD AFTER SEPTEMBER 11

With the introduction of the philosophy of Great Power Pragmatism, the West remained at the center of Russia's foreign policy. The new policy was, however, to reengage the West in order to acquire its recognition for Russia as a great power. Therefore, while insisting on Russia's own interests in many areas of world politics, Putin sought to frame those interests as consistent with strategic commitments to Western values, such as international law, personal freedoms, and a market economy. His strategy of engaging the West was to propose a new agenda, the implications of which might be more far reaching than those stemming from addressing the old issues of NATO expansion or the missile defense system. While not giving up on the old issues easily, Russia's leader did not want to be cornered on those issues. He therefore proposed some new areas in which Russia could develop some long-term advantages. Two of these areas were counterterrorism and energy cooperation. As a result, while preserving a large space in which to maneuver in dealing with his domestic critics, Putin has proven to be more efficient in engaging the West than was his most pro-Western predecessor, Kozyrev.

Reengaging the United States

Putin's efforts to engage the United States predate the September 11 attacks. The new leader wanted to start fresh after the Kosovo experience that had considerably soured Russia-West relations, and he began to cultivate ties with the American administration soon after he came to office. Washington's initial reaction was cold. The new administration in the United States made it clear that it did not foresee any breakthroughs in relations with Russia. It made public the arrest of FBI agent Robert Hanssen, who had spied for the Russians, and it subsequently ordered fifty Russian diplomats to leave the United States. It threatened to end any economic aid except for nonproliferation projects and—through Secretary of Defense Donald Rumsfeld—accused Russia of proliferating nuclear materials and weapons technologies. As late as February 2001, Bush's national security adviser Condoleezza Rice insisted that Russia was a threat to America and its European allies. Putin persisted and finally got his break when he met with the American president in Ljubljana, Slovenia, in the summer of 2001. The relationship began to change, largely thanks to personal chemistry between the two leaders. It was after the summit that Bush made his famous remarks on Putin: "I was able to get a sense of his soul."[24]

September 11 presented Putin with a unique opportunity to implement his new vision of national interest. Soon after the terrorist attacks on the United States, he offered that country's leaders broad support for antiterrorist operations in Afghanistan. The measures included intelligence sharing, opening Russian airspace to relief missions, taking part in search-and-rescue operations, rallying central Asian countries to the American cause, and arming anti-Taliban forces inside Afghanistan. As our earlier analysis indicates, the domestic public was wary of rapprochement with the United States, and that constrained Putin's freedom of action. Determined, he pressed forward by stressing the positive potential of the new Russia-U.S. relations. In particular, beginning with his interview in the *Wall Street Journal* in February 2002, he emphasized Russia as a reliable alternative to traditional Middle Eastern sources of oil and natural gas. Russia was the world's single largest non-OPEC oil exporter, with 10 percent of the known oil reserves and 9 percent of the world output. Yet this oil accounted for only 1 percent of American imports in 2001.[25] Putin projected for Russia to increase production of crude oil at the rate of 9 percent per year, much of it intended for export, with a considerable part for the United States. The subsequent events demonstrated the existence of reinforcing interests in this aspect of Russia-U.S. relations on both sides. In May of the same year at their summit in Moscow, the U.S. and Russian presidents signed a joint declaration on energy cooperation. Then followed the Houston "energy summit" in October, where Russian officials said that they could export as many as a million barrels a day to the United States within five years. The *Economist* summed up all these efforts at the time: "America's relations with Russia are now better than at any time since the end of the Second World War and are improving."[26]

Eager to engage the United States, Putin was careful not to overplay his opposition on traditional issues, such as NATO, the Balkans, and the ABM Treaty. Rather than insisting on Russia's membership in NATO or the alliance's not admitting new members—both demands being entirely unrealistic although not uncommon for previous diplomacies—Putin moved to organize security relations with Western countries on the common basis of counterterrorism. After initial support for Slobodan Milošević, he opted to minimize involvement in the affairs of the post-Kosovo Balkans. In August 2003, Moscow withdrew its peacekeeping mission from Bosnia and Kosovo. And, despite formidable domestic resistance, he made little of his opposition to the U.S. desire to abandon the ABM Treaty that had prohibited the unilateral building of a nuclear missile defense system. The United States' administration made it clear that it would be withdrawing from the treaty, regardless of the reaction from Russia. Putin's reaction was mute and nonthreatening, despite some expectations of a possible confrontational response. In his opinion, the United States' decision was a "mistake," but it presented no threat to the national security of the Russian Federation.

Capitalizing on Ties with Europe

In addition to developing the new relations with the United States, Putin put a new emphasis on ties with European partners, especially Germany, France, and Italy. Russia's energy markets were primarily in Europe—they accounted for 40 percent of Russia's foreign trade relative to a mere 5 percent of trade with the United States. In fact, if Europe is understood in the wider sense—as the one that includes the EU, Central and Eastern Europe, Norway, and Switzerland—then the share of Russia's trade went up to 55 percent.[27] In June 2003, Putin also sealed a joint venture with British Petroleum worth over $6 billion. His vision of global security, too, proved to be quite compatible with those of large European nations. During the crisis over the American decision to go to war against Iraq, Russia joined the antiwar coalition and argued that the United Nations was the only legitimate body to sanction the use of force. In siding with the Europeans, Putin was firmly supported at home, but he was also careful not to present his views as anti-American, positioning himself instead as a voice of moderation and even reconciliation between the American and the European side in the West. Putin continued making efforts to bring Russia and Europe closer culturally. During the celebration of St. Petersburg's three-hundred-year anniversary, he went as far as to suggest that visas between EU countries and Russia be abandoned altogether by the year 2006.

As was the case with Russia's new relations with the United States, Putin's efforts to demonstrate his commitment to European values were unmistakably pragmatic. In those issues where the new leadership perceived European powers to be infringing upon Russia's interests, the Kremlin preferred to maintain a distance from Brussels. Most symptomatically, for all the rhetoric of developing closer relations with the EU, there was relatively little cooperation in the area of security. For instance, Moscow continued to be mistrustful and rejected European ideas for joint peacekeeping missions in the former Soviet states, such as Moldova. It also shut down the OSCE mission in Chechnya. In addition, Putin's government decided to put an end to the activities of U.S. Peace Corps volunteers in Russia; this action became a source of irritation in relations with the United States. All this indicated that Russia continued to differ from its Western counterparts in its evaluation of national interest and security threats. Consistent with the earlier specified strategy of modernization, Russia continued to be interested primarily in economic cooperation with Europe, defined in terms of growing investments and sales of energy and weapons abroad.

In their turn, Europeans continued to be suspicious of Russia's often treating Europe, in the perception of Putin's adviser, as a "mischievous student in the school of democracy."[28] Some of these suspicions were visible in discussions about the issue of visas for Russian transit travelers to and from Kaliningrad. Kaliningrad was the Russian enclave that became surrounded by EU members after Lithuania's admission into the EU in May 2004. The Europeans were especially worried about corruption of the local administration in the Kaliningrad region as well as the miserable economic situation there. On that basis, they declined Russia's proposal to have a visa-free arrangement, but the two sides reached a compromise agreement in Luxembourg on April 2, 2004. The agreement spelled out measures aimed at ensuring the free transit of goods from Russia to Kaliningrad, and it ensured that Russian train travelers to the Kaliningrad enclave were to obtain a Lithuanian permit only. More broadly, the historical enlargement of the EU and the incorporation of ten new members on May 1, 2004, underscored the policy of constructing Europe without any meaningful role for Russia. As one observer put it, "A chagrined Russia finds itself not the architect of this new creation, or even a member, but an outcast relegated to a sideline role."[29]

Supporting the United States in Afghanistan, but Not in Iraq

The pragmatism in defining national interest helps to interpret Russia's divergent foreign policy responses toward two major military crises after September 11—Afghanistan and Iraq. Putin's support of America after 9/11, on the one hand, and his decision to oppose the war in Iraq, on the other, were both shaped by a sober calculation of payoffs in state power and autonomy.

The pragmatism of Putin's support for the United States' war against the Taliban regime in Afghanistan was quite obvious—for a long time, Russia supported the Northern Alliance and was eager to have its long-term rival removed from power without a single shot fired. While offering his support, Putin made it clear that he would not commit Russian troops to operations inside Afghanistan because the Russian constitution proscribed such operations and the United Nations had yet to authorize them. Another expected payoff from the extended intelligence cooperation was the American support for Putin's policies in Chechnya, the absence of which had been complicating Russia's efforts to develop a positive image in the eyes of the West. Other expectations were of an economic nature and related to Moscow's plans to increase energy sales abroad. Finally, Putin had in mind to eventually gain membership in the World Trade Organization (WTO), but on relatively favorable terms. On all these accounts, the president was counting on the support of the United States.

The war in Iraq was a different matter, however. Here, Putin decided to join the coalition of those opposing the war on American terms. Along with Russia's foreign policy officials, he warned against going over the head of the United Nations, which would authorize the use of force. The same vision of national interest underlined Putin's decision. As in Afghanistan, he wanted to reduce terrorist threats to Russia, and he wanted to provide his country with better conditions for economic modernization. Not convinced by arguments about the existence of a nuclear program in Iraq and links between Saddam Hussein's regime and the Al Qaeda terrorist network—both being the key arguments of the Bush administration—he saw the war as a deviation from the global war on terrorism. Along with many others in Russia's political circles, Putin believed that terrorism, as a stateless phenomenon, was a challenge to the very system of states. In his view, terrorism could be defeated only through the coordination of state efforts, and not through taking on relatively established states, such as Iraq.

The economic modernization consideration was also prominent in Putin's calculations. This consideration included Russia's ties with Europe and Iraq. The strategy of great power pragmatism assumed cooperation with the United States, but not at the expense of ties with Europe, the latter being far more extensive. In addition, Russia had important oil interests in Iraq, and Saddam Hussein skillfully exploited those by promising to Russian private companies more lucrative contracts. In the wake of the military intervention, many Russian experts forecasted a drastic fall in world oil prices in the near future—another nightmare for Russia, where a considerable part of revenue came from exporting natural resources. There was also the issue of Iraq's sizable debt to Russia—$7–8 billion, by different calculations—and Russia was worried it would never see the money as a result of the war.

The two divergent decisions found support at home. If Putin had lost any of his credibility for throwing his support behind American intervention in Afghanistan, he certainly regained it all during his opposition to the war in Iraq. Russian elites grew highly skeptical of the idea of siding with the United States. Even some of the Westernizers viewed the war in Iraq as a dangerous precedent of jeopardizing the role of the United Nations. Very few supported the war, insisting on the primacy of Russia's "strategic partnership" with the United States and Russia's future role in Iraq. Statists and Civilizationists, predictably, saw the war as George W. Bush's drive for global hegemony and warned of his appetite for Russia's resources and territory. For instance, a former defense minister,

General Igor' Rodionov, in typical remarks referred to Russia as an "occupied country" defeated by the United States. At the conference marking the anniversary of the Nazi invasion of the Soviet Union, he went on to argue that "our geopolitical enemy has achieved what Hitler wanted to."[30]

As far as the general public was concerned, although many in Russia felt sympathy for America following the September 11 terrorist attacks and had little support for Saddam Hussein, Russian public opinion turned sharply against Washington's intervention in Iraq. In April 2003, only 2 percent approved of the U.S. military action, while 83 percent were opposed. This was a matter of anti-American, not pro-Iraqi, feeling. Only 45 percent sympathized with the Iraqis, whereas 46 percent were undecided and a mere 5 percent supported the Americans. And 71 percent of the Russian public felt threatened by the United States and was afraid of being next on the list of American targets for military intervention.[31] In addition, Putin's decision to oppose the war in Iraq rested on firm support abroad. In addition to France and Germany, the world outside Russia overwhelmingly—as the Pew Global Attitudes survey demonstrated—held a negative image of the United States and its actions in the post–September 11 era (table 5.6 demonstrates the degree to which different nations, including Russia, held negative views about the United States over time).

Outside the West: Economic Modernization at Any Cost?

Putin's view of the world outside the West was shaped by the same belief that Russia must do everything in its power to conduct successful economic modernization. Like Primakov, he believed in the necessity for Russia to have a strong presence on the world political scene, but he chose a different method of achieving that goal. The issues that for Primakov had the political signifi-

Table 5.6.   Favorable View of the United States (%)

	1999/2000	March 2002	March 2003
Britain	83	75	48
France	62	63	31
Germany	78	61	25
Poland	86	79	50
RUSSIA	37	61	28
Turkey	52	30	12

The surveys were conducted among 38,000 respondents of forty-four nations. They found that "despite an initial outpouring of public sympathy for America following the September 11, 2001 terrorist attacks . . . images of the U.S. have been tarnished in all types of nations: among longtime NATO allies, in developing countries, in Eastern Europe, and most dramatically, in Muslim societies."
Source: *What the World Thinks in 2002*. Washington, DC: Pew Research Center for the People and the Press, December 4, 2002; *America's Image Further Erodes, Europeans Want Weaker Ties*. Washington, DC: The Pew Research Center for the People and the Press, March 18, 2003, at www.people-press.org.

cance of balancing the American power were reduced to considerations of economic recovery under Putin. Unlike his predecessor, Putin was not a committed Eurasianist and did not seem to have much trust in the East. In some ways, his thinking about Russia's Asian neighbors was similar to that of Westernizers and was marked by fear and defensiveness. For example, he shared the Westernizers' concern that if Moscow failed to improve the economic situation, neighboring nations could exploit Russia. In one of his speeches, the president issued an explicit warning, "I do not want to dramatize the situation, but if we do not make every real effort, even the indigenous Russian population will soon speak mostly Japanese, Chinese, and Korean."[32] Putin was also not particularly careful in some of his statements on Chechens; these statements further revealed his ethnocentric bias. Insistence on Russia's belongingness to Western European culture described his beliefs better than attempts to cast himself as a supporter of Eurasianist identity. In his own words, "Above all else Russia was, is and will, of course, be a major European power."[33]

Therefore, Putin's policies outside the West, as active as they were, are best understood as serving the purpose of modernizing Russia, rather than developing strategic diplomatic alliances or deep cultural affinities. In building ties with Asian neighbors, Russia was especially determined to win markets in arms and energy. It was interested in selling its arms in the West as well, but many Western forces dismissed Russian products as inferior. China and India, on the other hand, had emerged as Russia's largest buyers. Given that the two countries had been the world's largest and second-largest arms importers, the economic prospects of cooperating with them were quite promising. For Russia, the additional incentive came from the military industrial complex's overcapacity relative to almost nonexistent domestic orders. As a result, the arms exports rose dramatically, particularly in 2001 and 2002. During 1997–2001, Russia exported over $17 billion in arms, relative to the United States' share of almost $45 billion. Characteristically, while promoting weapons sales in Asia, at no point did Putin raise the issue of balancing the United States or creating some new strategic "axis" to serve this purpose. Even in the midst of signing a friendship treaty with China and knowing Russia's opposition to U.S. plans for a national missile defense, Putin stressed that "Russia plans no joint actions with other states in this sphere, including China."[34]

While selling arms, Putin was typically dismissive of Western concerns about weapons proliferation. He argued that these concerns merely reflected commercial interests to drive Russia out of competitive markets. On a number of occasions, the president demonstrated that he was not willing to bow to Washington's pressures that Russia stop cooperating with "dangerous regimes," such as Iran. Western officials and researchers argued that Russia was engaged in the proliferation of nuclear technology by helping India's nuclear program and building a nuclear reactor in Iran. However, Russia's president was convinced that his country's actions were perfectly legitimate. Russia pledged to build two more nuclear reactors in Iran and signed an $800 million deal with the Iranian government. The deal had been signed before Putin visited the United States in September 2003, and President Bush's efforts to change Putin's mind produced no results. In his interview with Western journalists, the Russian president stated, "According to our information, many western European and American companies cooperate with Iran—either directly or through intermediary organizations—in the nuclear sphere."[35] To substantiate the Kremlin's claims about the commercial nature of Washington's pressures, some Russian analysts argued that, in the absence of official contracts, the U.S.-Iranian trade turnover was around $1 billion, which was higher than that of Russia, despite the Russian-Iranian strategic partnership agreement. These analysts recalled that immediately before the Islamic revolution in Iran, Washington and Tehran had signed a $24 billion contract, which provided for U.S. assistance in constructing eight nuclear power plants in Iran within ten years.[36]

Another key concentration of Russia in Eurasia was energy and transportation projects. Here again, Russia was closely cooperating with China, Japan, Iran, and India. In the south, one key idea had been to build the so-called north-south transport corridor that would pave the way for the delivery of goods from India and the Arabian Peninsula through Iran and the Caspian region to Russia and Europe, and vice versa. In September 2000, Russia, India, and Iran signed the agreement, according to which all signatories would get relief from import tax and customs duties. The transportation route was expected to reduce transport costs by 20 percent, and delivery times by fifteen to twenty days compared with the old route via the Suez Canal. According to estimates by Mikhail Margelov, the head of the Federation Council's Foreign Relations Committee, Russia expected to make an additional $5–6 billion a year in transport revenues from the new route.[37]

In the east, Russia was planning to capitalize on Siberian rich oil reserves by building pipelines to the neighboring countries. During 2003–2004, Russia's government was deciding between a shorter Chinese route and a longer route that would connect Siberian oil sources with Japanese markets. The Chinese Angarsk-Daqing project was agreed on by Russia's Yukos and China National Petroleum; and in May 2003, the twenty-five-year oil-supply deal was signed by the new Chinese president, Hu Jintao, on his first trip to Russia. The alternative project would connect East Siberia to Nakhodka and, from there, to Japan. It was extensively lobbied by the Japanese side, which promised to finance the whole project if Russia agreed to it. The oil pipeline issue was being discussed along with the issue of northern territories and a possible peace treaty with Japan. Russian fears of China's gaining control over parts of Siberia continued to figure in Moscow's decision process, particularly since Beijing wanted the right to bring in tens of thousands of Chinese workers to build the pipeline. An additional complication for Russia was that China also wanted outright control over oil and gas, but offered to pay Russia only as much as Moscow sold gas for domestically.

5.4. PRAGMATISM IN THE FORMER SOVIET WORLD

Putin's approach to the former Soviet region was in line with his overall foreign policy philosophy of pragmatic modernization. Along with Primakov, he valued the region's political and geostrategic significance, but he placed the key emphasis on post-Soviet Eurasia's "advantage on the scale of global economic competition."[38] The new vision of the region assumed a more open, multilevel politicoeconomic space planned by the Russian state, but built with the close participation of the Russian private sector. In addition, Putin stepped up cooperation on issues of counterterrorism and attempted to assemble his own coalition of the willing in the region.

The New Westernist-Statist Consensus

The new vision rested on firm social support at home. Various media and political forces had long expressed their dissatisfaction with Primakov's grandiose foreign policy philosophy that had the "integration" of the former Soviet area as its key component. Westernizers were critical of the "integration" strategy for its underestimation of domestic business interests and for continuing what they saw as harmful practices of paying the former republics in exchange for their political loyalty to Russia. Boris Berezovski, a prominent oligarch and a onetime CIS executive secretary, attacked the Primakov-inspired vision for its "antimarket spirit." Scholars pointed to the pro-integration efforts running in a fundamentally different direction from the real economic interests of most of the former Soviet republics.[39] Liberal politicians, such as Grigori Yavlinski, opposed the government's attempts to entice Ukraine and Belarus into a closer relationship by subsidizing their energy payments and being soft on their debts to Russia. As early as 1994, pro-Western reformers such as Economics Minister Yegor Gaidar and Finance Minister Boris Fedorov resigned, due partly to their opposition to the negotiations over an economic union with Belarus. To Westernizers, the former republics were unreliable partners—too corrupt and conservative to develop economic relationships with Russia.

Some of Primakov's Statist-oriented supporters, too, began to withdraw their support for the strategy of post-Soviet integration. Driven by nationalist rather than free-market considerations, they spoke against what they saw as Russia's one-sided concessions and unwarranted exploitation of its resources. For instance, Andranik Migranyan, once a prominent critic of Kozyrev's isolationism and a promoter of Russia's "Monroe Doctrine" in the former Soviet area, now saw the CIS-centered integration as too costly and argued against Russia's remaining a leader in such an integration. As he stated in his reevaluation, "During the several last years, it became absolutely clear that all the attempts to integrate the post-Soviet space have led to nothing. The CIS is barely able to function."[40]

The new liberal-nationalist consensus was summarized in the document of the influential Council for Foreign and Defense Policy entitled "Strategy for Russia: Agenda for President—2000." Both Westernizers, such as Deputy Foreign Minister Anatoli Adamishin, and Statists, such as the chairman of the Duma's Committee on the CIS Affairs Konstantin Zatulin, collaborated in writing the final draft of the document. They found Primakov's vision of a multipolar world to be outdated, expensive, and potentially confrontational. Instead, the authors proposed the concept of "selective engagement," which they compared with Russia's nineteenth-century policy of "self-concentration" after its defeat in the war in the Crimea and with China's policy since Den Xiaoping. Regarding the former Soviet area, the authors recommended a "considerable revision" of policy, which would involve abandoning the "pseudointegration at Russia's expense" and "tough defense of our national economic interests."

> We must begin by changing the very concept of integration. It should be built not from above, but from below—on the basis of supporting the integration of various markets of separate goods and services, creating transnational financial-industrial groups . . . exchanging debts for assets' ownership. The state policy of cooperation and integration should be directed at supporting exactly this kind of activities.[41]

The Russian public seemed to favor such a view: it supported measures to boast economic development and questioned military solutions in the region.[42] This is not to say that there were no groups within the Russian political class supportive of a far-reaching integration in the former Soviet region, including one that would have involved military intervention. Such groups continued to exist and advocate their views, but they had been effectively marginalized by the new consensus.

The Vision of Three-Level Ties in the Region

Consistent with the newly formed consensus, the new leadership adopted the rhetoric of pragmatism and self-concentration regarding the former Soviet area. In February 2001, the secretary of the Security Council, Sergei Ivanov, publicly announced the new course, acknowledging that it would mean a serious rethinking of Russia's previous policies in the region. Almost repeating the lines of Primakov's critics, he announced that previous attempts to integrate the CIS had come at a very high price and that Russia must now abandon the integration project in favor of a "pragmatic" course of bilateral relations. By the time of this announcement, the debt of the CIS states to Russia had reached $5.5 billion.[43] Vice Premier Viktor Khristenko clarified the new approach by emphasizing its reciprocal nature:

> The essence of the current policy of Russia toward the CIS states is an energetic bilateral cooperation based on pragmatism and a reciprocal account of interests. We develop multilateral contacts only in those spheres that received support from the parties. Based on such an approach, we move to more advanced forms of cooperation mainly with those partners who express a genuine interest in a tighter integration.[44]

In the words of the parliament's CIS committee member Igor Glukhovski, Russia's relations with the former Soviet states would now exist on three separate levels—bilateral, subregional, and regional. In addition to bilateral relations, Russia would participate in subregional arrangements, such as the Collective Security treaty signed by Russia, Belarus, Armenia, Kazakhstan, Kyrgyzstan, and Tajikistan. Another subregional arrangement was the Eurasian Economic Union, which was formed by Russia, Belarus, Kazakhstan, and Kyrgyzstan with Ukraine joining in October 2003. Finally, Russia would develop regional forms of participation, particularly when it came to defending the region from international terrorist threats.[45]

New Bilateral Relations

Putin's objective of strengthening Russia's economic presence in the region materialized in aggressively asserting control over the ex-republics' strategic property and transportation. For example, in Georgia, Russia's state electric company obtained the right to be the main electricity provider, which provided it with a formidable opportunity to influence Georgian economic development. In Armenia, Russia obtained several strategic assets, such as an atomic electric station to offset a debt of $40 million. Outside the Caucasus, Russia was covering 30 percent of the energy needs in Belarus, and the head of Russia's state electric company Anatoli Chubais also expressed an interest in participating in energy privatization in Ukraine and other states of the former Soviet region. Chubais went on to announce that Russia's main goal in the twenty-first century should be to develop "liberal capitalism" and to build up a "liberal empire" through strengthening its position in the former Soviet Union.[46] Empire or not, Russia continued to press for control of oil pipelines in the Caucasus, central Asia, Ukraine, and the Baltics. Its most important achievement was a strategic energy accord with Turkmenistan, under which virtually all of Turkmenistan's gas fell into Russia's sphere of influence for the following twenty-five years. The accord effectively eliminated the plans to utilize Turkmenistan's gas fields for laying pipelines through Afghanistan with the assistance of the United States.

This strategy of economic domination also implied Russia's cultivation of relationships with the already-existing political regimes in the former Soviet Union, however democratic or authoritarian they were. In the fall of 2003, Russia quickly endorsed elections in Azerbaijan and Armenia, despite their questionably democratic nature. The transformation in relations with Azerbaijan was especially interesting given that previously Russia had perceived it with suspicion for developing ties with NATO and GUUAM. Putin's emphasis on economic ties assisted here as well. In late September 2003, he visited Azerbaijan to sign an agreement dividing the two countries' rights to Caspian oil and gas, which mattered greatly to Azerbaijan. Russia also secured continued use of the Gabala radar station, which was located in Azerbaijan and which Russian media speculated Moscow was using to monitor the United States–led war on Iraq. In Georgia, Russia chose not to comment on another fraudulent parliamentary election that eventually caused president Eduard Shevardnadze to resign, and it quickly moved to start afresh with the newly elected president, Mikhail Saakashvili. Here, in addition to economic interests, Russia wanted to secure the border with Chechnya and, especially, the Pankisi Gorge, which was long recognized as a transit point for terrorists.

In central Asia, Putin actively coordinated counterterrorist efforts with the local regimes, and he provided them with substantial military assistance in exchange for Russia's expanded military presence. He secured strategic partnership with Kazakhstan, in part through the division of Caspian resources. As a part of the gas deal with Turkmenistan, he also promised President Sapurmurat Niyazov some unspecified extra security services "to combat international terrorism." In Ukraine, Putin decisively supported the incumbent president Leonid Kuchma in his conflicts with the opposition. Here, too, the expectation was that the next president would continue Kuchma's policies of cooperation with Russia, and Russia would therefore continue to expand its economic presence in the country. In his turn, Kuchma agreed to sell Russia parts of Ukraine's natural gas transit system to offset the debt of roughly $2 billion to Moscow for energy deliveries. Finally, in Belarus, Russia continued to support President Aleksandr Lukashenko and supply energy at a discounted rate, but raised new demands regarding further steps to develop the Russia-Belarus union.

In addition to developing its economic presence in the region, Moscow sought to offset the growing geoeconomic influences of the West. Joint U.S.-British companies controlled 27 percent of the Caspian's oil reserves and 40 percent of its gas reserves. The United States also supported the Baku-Ceyhan oil pipeline, which passed through Georgia and Turkey to Europe and by-passed Russia. It provided resources for GUUAM, an economic and security group of five former Soviet states—Georgia, Ukraine, Uzbekistan, Azerbaijan, and Moldova—established in 1998 as a counterweight to Russian influence. And after September 11, it opened military bases in several central Asian states. Russia responded to these developments by preserving and strengthening its military presence in the Caucasus, central Asia, and Belarus through bilateral and multilateral efforts. Bilaterally, it negotiated the establishment of a new air force base in Kyrgyzstan and a base in Tajikistan, in addition to the already-existing other arrangements, such as the Baikonur Cosmodrome, the ballistic-missile testing range in Kazakhstan, and a major early-warning radar in Tajikistan. Russia also moved to consolidate its naval supremacy on the Caspian Sea with the planned induction of dozens of new warships in its Caspian flotilla over the next few years.

Pragmatic Multilateralism

Although Putin abandoned the Primakov-like effort to revive the CIS, he did not give up multilateralism as a way to strengthen Russia's position in the region. Through both economic and security multilateralism, Putin was patiently assembling his own coalition of the willing. In the economic area, a notable development was the creation of an economic agreement with Belarus, Kazakhstan, and Ukraine, which aimed at eliminating trade barriers and devising shared energy-transport policies. In the security realm, Russia concentrated on counterterrorist activities by developing the Shanghai Five, with China as a prominent member, and rebuilding the old Tashkent Collective Security Treaty. The Shanghai Five, or the Shanghai Cooperation Organization (SCO), emerged out of a Russia-China treaty on significant reduction of the number of border troops. The treaty was signed in 1997 along with Kazakhstan, Tajikistan, and Kyrgyzstan. After September 11, both Russia and China reactivated the SCO to address terrorism and a security vacuum in central Asia. A perceived threat of Islamic separatism was a matter of concern for Beijing, due to outbreaks of unrest among the Muslim Uighur minority—a Turkic-speaking group in China's Xinjiang region that borders central Asia, Afghanistan, and Pakistan. Even Uzbekistan, once the central Asian state most interested in reducing Moscow's power in the region, was now more inclined to cooperate with Russia. Uzbekistan joined the Moscow-created center to fight terrorism and called Russia "not only the guarantor of our security, but also a reliable strategic partner." Uzbekistan joined the SCO in late 2001, and in June 2004, it went so far as to sign a strategic cooperation agreement with Russia that included some important economic and military dimensions.

In addition, Russia's long-advocated collective security action to deal with perceived threats in central Asia found its expression in transforming the old Tashkent treaty into a full-fledged regional defense pact. In April 2003, six states—Russia, Belarus, Kazakhstan, Kyrgyzstan, Tajikistan, and Armenia— formed the Collective Security Treaty Organization (CSTO), pledging to pool their resources to fight terrorism in the area. The organization sought to mimic the Cold War–era Warsaw Pact in Eastern Europe, complete with a joint headquarters and armed forces, and a written commitment to respond to aggression against any member state.

Transportation Initiatives

Accelerating the development of a transportation system through transnational and transregional projects was an especially prominent focus of Putin's activities in the post-Soviet region. Most of these projects involved transporting oil and gas, of which Russia is one of the world's largest producers. In response to the rising oil prices, Russia stepped up its production considerably and, some analysts speculated, was on a course to pose a rivalry to Saudi Arabia by the end of the decade.[47] The Caspian Sea was a particularly prominent area of attention of the Russian state. Here, the idea was to quickly establish a gas supply network to Turkey and Europe in order to undermine some Russia-competitive pipelines in the region. One such pipeline—from Baku to Ceyhan—was completed in May 2005, and by connecting northern Caspian structures to the Russian oil pipeline system, Russia would emerge as more competitive. Another pipeline was under discussion. It was of a trans-Caspian nature, and it meant to bring oil underwater from Aktau in Kazakhstan to Baku and then to outside markets via the Baku-Ceyhan line. In February 2002, the Russian president also proposed an ambitious "gas OPEC" project that would involve Russia's pooling its natural gas resources with those of the central Asian states for the purpose of dominating the world markets.

Russian policymakers have been actively promoting transregional projects besides those related to the Caspian Sea. One of these projects is the Trans-Siberian Railroad, both an east-west route and a north-south one. The Russian Transportation Ministry has strongly lobbied for the Trans-Siberian project, which involves a completion of the 8,500 miles of railroad for transporting up to 100 million tons of cargo a year. While developing the project, the Russian government sought to be globally competitive, with potential competition coming from TRASEKA, the Brussels-planned international transportation corridor for connecting Europe, the Caucasus, and Asia. In addition to the Trans-Siberian route, Moscow's plans included developing a China–Kazakhstan–Russia–Europe route (east-west) and one that would connect Russia with India, Iran, Kazakhstan, Turkmenistan, and other Persian Gulf states (the north-south route). More recent initiatives included the April 2005 agreement between Russia and Germany on a project to deliver Russian gas directly to Germany by a pipeline under the Baltic Sea, bypassing the Baltic states and Poland.[48]

Many of Putin's efforts were improvisations, and it remains to be seen whether they will be more successful than previous policies of disengagement and integration in the region. In the meantime, some critics raised concerns that these efforts were of an ad hoc nature and not very well thought out, and that they overestimated the power of the Russian private sector. These critics feared that the new policy of pragmatism was about to repeat Kozyrev's errors of disengagement that might eventually cost Russia its dominant presence in the region. Furthermore, they urged Putin not to give up the CIS as a vehicle for preserving Russia's influences.[49]

Yet the new vision was hardly an example of disengagement. It assumed that post-Soviet Eurasia is a relatively economically open region, but one in which Russia occupies a central role and derives considerable economic, as well as political, benefits. The Russian foreign policy community had been debating the benefits of such geoeconomic thinking for quite some time. For instance, in his Eurasian Strategy for Russia, Sergei Rogov proposed that Russia focus on building the "communicational bridge" linking its southern, western, and eastern peripheries through the development of ground, air, and electronic transportation routes.[50] Economically, the project could, in the author's view, decrease by half the length of networks of communication that were linking Europe and East Asia, and this would be mutually beneficial for all participants. In addition, Eurasia was meant to be preserved as a politically stable and cohesive region. Although market oriented, this vision meant to preserve Russia's leadership in the region and was broadly supported by various political movements, as well as a regionally oriented private sector. It bore little resemblance to Kozyrev's philosophy of integration with the West at the expense of Asian and former Soviet partners.

5.5. NEW CHALLENGES FOR GREAT POWER PRAGMATISM

Soon after his reelection in March 2004, Putin was confronted with a series of new challenges. An intensification of terrorist activities in the northern Caucasus, the Orange Revolution in Ukraine, destabilization of central Asia, and refusal by some European states to celebrate the sixtieth anniversary of the victory over fascism in Moscow became important tests for the survival of Great Power Pragmatism. Great Power Pragmatism defended the enhancement of Russia's influences in the world by cooperating with Western nations on a variety of economic and security issues. Putin's Russia wanted to be a normal great power or the one recognized by the outside world. As the country faced new challenges, the course came under criticism at home. Some Statists insisted that cooperation with the West was not paying off, and Russia had to defend its interests more aggressively because its own survival was at stake. On the other side of the spectrum, liberal Westernizers argued the need to give up great power ambitions and pursue greater economic and political liberalization. In addition, the domestically questioned course had to be defended in the context of intensified efforts by Western nations, particularly the United States, to influence developments in the former Soviet region.

Washington's Regime-Change Strategy in the Former Soviet Region

Although many in Russia saw the American invasion of Iraq as driven by an appetite for Middle Eastern oil, Washington also had the objective of democratizing the region by establishing a new pro-Western regime at its heart. Soon, it became apparent that the strategy of changing regimes and expanding liberty was not limited to the Middle East. President Bush's inaugural address in January 2005 made the spread of freedom and democracy the center of the United States' political strategy in the "war on terror," and his State of the Union speech in February continued the theme: "The attack on freedom in our world has reaffirmed our confidence in freedom's power to change the world."[51] The so-called Rose Revolution in Georgia in November 2003 replaced the old regime by popular protest over a rigged parliamentary election and emboldened Washington to apply the strategy in the former Soviet region as well. While the military option was excluded, the emphasis was still on providing opposition with relevant training and financial resources for challenging the old regimes in power.[52]

The Kremlin's reaction to the new strategy was consistent with that to the intervention in Iraq. Moscow did not view terrorism as a state-based phenomenon, and it wanted interstate cooperation, not regime change, to be the basis for solving the problem. It therefore perceived the new American effort to reshape the post-Soviet space with suspicion, as a threat to Russia's own influence in the region.[53] For example, when America and other Western nations stepped up their support for the opposition in the October 2004 Ukrainian presidential election, the Kremlin threw all its weight behind the candidate of the ruling regime. Russia also maintained close relationships with existing leaderships in Belarus, Armenia, and the central Asian countries, despite their growing criticism by the United States and the EU. Few were willing to question the Kremlin's reaction or to lend support for the regime-change strategy adopted by Washington. The majority of the political class and general public remained wary of Western intentions, and this made it easier for the Kremlin to articulate its concerns and pursue the chosen course.

Moscow's response to Washington's regime-change strategy was therefore domestically sustainable. Two additional considerations reinforced the reaction by the Kremlin. First, supporting the opposition in those countries where existing regimes remained fully in control was hardly a viable option. Second, the Kremlin had reasons to suspect geopolitical motivations behind the regime-change strategy, which included a long-term geostrategic presence and greater control over natural resources in the region.[54] Russia therefore continued to defend its distinct interests, while developing relationships with Western nations in the areas of mutual concern. Despite some serious setbacks, this course survived tests of new challenges.

Beslan and Terrorism in the Northern Caucasus

Domestically, the most serious challenge to Great Power Pragmatism came in September 2004 when, after downing two civilian airliners, terrorists took more than a thousand people hostage in a school in Beslan, North Ossetia. Chechen field commander Shamil Basayev took responsibility for the incident, demanding the withdrawal of Russian troops from the territory of Chechnya. Ultimately, as the terrorists were in the process of releasing hostages, hundreds of women and children died. In the long list of terrorist attacks on Russian civilians, this was the worst. It also came in the middle of the Kremlin's efforts to stabilize the situation in Chechnya and to present it as considerable progress in fighting terrorism. The attacks seemed to have been spreading across the greater northern Caucasus, and people felt increasingly less, not more, protected from the threat. This reaction was a major blow to Putin's promises to "eradicate terrorism," which had helped him to win the March 2000 presidential election.

The Kremlin's initial reaction was hardly in line with the pragmatic Westernist course. In his first public statement, Putin admitted that Russia had inadequate defenses, but also he relegated partial responsibility for the Beslan incident to some unspecified foreign forces. In a thinly veiled reference to the West, Russia's president said, "Some want to tear off a big chunk of our country and others are helping them. They are helping them in the belief that Russia, as one of the greatest nuclear powers of the world, still poses a threat to them and, therefore, this threat has to be eliminated. Terrorism is their only tool."[55] Soon, Putin came under heavy attacks at home from both nationalist and liberal forces for not being able to prevent the terrorist attack and for choosing "wrong" ways of dealing with the threat. Nationalists blamed him for not building a more strongly centralized power, while liberals faulted Putin for missing a chance to negotiate with some elements within the Chechen separatist movement. Liberals also insisted that only international involvement similar to the one that stopped the escalation of violence in Northern Ireland would bring an end to violence.[56]

Gradually, the Kremlin gained composure and proposed a series of steps that included a far-reaching reform of the political system. At the heart of the proposed reform was the idea of further centralization of decision making. Local governors were no longer to be elected; instead, they were to be nominated by the president and confirmed by local legislative bodies. In addition, the Kremlin stepped up its counterterrorist activities and promised to hold new parliamentary elections in Chechnya. Finally, although suspicions of the international role persisted, Russia made efforts to reengage the West. After the September hostage taking in North Ossetia, Russia asked for a special session of the UN Security Council. It also provided an opening for a more positive Western role in the region by informing German chancellor Gerhard Schroeder of its desire for active Western involvement in the economic development of the North Caucasus region.[57] It remains to be seen, however, whether these measures will prevent terrorism from spreading across the northern Caucasus and other Russian territories.

Velvet Revolutions and the Test of Ukraine

Georgia's peaceful change of power following the fraudulent parliamentary election was not the only velvet revolution in the former Soviet region. The next and most important one took place in Ukraine. In November 2004 under pressure from both the Ukrainian opposition and the West, the results of the rigged presidential elections were renounced. The Kremlin's favored candidate, Viktor Yanukovich, was subsequently defeated. Putin lost his sought-after political influence, but found a way to retreat and to remain engaged with Ukrainian leadership and the West.

Putin's support for Yanukovich never amounted to an effort to build a new empire or to incorporate Ukraine into Russia. The Kremlin did not seek to incorporate Ukraine, just as previously Putin had not sought to incorporate Armenia, Azerbaijan, or Belarus, countries that had held similarly flawed elections. Although the Russian president badly miscalculated Yanukovich's chances of winning, and although he provided strong support for Yanukovich's election,[58] Putin was never willing to sacrifice his relations with the

West over the crisis in Ukraine, and he did not let his readiness to stand for Russia's strategic interests be turned into confrontation. This behavior was consistent with past experiences that showed that Russia's president was not a poor loser and usually had an exit strategy prepared. For instance, he had no confrontational response when the Bush administration made it clear that it would be withdrawing from the ABM Treaty. Putin's reaction was muted and nonthreatening. In his opinion, the United States' decision was a "mistake," but presented no threat to the national security of the Russian Federation.

In handling the crisis and developing relationships with the new Ukrainian leadership, the Kremlin did not follow the advice of hard-line Statists who recommended applying economic sanctions or supporting separatism in Ukraine.[59] Although the general public in Russia overwhelmingly supported Yanukovich and many members of the political class felt cheated and betrayed by the West,[60] Putin sought an asymmetrical response. Immediately before the anticipated victory of Viktor Yushchenko, he issued a statement welcoming any winner in Ukraine's rerun of its presidential election and asserted that Russia had no objections to Ukraine's joining the European Union. Rather than coercing and applying pressures, the Kremlin planned to co-opt Yushchenko by mobilizing Russia's soft power and the two nations' economic, cultural, and institutional interdependence.[61]

At the same time, Putin did not accept the advice of liberal Westernizers to side with Yushchenko in the disputed election. He supported a candidate whom he perceived as pro-Russian, and he challenged Western leaders not to "meddle" in Ukrainian elections. He attributed the crisis to the West's heavy involvement in the elections and he is likely to continue to protect Russia's interests in Ukraine by exerting great power influence in that country. The presence of the Russian fleet in the Crimea, conditions for ethnic Russians and for Russian business, and Ukraine's foreign policy orientation will continue to be of great concern to Russia. Although a pragmatist in his beliefs, Putin may opt to respond to domestic nationalist pressures as a way to maintain his legitimacy and power base. If the Ukrainian leadership proves unwilling to meet the Kremlin halfway, applying pressure cannot be entirely excluded. Russia's way of handling Georgia is a case in point. Putin assisted the new Georgian leadership in negotiating a way out of the elections crisis and in ending separatism in Adjaria. In return, he expected Russia's interests in the Caucasus to be honored and not to be rushed in dismantling Russia's two military bases on Georgian soil. When Putin had seen what he perceived as a lack of reciprocity on the Georgian side, he changed tactics. After Tbilisi had attempted to subjugate the separatist South Ossetia by force and pressured Russia to withdraw, Putin retaliated. He stopped short of formally recognizing the separatist South

Ossetia and Abkhazia, but extended some support to them[62] and kept a visa regime on the border with Georgia.

The Destabilization of Central Asia

The next challenge to Russia's new foreign policy came with the destabilization of central Asia. In March 2005, Kyrgyzstan went through a change of power that involved mass protest. Similarly to what already had happened in Georgia and Ukraine, the opposition in Kyrgyzstan challenged the regime of Askar Akayev over the process and results of the parliamentary election by forcing Akayev to leave office. Unlike in Georgia and Ukraine, however, the Kyrgyz "revolution" was not "velvet." Although the regime refused to apply force, the protests were far from orderly and were accompanied by violence and looting. An even worse development occurred in Uzbekistan in May 2005, when thousands of demonstrators challenged the state decision to imprison several prominent businessmen in Andijan and used force to help them escape. The government, too, used force, justifying it as a need to confront the growing threat of Islamic extremism in the region. Several hundreds protesters died.

Both events had the potential to spread greater violence in the region. In both countries, Russia had a considerable military presence and well-established relations with the ruling regimes. In response to the crises, the Kremlin emphasized the importance of preserving legality and order in Kyrgyzstan, and it backed Uzbekistan's president in handling the crisis. Foreign Minister Sergei Lavrov blamed the involvement of "outside extremist forces" from Afghanistan, including the neo-Taliban, and supported the use of force to suppress the protests.[63] Although there was little opposition to the Kremlin's policies in Kyrgyzstan, the Russian public actively discussed Moscow's response to the violence in Uzbekistan. Comments by politicians and analysts ranged from unconditional support to strong criticism of the Uzbek crackdown on protesters in Andijan. Civilizationists and some Statists blamed the protest on the U.S. military presence in the region and fully supported the crackdown. Liberal Westernizers, however, warned against Russian support for the Karimov regime, which could trigger civil war in Uzbekistan. For instance, Boris Nemtsov, of the Union of Right Forces, argued that the Karimov regime was doomed and that by supporting Karimov the Kremlin had picked a losing scenario, as it had in Ukraine.[64]

At least in the short run, Russia's response to the central Asian crises was warranted and within the framework of Great Power Pragmatism. In Kyrgyzstan, Moscow abstained from interference and quickly established relations with the new leadership by providing a continuity in policy. In Uzbekistan, Russia did not have the option not to lend some support to Karimov. While exercising considerable influence in the region, the Kremlin did not have the ability to change regimes in the region and viewed such an approach as revolutionary and destructive. In the absence of policy leverage, it had little choice but to maintain relationships with the ruling regimes even when such regimes were mired in corruption and resorted to force and nondemocratic practices. Although building relationships with the entire political spectrum of neighboring countries may be desirable, as the Orange Revolution demonstrated, central Asia was no Georgia or Ukraine. As one Western expert commented, in Uzbekistan "there is no Saakashvili or Yushchenko waiting in the wings,"[65] and therefore a change could come only from inside the regime. Not unimportantly, Russia's reaction to the central Asian developments was not fundamentally at odds with that of the West. The Western nations called for an investigation of the events in Andijan, but refrained from calling for Karimov's resignation. Looking out for its interests in the region and cooperating with the West in the areas of mutual concern seem to have continued to work for Russia.

A Contested Victory Celebration and Relations with the New Europe

Finally, Russia's strategy of developing relations with Western nations while preserving its own vision of national interests was challenged by some of the former Eastern European nations. When the Kremlin invited more than fifty foreign leaders to come to Moscow on May 9, 2005, to celebrate the victory over fascism, several nations refused. Among them were two Baltic states, Lithuania and Estonia, which saw the end of World War II as the beginning of their occupation by the Soviets. Separating the victory over fascism and the occupation by the Soviets, for which many in Russia called, did not turn out to be possible for the small East European nations.

Russia's officials and political elites, as well as many common people, viewed the perception by new European nations as an insult and an attempt to undermine Soviet Russia's paramount role in destroying Hitler's regime. For instance, the nationalist Duma faction Rodina decided to boycott the official ceremonies in Moscow, protesting statements about the end of the war made by Latvia's president Vaira Vike-Freiberga and officials of other Baltic states.[66] The insistence by new European leaders on their version of history presented Russia as unable to relinquish its "imperial ambitions" and called into question Russia's policies of improving relationships with the European Union. The United States exerted additional pressures on Russia by supporting these claims. For instance, the American president, while traveling to the region and visiting Latvia, strongly condemned the Soviet annexation and occupation of the Baltic republics as a result of World War II.

The Kremlin stood firm and did not yield to pressures to frame the issue in terms of responsibility for Stalin's occupation of the Baltic states. Overall, despite the clashing interpretations of the end of World War II, Russia reached its two most important objectives. It reconfirmed its role in liberating the world from fascism, and it did so in the presence of fifty foreign leaders, including U.S. president George W. Bush, UN secretary-general Kofi Annan, Japanese prime minister Junichiro Koizumi, German chancellor Gerhard Schroeder, Italian prime minister Silvio Berlusconi, and Israeli president Moshe Katsav. Symbolically, the event assisted Russia in legitimizing its status as a Westernizing great power.

5.6. PUTIN'S LESSONS FOR THE FUTURE

Russia's Great Power Pragmatism continued and changed the previous course of Great Power Balancing. Putin picked up where Primakov left off and remained focused on the objective of preserving great power status. Yet the new leader abandoned the old strategy of achieving the objective. A multipolar world and post-Soviet integration—key tenets of Primakov's thinking—were replaced by more pragmatic means of asserting Russia's interests in global politics. This foreign policy transformation became possible due to a reshaped structure of domestic interest groups and their favored identity visions, as well as changes that had taken place in the international arena. The political context for foreign policymaking had been principally altered, and the new president took advantage of it. This section offers an evaluation of Russia's foreign policy record based on developments up to June 2005. I also briefly speculate on some foreign policy dilemmas that the course of Great Power Pragmatism is likely to encounter in the future.

An Evaluation of Putin's Foreign Policy

Vladimir Putin's first four years showed his commitment to the newly chosen course. Having started as a Primakovite, the new leader quickly evolved in the direction of engaging the West in a new global project. His strategy bore some similarity to that of Mikhail Gorbachev. What Gorbachev saw as a crisis of human civilization that had resulted from arms races, poverty, and environmental destruction during the Cold War, Putin sought to frame as the global threat of terrorism. Both politicians attempted to engage the West in a commonly shared understanding in order to achieve a better recognition and open a way to a joint search for solutions to the world's problems. Yet both sought to preserve what they saw as Russian national interest and special characteristics. Gorbachev defined such interest in terms of preserving "socialist values," while Putin demonstrated his commitment to the idea of great power. While Gorbachev lost his battle, Putin seems to have learned to be aware of the dangers of making too many concessions to the West.

As tentative as this evaluation can be, the overall record of Great Power Pragmatism is generally positive. Although there is much work ahead of Russia, one can register considerable progress in terms of meeting the foreign policy criteria of security, welfare, autonomy, and identity. The new course was encouraging in terms of addressing its welfare dimension. Relative to the pre-1999 period, the country's economic and social standing improved considerably. Critics argued that this improvement reflected the increased world oil prices. This, however, was only one part of the story; the other part had to do with having the leadership ability to make the best of the favorable global conditions. In order to press forward with economic reforms at home and gain membership in vital international institutions, such as the WTO, and to increase Russian market share in the world economy, leadership was crucial. Capitalizing on new economic opportunities, Putin managed to considerably improve relations with the United States, Europe, and the former Soviet states. Some examples of this include the energy summit in Houston, where Russia pledged to radically increase its oil supplies to the United States, and where it forged a joint venture with British Petroleum worth $6 billion. In 2003, Russia increased its oil production 11 percent and—in order to improve its bargaining position—it entered into a deal with Saudi Arabia. The five-year deal pledged cooperation between the Russian and Saudi energy sectors and in setting the international price of oil. As some observers noted, Russia was a net beneficiary of the deal because of its ability to further enhance its market power.[67] Renewed activism in winning energy and transportation markets in the former Soviet region added to the impression that the government was serious about economic modernization as its key foreign policy objective.

Table 5.7. summarizes the record of Putin's defensive pragmatism.

The new foreign policy course also improved Russia's decision-making autonomy. Partly as a result of Russia's changed economic standing, its improved relations with Western nations did not come with strings attached. Russia was

Table 5.7. The Record of Defensive Pragmatism

Security	Remaining problems with terrorism
Welfare	Improved economic and social standing
Autonomy	No external assistance needed
Identity	Engaged Western and Statist dimension of Russian values

able to pay its debt obligations on time and was no longer in need of additional external assistance. New engagement of the West on counterterrorism and energy issues did not mean that Russia's power to defend its own perceived interests at home and in the region was to be seriously curtailed.

Did Russians appreciate the foreign policy shift toward state pragmatism and economic modernization? Most polls indicated so, although there was still an expectation of greater improvement. Many supported Putin's efforts to improve the economy and strengthen Russia's position in the world. No less importantly, the Russian public seemed to back Putin's emphasis on state-driven modernization, which is one policy that would have preserved independence and not resulted in a loss of policy autonomy to the West or domestic commercial groups. For instance, in November 2001—immediately after the terrorist attacks on the United States and at a time when Russians felt a strong sympathy toward Americans—only 30 percent agreed with the statement that cooperation with the West was the main condition of Russia's economic prosperity. At the same time, 61 percent supported the idea that it was necessary to first develop the economy and only then to improve ties with the West.[68]

Putin's record in responding to Russia's security needs was weaker. The president made the correct decision by supporting the U.S. military operation against the Taliban regime in Afghanistan. For years, Russia had been supporting the Northern Alliance without particular success, and it would have been unwise to pass on the opportunity to remove a key cause of instability in the region. Also in order to fight terrorism, Putin had been patiently assembling a coalition of the willing from the former Soviet states. Working both bilaterally and multilaterally, he made progress in pooling available military and intelligence resources in the region. However, he was much less successful in defusing a key source of terrorism on his own territory, in Chechnya. Granted, he had been left with a tough legacy after the years of lawlessness in the republic and had little choice but to apply military force. But the improvement of the situation remained marginal, with terrorist attacks continuing and the Russian public expressing reservations about the effectiveness of Putin's policies. Although people continued to have trust in the president, many increasingly felt that he failed to deliver on his promise to eliminate the resistance in Chechnya. For instance, in December 2003, one poll registered as many as 68 percent expressing their frustration with the situation.[69]

Finally, the record of Great Power Pragmatism in addressing the Russian people's identity needs was both positive and ambivalent. The new course was successful in engaging both the Westernist and the Statist components of Russian national psychology. It did not neglect the relevance of national experience, as did Kozyrev's Westernism. Nor did it encourage anti-Western themes in national consciousness, which had been a result of Primakov's foreign policy. The new course therefore provided the space necessary for reformulating Russia's national identity and moving beyond the post-Soviet identity crisis. Yet that space was yet to be filled with some creatively defined national idea, and the government was yet to engage some of the Russians' key cultural concerns. For instance, polls consistently demonstrated that Russians supported the need to maintain strong ties with the former Soviet republics. Previous efforts to maintain such ties by encouraging the post-Soviet states to adopt dual-citizenship policies with regard to ethnic Russians had been a failure, but no other initiatives came to replace those policies.

Can Great Power Pragmatism Be Sustained?

The course of Great Power Pragmatism is still a work in progress, and it remains to be seen whether it will be sustained in the future. Although the effort to seize the middle ground between the old-style Statism and Westernism has been generally successful in responding to the nation's foreign policy challenges, it is bound to face some critical dilemmas in the future.

One such dilemma is how to improve Russia's security without becoming overly dependent on traditional Statists tools, such as buying political supporters, using force against opponents, and maintaining relationships with dictatorial regimes. In the past, Russia tried these tactics in the former Soviet region with only limited success. Fighting terrorism using the same tactics has its limitations. Use of force can no longer solve the Chechnya problem. Nor can it stabilize Georgia, Moldova, Uzbekistan, or other neighboring states. Offering money to leaders in central Asia or the Caucasus in exchange for a more extended military presence can help only in the short run. Extending support to regimes that violate their citizens' rights is an extreme measure, and it should not become a common policy practice. More robust solutions would require the development of greater leverage for influencing neighboring states in the region. Such solutions might include the mobilization of ties with societies, rather than states only, through greater use of Russia's soft power and establishment of contacts with the entire political spectrum in the neighboring nations. They might also include adopting similar standards of behavior across the region and building international security institutions to deal with terrorist challenges.

Another dilemma has to do with the necessity to deepen cooperation with Western nations. Westernization has its costs, as Kozyrev's foreign policy has shown all too well, and it is important to preserve the ability to defend Russia's own interests. Yet without moving in this direction, Russia will remain provincial in economic and political dimensions. Russia has had to constantly maneuver between its military deals with China, Saudi Arabia, or former Soviet states, on the one hand, and chances to develop a better image or institutional presence in the West, on the other. In the past, Putin's unprecedented policy activism was helpful in squaring this circle. But preserving this policy line in the future may prove to be more difficult if Russia's partners outside the West will continue to be autocratic and if the West grows less patient with Russia's pragmatism. Some symptoms of a growing rift between Russia and the West include geopolitical rivalries in the former Soviet region and Putin's reluctance to travel abroad to meet his Western European "partners" in 2004. For instance, he put off important visits to the EU in 2004 in favor of summits with the leaders of Brazil, China, and India. In addition, Europeans themselves continue to be wary of strengthening ties with Russia, despite some obvious gains from doing so.[70] Without consistent policy engagement from both sides, the course of Great Power Pragmatism is likely to degenerate into the old-style Great Power Balancing.

Furthermore, Great Power Pragmatism has been supported by a delicate domestic coalition that, absent of strong leadership, may fall apart. Putin's way of dealing with Khodorkovski and other oligarchs alienated many Westernizers from his course. On the other hand, his military reform and removal of some key generals strained his relations with the military. The more he presses forward with the military reform, the less likely he is to lose the support of elites. While state capacity and autonomy are important in foreign policymaking, losing such support should not be equated with it. At home, Great Power Pragmatism is likely to run into difficulties with the political elites, and it will need, more than ever, the support of the general public.

Finally, Russia's continuing identity crisis may yet again pose the question of how to assist the nation in improving its sense of cultural confidence without resorting to some hard-line ideology. Many Russians continue to feel the identity void, yet the course of Great Power Pragmatism has not done enough to address it. Putin will have to find a way to respond to Russia's needs to see itself as a civilization, not just as a great power, if he wants to defuse the appeal of hard-line Civilizationists. It would be important to take into consideration the recent failure of the civilizational vision of "Eurasia" and reemphasize the European quality of Russia's cultural roots.[71] The European and great power components of Putin's vision must be bridged more forcefully, not separated from one another. Ukraine's 2004 presidential elections showed, among other things, the danger of separating the two. If Russia is going to develop a viable civilizational identification, it should reconfirm its commitment to democratic and institutional, rather than merely geopolitical, objectives of its foreign policy. Although Russia's success is also predicated on Europe, in the absence of renewed democratic commitment, its civilizational perspective is in danger of becoming a hostage of a narrowly defined and state-driven modernization.

NOTES

1. Vladimir Putin, "Poslaniye Federal'nomu Sobraniyu Rossiyskoi Federatsiyi," March 16, 2003, at www.kremlin.ru; Vladimir Putin, *First Person: An Astonishingly Frank Self-Portrait by Russia's President* (New York: Public Affairs, 2000), 169.

2. Philip Hanson, "Joining but Not Signing Up? Russia's Economic 'Integration' into Europe," *Russian and Eurasia Review* 2, no. 6 (March 18, 2003); Julien Vercuil, "Opening Russia? Contemporary Foreign Trade," *Russian and Eurasia Review* 2, no. 4 (February 18, 2003), www.jamestown.org.

3. Richard Rose, "How Floating Parties Frustrate Democratic Accountability," in *Contemporary Russian Politics*, ed. Archie Brown (Oxford: Oxford University Press, 2001), 221–22.

4. Vladimir Putin, "Rossiya na rubezhe tysyacheletiy," *Nezavisimaya gazeta*, December 1999.

5. Putin, "Rossiya na rubezhe tysyacheletiy." In Putin's most revealing words, "If by democracy one means the dissolution of the state, then we do not need such democracy" (Interview, *Washington Post*, September 26, 2003).

6. Vladimir Putin, "Poslaniye Prezidenta Federal'nomu Sobraniyu Rossiyskoi Federatsiyi," *Mezhdunarodnaya zhizn'* 5 (2002): 4–5.

7. Peter Rutland, "Putin and the Oligarchs," in *Putin's Russia: Past Imperfect, Future Uncertain*, ed. Dale R. Herspring (Lanham, MD: Rowman & Littlefield, 2003), 148.

8. Dale R. Herspring, "Putin and the Armed Forces," in *Putin's Russia*, 170.

9. Putin, "Rossiya na rubezhe tysyacheletiy."

10. William Wohlforth, "Russia," in *Strategic Asia 2002–03: Asian Aftershocks*, ed. Richard J. Ellings and Aaron L. Friedberg (Washington, DC: National Bureau of Asian Research, 2003), 199.

11. Grigori Yavlinski, "Druzhba na vremya ili soyuz navsegda?" *Obschaya gazeta*, January 24, 2002; Grigori Yavlinski, "Dver' v Yevropu nakhoditsya v Vashingtone," *Obschaya gazeta*, May 16, 2002.

12. Aleksei Kara-Murza, "Na perekrestke politiki i nauki," *Polis* 6 (2001).

13. Thomas Friedman, "World War Three," *New York Times*, September 19, 2001. For similar arguments made by Western conservatives, see Fukuyama, "Their Target: The Modern World"; Margaret Thatcher, "Advice to a Superpower," *New York Times*, February 11, 2002.

14. A. Buzgalin, "Russia and America: A New Twist in the Confrontation?" *Prism* 8, no. 2 (2002), at www.jamestown.org (accessed April 2, 2002).

15. Valeri Fedorov, "Vpered, k ideologiyi?" *Nezavisimaya gazeta*, February 18, 2002. Dmitri Furman argued that Putin's pro-Western choice might help to preserve the essentially nondemocratic regime in Russia, just as an American alliance with the central Asian states and Pakistan does not mean to make these states more friendly to human rights (Dmitri Furman, "Polyet dvuglavogo orla," *Obschaya gazeta*, May 30, 2002).

16. See, for example, Graham Allison, Karl Kaiser, and Sergei Karaganov, "The World Needs a Global Alliance for Security," *International Herald Tribune*, November 21, 2001.

17. Putin, "Poslaniye Prezidenta," 18. The European emphasis was made the key theme of Putin's address to the Federation Council in April 2005.

18. Yevgeni Primakov, *Mir posle 11 sentyabrya* (Moscow: Mysl', 2002), 106–7.

19. Sergei Kortunov, "Rossiysko-Amerikanskoye partnerstvo?" *Mezhdunarodnaya zhizn'* 4 (2002): 69.

20. See, for example, Aleksandr Panarin, "Ontologiya terrora," in *Geopolitika terrora* (Moscow: Arktogeya, 2002), 46; Aleksandr Prokhanov, "Ameriku potseloval angel smerti," *Zavtra*, September 18, 2001; Dugin, "Terakty 11 Sentyabrya: Ekonomicheski smysl," in *Geopolitika terrora*.

21. *RFE/RL Newsline*, January 16, 2002; Katrina Vanden Heuvel and Stephen F. Cohen, "Endangering US Security," *Nation*, April 15, 2002.

22. Sergey Ptichkin and Aleksei Chichkin, "From Where Russia Is Clearly Visible," *Rossiyskaya gazeta*, January 22, 2002; Evgeny Mikhilov, "The Art of Wiping Things Out," *Versty*, January 24, 2002 (as translated by *CDI Russia Weekly*, no. 190, January 25, 2002).

23. A. Oslon, ed., *Amerika: Vzglyad iz Rossiyi* (Moscow: Institut Fonda "Obschest-vennoye mneniye," 2001), 27. Another 64 percent of respondents perceived Washington's military activities in Afghanistan as dangerous for Russia (*Amerika: Vzglyad iz Rossiyi*, 124). At the same time, Russians continued to show strong support for Putin's decision to side with the West (*Amerika: Vzglyad iz Rossiyi*, 34, 124; "Rossiyani podderzhivayut sozdaniye soyuza RF i SshA v bor'be s mezhdunarodnym terrorizmom," *Nega-Set*, November 18, 2001).

24. As cited in Dale R. Herspring and Peter Rutland, "Putin and Russian Foreign Policy," in *Putin's Russia*, 237.

25. Leon Aron, "Russian Oil and U.S. Security," *New York Times*, May 5, 2002.

26. "Bush's Russian Romance," *Economist*, May 22, 2002.

27. Hanson, "Joining but Not Signing Up?"

28. Sergei Yastrzhembsky, "Russophobia Still Rampant," *New York Times*, April 24, 2002.

29. Stephen Foye, "The EU's Enlargement; Russia Plays Bridesmaid," *Eurasia Daily Monitor*, May 3, 2004, at www.jamestown.org.

30. "Ex-defense Minister Accuses US of Seeking to Dominate Russia," Associated Press, June 19, 2003 (as cited by *CDI Russia Weekly*, no. 262 [June 2003]).

31. A poll taken in April by the All-Russian Center for Public Opinion Studies (VT-sIOM), as quoted in Nikolai Petrov, "The War in Iraq and the Myth of Putin," *Russia and Eurasia Review* 2, no. 8 (April 15, 2003), at www.jamestown.org; The Pew Research Center for the People and the Press, September, 2003, at www.people-press.org.

32. Vladimir Putin, "Vystupleniye na soveschaniyi 'O perspektivakh razvitiya Dal'nego Vostoka i Zabaikalya,'" Blagoveschensk, July 21, 2000, at www.kremlin.ru.

33. Vladimir Putin, "Annual Address to the Federal Assembly" (The Kremlin, Moscow, April 25, 2005), at www.cdi.org/russia/johnson/9130-1.cfm.

34. Wohlforth, "Russia," 201–2.

35. "Putin's Interview," *Washington Post*, September 26, 2003.

36. Marianna Belenkaya, "America's Iranian Policy and Russia's Interests," Russia's Information Agency, as cited by the Center of Defense Information *Russia Weekly* 259, no. 6 (May 29, 2003), at www.cdi.org/russia/259.cfm.

37. *RFE/RL Newsline*, February 28, 2002, at www.rferl.org.

38. Vladimir Putin, "Vistupleniye Prezidenta na rasshirennom zasedaniyi s uchasti-yem poslov Rossiyskoi Federatsiyi v MID Rossiyi," July 12, 2002, at www.kremlin.ru.

39. Boris Berezovski, "SNG: Ot razvala k sotrudnichestvu," *Nezavisimaya gazeta*, November 13, 1998. For a representative summary of Westernist scholarship on the subject, see *Blizhneye i dal'neye zarubezh'e v geoekonomicheskoi strategiyi Rossiyi*, ed. Yuri V. Shishkov (Moscow: IMEMO, 1997). Already in 1994, Andrei Zagorski argued that the diverging economic interests of Russia and other former republics would prevent Primakov's integrational efforts from becoming permanent. See his *SNG: Ot dezintegratsiyi k reintegratsiyi?* (Moscow: MGIMO, 1994).

40. Andranik Migranyan, "Rasstavaniye s illuziyami," *Nezavisimaya gazeta*, October 27, 2000.

41. *Strategiya dlya Rossiyi: Povestka dlya prezidenta—2000* (Moscow: Sovet po vneshnei i oboronnoi politike, 2000), at www.svop.edu.

42. Susan Birgerson, *After the Breakup of a Multi-Ethnic Empire* (New York: Praeger, 2002), 89.

43. Alan Kasaiev, "Sovet Bezopasnosti Rossiyi reshil zakryt' SNG," *Nezavisimaya gazeta*, February 7, 2001.

44. As cited in Yekaterina Tesyemnikova, "Preimuschestva sodruzhestva dlya Rossiyi ochevidny," *Nezavisimaya gazeta*, August 2, 2001.

45. Igor Glukhovski, "Mnogovektornaya integratsiya kak otvet novym vyzovam," *Nezavisimaya gazeta*, February 13, 2001.

46. Anatoli Chubais, "Missiya Rossiyi v XXI veke," *Nezavisimaya gazeta*, October 1, 2003.

47. Edward L. Morse and James Richard, "The Battle for Energy Dominance," *Foreign Affairs* 81, no. 2 (2002).

48. Vladimir Socor, "Schroeder-Putin Gas Deal Undercuts Both New and Old EU Member Countries," *Eurasia Daily Monitor*, April 13, 2005, at www.jamestown.org.

49. Kasaiev, "Sovet Bezopasnosti Rossiyi reshil zakryt' SNG."

50. Sergei Rogov, *Yevraziyskaya strategiya dlya Rossiyi* (Moscow: Institut SshA i Kanady, 1998); also, Rogov, "Izolyatsiya ot integratsiyi," *NG-Dipkuryer*, December 7, 2000.

51. As quoted in: Anatol Lieven, "Bush's Choice: Messianism or Pragmatism," OpenDemocracy.net, February 22, 2005, at www.carnegieendowment.org.

52. For some evidence and discourse of such strategic calculations, see, for example, Stephen Blank, "Georgia: A Study in Democracy Exportation," *Asia Times*, December 6, 2003, at atimes.com; Graeme P. Herd, "Colorful Revolutions and the CIS," *Problems of Post-Communism* 52, no. 2 (2005).

53. Igor Torbakov, "Different Understanding of Democracy May Put Bush and Putin on Collision Course," *Eurasia Daily Monitor*, February 25, 2005, at www.jamestown.org.

54. See, for example, Anatoli Gordienko et al., "Zastolbili Kaspi," *Nezavisimaya gazeta*, April 15, 2005.

55. "Putin Says Russia Faces 'Total War' with Terrorism," *RFE/RL Newsline*, September 7, 2004, at www.rferl.org.

56. Charles Gurin, "Observers Say Terror Attacks Eroding Putin's Legitimacy," *Eurasia Daily Monitor*, September 7, 2004, at www.jamestown.org; Robert Coalson, "Russia Girds Itself for War," *RFE/RL Newsline*, September 3, 2004, at www.rferl.org.

57. Fiona Hill, Anatol Lieven, and Thomas de Waal, *A Spreading Danger: Time for a New Policy toward Chechnya* (Washington, DC: Carnegie Endowment for International Peace, March 2005), 2.

58. Europe and the United States, in their turn, did not limit themselves to political statements about the "unacceptability" of the election's results—a step in itself unprecedented in the light of their previously much calmer reaction to considerably less fair elections in central Asia and the Caucasus. Through the activities of various NGOs, the West also provided considerable financial assistance for Yushchenko's campaign.

59. The eastern regions of Ukraine, particularly Donetsk, Luhansk, and Crimea, vowed to pursue greater autonomy from Kiev after the nullification of Yanukovich's victory in the first presidential election. In Russia, nationalist State Duma members and Moscow Mayor Yuri Luzhkov visited eastern Ukraine to express their support for Yanukovich and for regional autonomy. It is not difficult to imagine how such autonomy claims might be manipulated to become a factor in Russian-Ukrainian high politics.

60. Levada-Tsentr, "Ukrainskiye sobytiya glazami rossiyan," December 16, 2004, at www.levada.ru/press/2004121601.html; Igor Torbakov, "After Ukraine Debacle, Kremlin Strategists Warn of Serious Rift with the West," *Eurasia Daily Monitor*, December 17, 2004, at www.jamestown.org.

61. Russian-Ukrainian interdependence has been well documented. See, for instance, Paul J. D'Anieri, *Economic Interdependence in Ukrainian-Russian Relations* (Albany: State University of New York Press, 1999); Andrei P. Tsygankov, *Pathways after Empire: National Identity and Foreign Economic Policy in the Post-Soviet World* (Lanham, MD: Rowman & Littlefield, 2001); Mikhail A. Molchanov, *Political Culture and National Identity in Russian-Ukrainian Relations* (Austin: University of Texas Press, 2002).

62. For instance, Russia extended its citizenship to many residents of South Ossetia and Abkhazia. Some analysts recommended that the Kremlin go much further and formally recognize the independence of the separatist republics (see, for example, Stanislav Belkovski, "Poslye imperii," *Komsomol'skaya pravda*, May 18, 2004).

63. "Moscow Accuses 'Outside Extremists,'" *RFE/RL Newsline*, May 16, 2005, at www.rferl.org.

64. Sergei Blagov, "Uzbekistan's Riots Yield Mixed Response in Russia," *Eurasia Daily Monitor*, May 19, 2005, atwww.jamestown.org.

65. Martha Olcott, "United States Helsinki Commission Briefing on Uzbekistan," May 19, 2005, at www.carnegieendowment.org.

66. "Nationalist Duma Faction Boycotts the Ceremonies," *RFE/RL Newsline*, May 16, 2005, at www.rferl.org.

67. Stephen Blank, "Moscow's Cosy Saudi Connection," *Asia Times*, September 13, 2003.

68. Vladimir A. Kolossov and Natalya A. Borodullina, "Rossiya i Zapad: Mneniye rossiyan," *Russia in Global Affairs* 1 (2003).

69. The poll of VTSIOM, as cited in "Support for Putin's Policies Is Weak, but He Is Still Popular," *RFE/RL Newsline*, December 2, 2003.

70. On this point, see, for instance, Alexander Rahr and Nicolai N. Petro, "Our Man in Moscow," *The Fletcher Forum of World Affairs* (Summer 2005), at fletcher.tufts.edu/forum.

71. Putin has attempted to move in this direction, as is seen in his 2005 presidential address to the Federal Assembly. Vladimir Putin, "Annual Address to the Federal Assembly" (The Kremlin, Moscow, April 25, 2005), at   www.cdi.org/russia/johnson/91301.cfm.

6

The U.S. Regime Change Strategy and a New Face of Great Power Pragmatism

One state and, of course, first and foremost the United States, has overstepped its national borders in every way. This is visible in the economic, political, cultural and educational policies it imposes on other nations. Well, who likes this? Who is happy about this?

... Russia is a country with a history that spans more than a thousand years and has practically always used the privilege to carry out an independent foreign policy. We are not going to change this tradition today

—Vladimir Putin, the Munich Conference on Security Policy, February 2007[1]

Soon after the colored revolutions in the former Soviet region, Putin's Great Power Pragmatism obtained a new dimension—assertiveness. Russia's foreign policy has not returned to the era of Primakov's balancing the United States' power in the world. Instead, Russia has sought to capitalize on its new economic recovery and energy competitiveness and break into Western economic markets, while maintaining political stability and an essentially defensive security posture. Putin's speech at the Munich Conference on Security Policy became a high point in Russia's new assertiveness and was extremely critical of the U.S. "unilateralism," yet it only meant to preserve and deepen achievements of cooperation with the West. It sent a strong signal to the Western nations that in the Kremlin's perception, the course of Russia's integration with the West was in jeopardy because of highly destabilizing policies of the United States.

6.1. RUSSIA'S NEW CONDITIONS AND WORLDVIEW

Washington's Regime Change Strategy and Russia's Security Vulnerabilities

The colored revolutions that took place in Georgia, Ukraine, and Kyrgyzstan during 2003–2005 did not improve cooperation between Russia and Western countries in what had become a key international objective after September 11, 2001—fighting terrorism. Indeed, there was a connection between Washington's strategy of regime change and growing terrorist violence and political instability in the world. After the U.S. invasion of Iraq, terrorism became more, not less, active in the Middle East. Iraq was in a stage of civil war with hundreds of thousands of people killed and misplaced and millions leaving the country.[2] Afghanistan, recently considered a successful antiterrorist operation, too showed multiple signs of growing destabilization and was quickly turning into a new safe haven for terrorists and members of the overthrown Taliban regime. Yet Washington seemed determined to press ahead with its strategy and even showed signs of preparing to attack Iran unilaterally. A number of policymakers believed in "an attempt to revive the concept of spreading democracy in the Middle East by creating one new model state."[3] The United States pulled military forces in the Persian Gulf, including aircraft carriers, and it increased the number of troops in Iraq by 20,000. Washington also warned Tehran not to "meddle" in Iraq. In addition to perceiving Iran as building a nuclear bomb, Washington viewed it as a regime that harbored terrorists and obstructed U.S. efforts to stabilize Iraq.

Russia also became more vulnerable because of the spread of political instability in its periphery. The so-called colored revolutions were strongly supported by the Western nations, but have been viewed as destabilizing by Russia and directed against the Kremlin's power and security. Georgia, Ukraine, and Kyrgyzstan failed to address the root causes of the revolution, such as poor living conditions and unpopular leadership. In dealing with separatist South Ossetia, Tbilisi increasingly relied on force, while pressuring Russia out of the region. In addition, Georgia and Ukraine expressed their desire to join NATO, which added to Russia's sense of strategic insecurity. In the aftermath of the NATO summit in April 2008, President Putin stated, "We view the appearance of a powerful military bloc on our borders . . . as a direct threat to the security of our country. The claim that this process is not directed against Russia will not suffice. National security is not based on promises."[4] The public, too, reacted overwhelmingly negatively to the alliance's expansion. Seventy-four percent of Russians polled in March 2008 said that Ukraine's possible accession to NATO posed a threat to the national security of the Russian Federation, and 77 percent expressed a similar attitude toward Georgia's possible membership in the organization.[5]

Moscow also had fear of a revolution inside Russia. In addition to growing instability in the region, the colored revolutions added to the perception within the Kremlin that Washington's chief objective was in fact to change the regime in Russia. Although the public support for a revolution was weak, the Kremlin's political technologists took the threat seriously, knowing that less than 1 percent of the population was really involved in the recent capitals-centered colored revolutions and that influential elites in the United States maintained contacts with some radical organizations in Russia. For instance, in April 2007, the U.S. State Department issued a report highly critical of Russia's political system and pledging various assistance to "democratic organizations" inside the country. In response, the Kremlin took a number of defensive steps. It trained its own youth organizations to defend what it saw as Russia's indigenous democracy, restricted activities of Western NGOs and radical opposition inside the country, and warned the United States against interference with Russia's domestic developments.

Finally, Russia felt vulnerable to radicalization of Islam in response to the U.S. style of fighting a war on terror. Although the situation in the Chechen Republic became more stable, North Ossetia, Ingushetia, Kabardino-Balkaria, and Dagestan were experiencing a growing number of terrorist attacks. Some of it, undoubtedly, could be attributed to Russia's own errors. A growing influence of radical Islamist ideologies, rising immigration from Muslim ex-Soviet republics, and attempts by some of Russia's authorities to address the problem by closing local mosques created a politically explosive environment. However, the other part had to do with the U.S. style of fighting a war on terror that was increasingly perceived in the Muslim world as a war of civilizations. What began as a counterterrorist operation in Afghanistan with relatively broad international support has increasingly turned into a "war of civilizations," or a U.S. crusade against Muslims and their style of living. Instead of engaging moderate Muslims, U.S. policies tended to isolate them and give the cards to radicals. In a global world, this translated into a greater support for Islamic radicals inside Russia.

Russia's Growing Domestic Strength

After the years of the post-Soviet depression, Russia's domestic conditions have changed dramatically. During 1999–2007, the economy caught up with the level of 1990 and continued to grow at the annual pace of about 7 percent (Russia's basic economic indicators are summarized in table 6.1). The overall size of the economy increased about six times in current dollars—from $200 billion to $1.3 trillion. Russia's per-capita GDP has quadrupled to nearly $7,000, and about twenty million people have been lifted out of poverty.[6] Russia's middle class now constituted about 25 percent of the population.[7] Over 2000–2005, the average Russian saw a 26 percent annual growth in income, relative to only a 10 percent rise in that of the average Chinese.[8] Direct foreign investments to the Russian economy skyrocketed, making it the first in the world among developing economies.[9] Although much of the economic recovery was due to high oil prices, the government continued to work to reduce a reliance on energy exports. In early 2008, for example, industrial production rose an annual 9.2 percent.[10] As a result, the number of Russians who thought that the chosen development course in Russia was correct had been growing year on year.[11] The economic recovery provided conditions for Russia's active business promotion in Europe, which accounts for 50 percent of Russia's foreign trade. The Kremlin insisted on long-term contracts with Europeans and greater integration with European markets in order to avoid a repetition of the 1985–1986 scenario when sharp decline in energy prices had considerably contributed to the breakup of the Soviet economy.

The Changed Identity Coalition

The persistent security vulnerabilities and improved economic conditions led to changes in Russia's identity coalitions. Security threats strengthened the position of the security class. As a result, in the coalition of oligarchs and *siloviks*, the latter gained a considerable prominence over the former. The security class did not become dominant, as some have suggested,[12] but it was affecting state decisions more than it had previously, and it gained a greater presence in commercial companies, especially those energy related. The state was not

Table 6.1. Russia's Basic Economic Indicators, 1999–2007 (%, annual change)

	1998	1999	2000	2001	2002	2003	2004	2005	2006	2007
Real GDP growth	−5.3	6.3	10.0	5.1	4.3	7.7	7.2	6.4	6.7	7.3
Real wages	−10	−22	18	20	16	11	11	13	13	16
Budget surplus (% of GDP)	−5.3	0.5	3.5	3.0	1.4	1.7	4.5	8.1	8.5	5.5
Urals oil prices ($/barrel)	12	17	27	23	24	27	34	50	61	69

Source: Peter Rutland, "Putin's Economic Record: Is the Oil Boom Sustainable?" *Europe-Asia Studies* 60, no. 6 (2008), 1052.

consolidated enough to isolate powerful security influences, yet it did not become a hostage to those influences. Liberals, such as Aleksei Kudrin and German Gref, stayed in the government and continued to make a case for more aggressive liberal economic policies. Members of the security class were unable to assert greater isolationism in economic matters by protecting large companies from international competition and in politics by forcing Putin to stay for the third presidential term.

Rather than staying for the third term, Putin designated Dmitri Medvedev—not known for his ties with members of the security class—as his successor. Despite predictions of the third term and assessments of Russia's political system as fundamentally unstable, the power transition went generally smoothly. With Putin's support, Medvedev decisively defeated his three rivals—the Communist Party's Gennadi Zyuganov, Vladimir Zhirinovski of the Liberal Democratic Party, and the Democratic Party's Andrei Bogdanov—winning the overwhelming majority of the popular vote in the first round of voting. Western media and election monitoring organizations, such as the OSCE, were critical of the elections, citing the lack of public debate among the candidates and harassment of the opposition.[13] Yet the United States and European governments preferred to work with the Kremlin and expressed a cautious support for Medvedev. The elections testified yet again that the state was not a hostage to ideologies of security-driven isolationism or liberal-minded openness and was in charge when deciding between them.

In economic matters, the state position has been to stake a middle ground between the two approaches by acquiring a greater prominence in economic affairs, yet using it for making Russia more open, not closed, to international competition. Ever since most of the powerful oligarchs, such as Boris Berezovski, Vladimir Gusinski, and Mikhail Khodorkovski, were stripped of their economic empires, the state has consistently asserted itself in other key areas. It increased its share in leading energy companies, such as Gazprom and Rosneft. It has renegotiated production-sharing agreements with Western companies in the most lucrative oil fields in Siberia and the Far East. Foreign energy giants, such as Royal Dutch Shell and British Petroleum, now had to play by different rules as introduced by the more assertive Russian state. In addition to the energy industry and military-industrial complex, the state announced plans to create "national champions" or state-supported companies in the banking, aerospace, automobile, and heavy machinery industries. Yet the state also argued that creation of such companies was necessary to position them for successful international competition.[14] Russian officials also insisted on expediting the country's entrance to the WTO. Furthermore, Putin's strategy of a state-dominant capitalism recognized the vital need of foreign investments for continuing high economic growth, particularly coming from Western nations.

The state assertiveness in the nation's political economy reshaped the previously loose coalition of oligarchs and *siloviks,* creating a more stable alliance that shared Putin's pragmatic vision of Russia as a "normal great power"—a strong state playing by internationally accepted rules and norms of behavior.

The Refined Vision of National Interest

The overall objectives of Russia's foreign policy stayed the same as they had been outlined in Putin's early programmatic speech "Russia at the Turn of Millenniums"—economic modernization, political stability, and enhancement of security.[15] Yet the context in which Russia had to act changed considerably, and that modified methods of pursuing foreign policy objectives.

In his response to new challenges and security vulnerabilities, Putin sought to reaffirm Russia's commitments to European values. In his programmatic speech delivered to the Federation Council in March 2005, Putin declared that he saw Russia moving toward the same values that are shared by others in the European continent—"the ideals of freedom, human rights, justice and democracy."[16] In the former Soviet region, this translated into the doctrine of "continuing the civilizational role of the Russian nation in Eurasia." Responding to charges of imperialism toward post-Soviet nations in the wake of the colored revolutions, Putin insisted that Russia seeks not the post-Soviet states' territory or natural resources, but the human dignity and the quality of life of its citizens, whom it regards as its own cultural compatriots.

Putin was clear, however, that while moving in the same direction of freedom and democracy with Europeans, Russia does so at its own pace and given its own conditions. In the same speech, referring to the Western role in the colored revolutions in Georgia and Ukraine, Putin insisted on Russia's right to "decide for itself the pace, terms and conditions of moving towards democracy," and he warned against attempts to destabilize the political system by "any unlawful methods of struggle."[17] The motive of noninterference in Russia's domestic developments from outside only became stronger over time, and in his addresses to the Federation Council in May 2006 and April 2007, Putin put an even greater emphasis on values of sovereignty and strong national defense.[18]

Putin's supporters interpreted his vision of Russia's identity using the idea of "Euro-Eastern" civilization, which should be differentiated from the earlier discussed "West" and "Eurasia."[19] Intellectuals and political consultants, such as Gleb Pavlovski, articulated three components of the new civilizational idea. First, the countries of Euro-East, such as Russia, Ukraine, and Kazakhstan, shared with Europe values of market economy and growing middle class. Second, because of their preoccupation with domestic economic and social modernization, the Euro-Eastern area had a special need for maintaining political stability. Growing middle class and political stability should not be viewed, however, as in conflict with development of democratic institutions. Rather, according to Pavlovski, each nation in the region should be given a right to experiment with its own democratic model that fits its national and international conditions. To him, Kazakhstan, a country that was typically viewed as lacking democracy, was in the process of finding its model of democratic development.[20] Third, domestic transformation of the Euro-Eastern nations requires preservation of political sovereignty and defense from attempts by outsiders to exploit internal resources of the nation of the region. Russia—by virtue of its size and capabilities—is in a special position to greatly contribute to providing the collective goods of security, sovereignty, and stability in the region.

The Kremlin's ideologists and theorists sympathetic to the official agenda have developed concepts of "sovereign democracy" and "sovereign economy,"[21] insisting on the need for Russia to protect its path of development and natural resources. "Sovereign democracy" implied a desire to defend an internally determined path to political development.[22] "Sovereign economy" indicated that the state was determined to have an upper hand in deciding conditions on which Western companies were to participate in Russia's economic development. In the world of growing energy prices, the emphasis shifted from providing a macroeconomic discipline and tough fiscal policies toward desire to capitalize on Russia's reserves of natural gas and oil. In addition, Russia insisted that a more assertive foreign policy would better protect its national security. Putin's speech in Munich[23] and a strong criticism of the U.S. "unilateralism" in world politics was especially noteworthy, serving as another reminder that Russia was not about to tolerate policies that it viewed as interfering with its sovereignty and security. Importantly, the speech was delivered to a European audience, and Putin's supporters long argued that insistence on sovereignty and security was not inconsistent with European values. In their perspective, by upholding values of sovereignty Russia was in fact preserving European values that Europe itself could not always sustain when confronted with political pressures from the United States.[24]

Overall, a new foreign policy consensus emerged that an assertive style of achieving the objectives of development, stability, and security suited Russia well at the moment. The new Foreign Ministry report entitled "A Review of the Russian Federation's Foreign Policy," commissioned by the Kremlin and released on March 27, 2007, further elaborated on the new face of Russia's Great Power Pragmatism. It indicated an important change in Russia's thinking since the 2000 Foreign Policy Concept. The report embraced the notion of multipolarity based on "a more equitable distribution of resources for influence and economic growth,"[25] which it said laid the ground for a more self-confident and assertive Russia. The document presented Russia as ready to actively shape international relations by challenging the actions of others, particularly the United States, if they were "unilateral" and disrespectful of international law. At the same time, the report was not anti-American and did not call for any concerted effort to undermine the U.S. global position. Instead, it defended the notion of collective leadership and multilateral diplomacy as the alternative to unilateralism and hegemony in international relations.

Russia's new president, Dmitri Medvedev, amplified Putin's assertive vision, seeking to position Russia as a global player and a maker of new global rules. Speaking in Berlin in June 2008 he proposed a broad perspective on Europe "from Vancouver to Vladivostok" and proposed a new all-European treaty to establish a new security architecture by moving beyond NATO expansion and the conflict over Kosovo.[26] In addition to expressing his dissatisfaction with the U.S. role in European security, Medvedev blamed the United States for generating the global financial crisis by trying to substitute for the global commodities and financial markets, and he proposed an overhaul of the international economic order.[27] By these criticisms Russia did not mean to pursue an anti-Western policy. On the contrary, it sought to re-engage the West on terms the Kremlin viewed comfortable—by strengthening membership within a U.S.-EU-Russia alliance, developing ties with growing powers, such as China and India, and sharing the world's economic benefits with poor non-Western nations (table 6.2 summarizes the new vision of national interest).

6.2. DOMESTIC DEBATE ON NATIONAL INTEREST

Advocates of Assertive Foreign Policy

The changed vision of Russia's identity remained consistent with Putin's overall foreign policy philosophy. Throughout his presidency, he advocated a greater integration with Western nations, while insisting on Russia's great power status and viewing such status as a necessary geopolitical condition for domestic economic and political development. While emphasizing Russia's

Table 6.2.   Assertive Pragmatism: View of National Interest

What?	A great power in the West-centered world
How?	Multilateralism among great powers Energy power Indigenous democracy

own interests in many areas of world politics, Putin sought to frame those interests as fully compatible with strategic commitments to Western values, such as international law, personal freedoms, and a market economy. A great power status was not a goal in itself for Putin; rather, the role of great power status was to create a necessary condition for Russia's more advanced engagement with the world. The term "normal" signaled support for Westernizers, whereas the concept "great power" spoke to the need to protect Russia's territorial integrity. Such vision was not principally new. For instance, in the late nineteenth–early twentieth century, the so-called new liberals, such as Pyetr Struve, Pavel Novgorodtsev, and Sergei Gessen, saw Russia as both a European and a distinctively strong socially responsible state. This vision differed from the one defended by the old liberals of primarily constitutionalist orientation, such as Boris Chicherin and Pavel Milyukov.[28]

As Russia was moving closer to its economic and social recovery, a new version of assertiveness made itself heard in political circles. Louder than before, some influential politicians and intellectuals voiced their support for a more expansionist foreign policy that would seek gains in power, not merely status quo maintenance. Such a policy, they believed, was warranted by Russia's full restoration of great power status. For instance, Minister of Defense Sergei Ivanov publicly proclaimed, "Russia has now completely recovered the status of a great power that bears global responsibility for the situation on the planet and the future of human civilization."[29] His article sought to justify the need for greater military expenditures, yet it also served to embolden those advocating greater separation from the West in areas such as energy supplies and relations with the former Soviet states. Energy analysts and geopoliticians insisted that Russia would be better off sharply redirecting its oil and gas supplies toward Eurasian countries, such as China and India, because it would assist the country in developing "energy-intensive goods" and in transforming its current status of a raw materials appendage of Europe.[30] Supporters of more aggressive policies in the former Soviet region proposed that Russia increase its power by recognizing separatist territories in "politically disloyal" Georgia, Moldova, and Azerbajian and demanding a greater independence of Crimea in Ukraine.[31]

This kind of assertiveness was more than a difference in style with Putin's foreign policy. Putin's perspective was still pragmatically focused on internal modernization, rather than directly challenging interests of the West, and the United States in particular, in the world. Increased toughness on America's "unipolar" actions, as indicated by the Kremlin's numerous public statements, did not mean to promote Russia's unilateralism or crude accumulation of power. Rather, it meant to draw attention to nonaddressed critical challenges of the post–Cold War world, such as terrorism, weapons of mass destruction, poverty, and political instability. It also meant to convey Russia's desire to be more integrated with the Western economy, and for these reasons, it was hardly a return to Primakov's policy of balancing the United States. Although a chance of moving in Primakov's direction remained, the policy course stayed focused on strengthening economic relations with the world, especially Europe,[32] not on building a strong security alliance with China and India or tightening the CIS under the Kremlin's leadership.

Pro-Western Critics

Russia's liberal Westernizers criticized Putin for his insistence on advancing a great power status. In their mind, there existed only two fundamental paths— pro-Western or great power nationalistic. Accustomed to viewing reality in terms of dichotomies, they followed the line of some Western analysts, insisting that if Russia is not a Western-style democracy, then it must be an empire,[33] or if it is a great power, then it must be an anti-Western one. Despite Putin's efforts to integrate with Western nations economically and in terms of addressing common security threats, Westernizers charged the Kremlin was becoming increasingly anti-Western in various aspects of its foreign policy. They blamed Putin for his lack of commitment to institutional integration with the West, and they insisted that Russia was becoming (1) increasingly imperialist toward its neighbors; (2) unnecessarily confrontational toward the West; and (3) obsessed with restoring great power at the expense of domestic modernization needs.

For instance, Liliya Shevtsova of Carnegie Moscow Center expressed a typical liberal view that the Kremlin became obsessed with insecurity and control over economic assets, as the situation was growing increasingly unpredictable. Rather than building a pluralistic political system and improving relations with the West, she argued, "the Kremlin's policies have in fact become a tool for the elite, composed of representatives of energy companies and force structures, to pursue its own interests—and this in turn has led to a worsening in Russia's relations with the West and with the new independent states, including its closest allies."[34] Energy-dependent nations, such as Ukraine, Moldova, and even the loyal ally Belarus, were now eager to escape Russia's embrace and look for alternative international ties. Members of the European Union, too, showed their reluctance to develop economic relations with Moscow. According to Shevtsova, the Kremlin also abandoned domestic modernization in favor of becoming a petrostate that "transforms market relations into affairs of state, and economic resources into political tools."[35] For these reasons, liberals believed, a sharp decline in oil prices would do Russia good, as it would push it toward modernization and democratization.

Table 6.3.   Assertive Pragmatism (AP): Contending Views

Civilizationists/Statists:		Westernizers:
AP is insufficient to achieve a political and cultural independence	VS.	AP provokes confrontation with the West

Table 6.3 summarizes contending views on Assertive Pragmatism.

Civilizationists and Social Democrats

Civilizationists showed their ambivalence toward the new, more assertive foreign policy advanced by the Kremlin. On the one hand, a greater assertiveness is what they had been advocating since the 1990s, challenging Russia to restore its hegemony in the former Soviet region and strong ties with the Soviet allies (see chapter 4). On the other hand, the assertiveness they defended served entirely different purposes and meant to support Russia's break with the West, not an appropriate place within the West-centered economic and political structures. For instance, Russian imperialists advocated a restoration of a "fortress Russia" able to resist powerful pressures from both Western and Eastern directions.[36]

A different group, Eurasianists, advocated a close alliance with China or Iran in order for Russia to return to its "cultural roots" and defend itself against influences from the West, seen as the most dangerous.[37] According to Eurasianists, if Russia had indeed fully recovered as a great power, it did not need to seek the West's approval of its actions and intentions. Russia had to create energy cartels and exclusive military alliances, and push arrogant Americans out of Eurasia once and for all. As a member in the Eurasian coalition, Russia would grow much faster, thereby creating a meaningful counterbalance to the West. Eurasianists also frequently argued against Russia's preoccupation with ethnonationalist ideas that were perceived as prone to violence and disruption of the region's ethnoreligious balance. Although Eurasianists kept a relatively low profile, their influence in the Kremlin and Russia's media space grew. Their philosophy was often shared by Putin's powerful deputy head administrator, Igor Sechin, who was in control of the state-owned oil company Rosneft, the second-largest in the country, and who had numerous allies in the media and political circles. Putin was not invulnerable to the group's pressures, and its members insisted on the president's third term hoping to continue consolidating their influence in his shadow.

All groups within the Civilizationist school of thinking agreed that Putin's foreign policy was lacking a "civilizational mission" or an "image of a future." Their criticism of the Kremlin's ideology of sovereign state was not a criticism of sovereignty as an outdated concept—something that a number of Western-izers were likely to agree with—but an argument that sovereignty itself must not be equated with state bureaucracy and its assets. Rather, Civilizationists argued, sovereignty is a tool of advancing a national sense of purpose, and before asserting its sovereignty Russia had to know first what it was culturally and spiritually.[38] In their assessment, the Kremlin's policies of energy independence and raising prices for Russia's neighbors and "loyal allies," such as Armenia and Belarus, were harmful to Russia's status of spiritual leader and protector of the region.[39]

Social democrats, too, were critical of the potentially bureaucratic nature of Russia's new foreign policy assertiveness and preoccupation with sovereignty. Unlike Civilizationists, however, this group concentrated on development of human potential, stronger social programs, and improvement of people's life rather than cultural mission as a key foreign policy objective.[40] Alternatively, at least some Eurasianists showed themselves to be mainly concerned with re-building Russia's power, not living standards. Sergei Pereslegin, for instance, defended a destruction of the newly emerged middle class and stimulation of social inequality in order to expedite economic growth and become an internationally powerful state. If Putin were serious in his critique of unipolarity, he had to bid farewell to the "hypocritical and stagnating" middle-class Europeans and embrace economic tigers in Asia and growing powers in the Middle East.[41]

Table 6.4 summarizes Russia's foreign policy discourse.

Support from the Larger Society

Overall, despite the diversity of elite perspectives on Russia's foreign policy, the larger society was very supportive of its official ideology and new assertive methods of advancing international objectives. Russians strongly supported

Table 6.4. Russia's Foreign Policy Discourse

	Kremlin	Westernizers	Civilizationists	Social Democrats
Main objective	Great power normalization	Westernization	Advancement of cultural values	Improvement of human capital and living standards
Geopolitical orientation	Euro-East	West	Independence or Eurasia	Europe
Foreign policy methods	Pragmatic assertiveness	Cooperation with Western nations	Independent assertiveness; cooperation with Eurasian nations	Cooperation with European nations

Putin and his outlined foreign policy objectives—economic development, political stability, and security from threats. Multiple polls demonstrated that society was well aware of considerable financial and political costs of embarking on imperial projects. Most respondents were convinced that the only way to regain the former great power status was through a successful development of the Russian economy and had no illusions about restoring the Soviet system. In a typical poll, about 60 percent expressed nostalgia about the system, yet only about 12 percent considered its restoration realistic, and 31 percent were against such a restoration.[42] In addition, only 34 percent wanted Russia to become a world power, while about 47 percent would have been content to see their country among the world's ten to fifteen most advanced economies and politically influential countries.[43]

Russians also valued political order and stability as a result of a successful foreign policy by expressing strong condemnation of revolutionary prospects in the country. One poll revealed, for instance, that Russians are most positive about such word symbols, as "order" (58 percent), "justice" (49 percent), and "stability" (38 percent). In the same poll, the word "revolution" was among the least popular ones, with 22 percent viewing it in a negative light.[44]

In addition, Russians showed their lack of strong identification with Europe or Asia—a disappointment for both liberal Westernist and Eurasianist hopes. In March 2007, only 38 percent saw Russia as a part of Europe, while 45 percent claimed Russia was a particular Eurasian civilization with interests of moving the East in the future. The poll should not be read as anti-European, however, as the notion "Europe" brought positive emotions of 77 percent of Russians, relative to 56 percent of those favorably predisposed to the notion "Asia."[45]

Finally, although the registered feelings hardly qualified the society as supportive of various Civilizationist projects, Russians showed their support for assertive tactics of advancing national interests in the world. One poll indicated that most of them approve Putin's tough approach and "welcome the readiness of the authorities to discuss energy matters with the neighbors from the position of strength." About 61 percent viewed Putin's course to be "well-considered and well-balanced," and only about 40 percent felt that another Cold War with the West was possible, while 48 percent did not think so.[46]

6.3. THE UNITED STATES AND EUROPE

Cooperation and Rivalry with the United States

In a number of areas, Russia's cooperation with the United States remained strong since establishment of the post-9/11 partnership. Both sides were committed to solving issues of nuclear proliferation and joined forces in encouraging North Korea and Iran to halt their movements toward producing a nuclear bomb. The United States supported Russia's proposal to reprocess spent nuclear fuel outside Iran as a way for the country to continue with its nuclear program for peaceful purposes. The two sides also coordinated numerous antiterrorist activities. For instance, in December 2006 U.S. intelligence alerted Russia to a potential terrorist threat of an explosion in the Moscow metro, which helped the Kremlin adequately respond to the threat.

Despite these positive developments, tensions between the two countries grew dramatically and concerned at least five issues—Iran, arms sales abroad, China, energy resources, and expansion of American military infrastructure toward Russia's borders. Elections of new presidents in both countries during 2008 did not eliminate the tensions over these issues. On Iran, Russia was against putting additional pressures on the Middle Eastern nation, favoring continuing negotiations. The Kremlin was not willing to support tough sanctions for two main reasons—its own interests and fear of U.S. unilateralism and potential use of force. First, it viewed the issue in a broader context of Russia's multiple economic, political, and security ties and what it viewed as an important neighbor. No other United Nations Security Council (UNSC) member has relations with Iran as deep and as extensive as Russia, and the Kremlin assumed that Ahmadinejad, with his regime and irresponsible policies, was temporary, while Iran was here to stay. Russia wanted to find the right balance between pressuring the top leaders of Iran and not disrupting important ties between Russian and Iranian societies, and such an approach was sure to dictate a foreign policy that would differ from those adopted by the United States, the EU, and China. Second, Russia's leadership signaled it was not optimistic about resolving the issue in the face of the U.S. policy to continue with threats to use force, while abstaining from initiating any nuclear reductions.[47] The Kremlin's leadership did not want to be seen as responsible for moving the issue down to the path of military confrontation and therefore participating in what it saw as another immoral act of aggression similar to those against Yugoslavia and Iraq.

An additional area of tension was Russia's sharply growing arms sales, including to regions of potential concern to the United States in the Middle East, China, and Latin America. In 2006 sales of arms and military hardware were up 20 percent over 2005, for a total value of $6.5 billion.[48] Although the United States protested against sales to such U.S.-unfriendly states, as Iran, Syria, and Venezuela, Russia's response was that those weapons systems were commercially important and of a defensive nature. By selling them, the Kremlin therefore did not violate any international agreements and only did what the United States was doing by selling its own weapons worldwide, including to areas of Russia's concern, such as Georgia and Azerbaijan.

Related to weapons sales was the issue of China, as the country was the single largest buyer of Russia's arms. Russia-China ties, however, were of concern to the United States for a host of other reasons, first and foremost geopolitical ones. Russia-China cooperation, particularly in addressing security issues in central Asia, was viewed in the light of the two nations' growing ambitions to challenge American interests. That could be achieved by creating a regional alliance of several countries that would make rules for its members but exclude the United States from participating. For example, the Shanghai Cooperation Organization, established by Russia, China, and central Asian states, added India and Iran as its associate members, yet refused to consider such status for the United States. The Kremlin remained suspicious, however, viewing the geographic region through the lens of competition, rather than potential cooperation. It felt that the United States was mainly interested in the region's abundant energy resources and geostrategic presence and was about to use Trojan Horse tactics: move in first and conquer second.

Another issue was that of Russia's energy interests in the former Soviet region and Europe. Russia's energy strategy—increasing state share in energy companies, often at the expense of Western capital, building pipelines in all geographic directions, raising energy prices for its oil- and gas-dependent neighbors, moving to control transportation networks in the former USSR, and coordinating its activities with other energy-producers—generated an anxiety in the American political class. Its members, such as Senator John Mc-Cain and Vice President Dick Cheney, issued multiple statements that indicated their concerns with Russia's new "imperialism" and energy "blackmail." The United States built the alternative Baku-Ceyhan pipeline and worked hard on persuading potential investors and central Asian nations to build the Trans-Caspian route under the Caspian Sea, circumventing Russia. In May 2007, Putin secured a commitment from Kazakhstan, Turkmenistan, and Uzbekistan to increase exports of central Asian energy via Russia's pipelines, which only served to heighten U.S. concerns. President Barack Obama's administration created the position of special envoy for Eurasian energy to support the United States' energy goals in the Eurasian region.

In Russia's perception, its actions were perfectly legitimate and only reflected its desire to capitalize on its energy reserves and improve its chances to serve as a reliable oil and gas supplier of the EU. Despite its increased state share in energy companies, Russia indicated it was still very interested in Western investments and technology. As for its attempts to control transportation networks and gain greater presence in European markets, these meant to ensure reliability of supplies and greater integration with the West. Finally, raising energy prices was necessary for commercial reasons, as a preparation for future membership in the WTO and as a practice fully consistent with market economy rules.

Finally, there was the issue of expanding American military infrastructure closer to Russia's borders, which was taking place within and outside NATO. The United States continued contacts with former Soviet states, such as Azerbaijan, Georgia, and Ukraine, who expressed their intent to join NATO. Outside NATO, Washington announced plans to deploy elements of a missile defense system against Iran and other unspecified dangerous states to the territory of Poland, Czech Republic, and, possibly, Georgia and Ukraine. Russia saw these developments as threatening its national security and indicated it was not satisfied with the United States' explanation.[49] At the summit in Bucharest in April 2008, Russia managed to block issuing Georgia and Ukraine Membership Action Plans (MAPs), and it further expressed a strong criticism of OSCE/NATO-based security system in Europe arguing again new "lines of division" between nations with a common history.[50] In addition, President Medvedev said Russia was "extremely disappointed" that the United States signed a deal to deploy part of a missile-defense system in the Czech Republic and would respond appropriately.[51] By then, the Kremlin had already tested new missiles capable of penetrating the missile defense system (MDS) and announced plans to re-equip its new single-warhead intercontinental ballistic missile (ICBM) Topol-M (SS-27) with multiple warheads.[52] In early 2009, the United States signaled its willingness to reconsider the issue of the missile defense system in exchange for Russia's cooperation on Iran, but the Kremlin reacted with a counteroffer of not delivering short-range missiles (Iskander) if the United States abandoned its MDS plans.[53]

Despite all these disagreements, Russia and the United States were not moving toward another Cold War. The newly elected leaders of the countries, Dmitri Medvedev and Barack Obama, remained interested in working together, which was further demonstrated by the U.S.-Russia summit in Moscow in July 2009. No less importantly, there was no ideological line dividing the two nations—they agreed on some issues while sharply disagreeing on others. Russia's new assertiveness expressed by Putin's Munich speech indicated frustration with lack of progress in developing ties with the West, not with the principle of Westernization as a foreign policy objective.

Russia's Energy Strategy and Relations with Europe

In relations with European countries, Russia's main focus was greater integration with the EU's economy, and it has concluded a number of important agreements to this effect. Russia's largest natural gas company, Gazprom, agreed to build a direct pipeline to Germany underneath the Baltic sea. It also negotiated an agreement with Hungary to extend Russia's Blue Stream pipeline from Turkey to Hungary via Bulgaria and Romania. Another important development was a new oil pipeline to Bulgaria and Greece projected to be build by 2010 with Russia owning 50.5 percent and the other two countries 24.5 percent each. In case of the latter, the oil supplies from Russia would be shipped through the Black Sea, bypassing the crowded Bosphorus.[54] Russia also managed to achieve greater integration with European economies by exchanging some companies' shares. Russia also made progress in political relations with the EU nations by developing a common understanding on solving the Middle Eastern conflict and the issue of Iran's nuclear program. Many Europeans shared the Kremlin's commitment to multilateralism and negotiations, rather than sanctions and force.

Still the strategy of integration with European countries faced important obstacles. Economically, Russia and the EU disagreed on what defines economic security. The EU perceived Russia's energy disputes with former Soviet republics as a threat to its own interests by insisting that Russia ratify the Energy Charter. The charter had been signed by Boris Yeltsin during the 1990s and stipulated access of third parties to Russia's energy pipelines. The EU also saw the issue in terms of market diversification principles and wanted to have room for changing energy partners should such an opportunity present itself. However, Russia was an energy producer, not a consumer, and it wanted to sign long-term contracts with Europeans, resisting access to its pipelines. Given the significance of high energy prices for its economic development, Russia wanted to avoid a repetition of the 1985–1986 scenario when a sharp decline in prices had undermined the Soviet economy. In addition, Russia was wary of European efforts to negotiate separate energy agreements with Azerbaijan, Turkey, and the countries of central Asia. Russia also had a limited success in gaining greater access to the EU retail markets and distribution networks, as well as shares in prominent European companies.

Other difficult issues with Europeans included the role of the OSCE in the former Soviet region and bilateral disputes with some Eastern European nations concerning, among other things, their decision to work with the United States in deploying elements of an antimissile system on their territory. Russia saw the OSCE as deviating from its main mission of solving security conflicts and concentrating instead on pushing a particular version of democracy in the region. The Kremlin indicated to the organization that it would withdraw its financial contribution should the practice continue. Russia also took a hard line on the antimissile defense system, claiming that in response it was considering withdrawing from the Intermediate Nuclear Missile Treaty and aiming some of its missiles at Poland and the Czech Republic, the nations that agreed to host the system on their territory. In addition, Russia refused to yield to pressures from Eastern European states to acknowledge responsibility for their post–World War II occupation or transport energy to Western European countries through their territory. Russia-EU summits in Samara (May 2007), Khanty-Mansiysk (June 2008), and Khabarovsk (May 2009) failed to secure a "strategic partnership" pact or produce any substantive agreements.

6.4. MIDDLE EAST AND ASIA

Opposing the "War of Civilizations" in the Middle East

Russia also demonstrated a renewed activism in the Middle East and the larger Muslim world. Aside from ambitious economic projects and weapons sales to India, Iran, Syria, and Palestine, the Kremlin encouraged an international conference on Iraq accompanied by American phased withdrawal from the country. In order to address growing suspicions of Iran's intent to obtain a nuclear bomb, it also encouraged Tehran to send its spent nuclear fuel to Russia. Acting independently from the UN-U.S.-EU-Russia quartet, the Kremlin also opened political dialogue with leaders of Hamas, who won the Palestinian elections but continued to refuse to renounce violence against Israel or recognize its right to exist as an independent state. In addition, Russia strongly condemned the publication in Denmark and some other European nations of cartoons satirizing the Prophet Muhammad as an "inadmissible" provocation against Muslims.

Russia's Middle East assertiveness had roots in both global and domestic developments. Globally, the Kremlin was reevaluating its relations with the United States. Many of Russia's post–September 11, 2001, expectations have not materialized. Military cooperation in central Asia and Afghanistan was now replaced by rivalry over controlling security space and energy resources. Instead of rebuilding Afghanistan, the United States launched a war in Iraq. The Kremlin no longer viewed Russia-U.S. cooperation in central Asia and the Middle East as primarily beneficial, and it thought the U.S. presence there invited terrorism rather than eradicated it. Russia's perception of the U.S. role in the region as destructive corresponded with perceptions by many Muslims across the world, who viewed the U.S. "war on terror" as a war on them.

For Russia's well-being, implications of the "war of civilizations" were fundamental. For a country with 20 million to 25 million Muslims, an involvement in such a war would mean inviting fire to its own home. Russia's domestic intercultural ties were far from balanced. A growing influence of radical Islamist ideologies, rising immigration from Muslim ex-Soviet republics, and poorly conceived actions of some of Russia's local authorities in failing to build ties with

Muslims created a politically explosive environment. Although the situation in Chechnya was much more stable, Islamic radicals were spreading violence and extremist ideology across the larger Northern Caucasus.

Although Russia's Eastern initiatives were not anti-Western, they signaled that the "war of civilizations" between Western nations and Islam was intensifying, as well as an understanding that Russia had no business participating in that war. Just as it was a tragic mistake to get involved in World War I in 1914, Russia felt it would be tragic to have a fully hardened Western-Islamic front today and to see Russia joining it. Russia's willingness to engage Iran and Hamas sought to compensate for blunders of Western policies in the region, such as calls to boycott elections in Iran or clumsy attempts to pressure Palestinian voters, and to find a way out of a developing intercivilizational confrontation. Implicitly, the new Kremlin initiatives also fully recognized that the threat of Islamic radicalism in Russia cannot be successfully confronted without reaching out to the Muslim world. The notion of a dialogue with the Muslim world was strongly endorsed by Russia's political class. Russia called for an "intercivilizational alliance" and "compromise" involving countries in the Middle East. For example, in March 2008 President Putin sent a message to the Organization of the Islamic Conference meeting in Senegal in which he said that "deeper relations of friendship and cooperation with the Islamic world are Russia's strategic course" and that "we share concerns about the danger of the world splitting along religious and civilizational lines."[55] Other officials presented Russia as a country, "which is on the junction of Europe and Asia and is a natural inter-civilization bridge" and expressed desire to have closer ties with the Islamic world.[56]

Imperatives of Modernization and Security in Asia

Although Russia saw itself as a country of European identity, it sought to take advantage of its strategic proximity to Asia for the purpose of modernizing the economy. It was highly symbolic that after being elected Russia's new president Medvedev chose China and central Asia as the first regions to visit. China and the Asia-Pacific region were important because of their potential for becoming a gateway for Russia's entrance to the global economy. With half of the population and one-fifth of global trade, the region was viewed by many as a success story of modernization/globalization. Rich in natural resources, Russia was poised to contribute to satisfying the region's growing demand for energy and modernizing its own domestic economy along the way. Russia moved from a primitive accumulation of capital to the stage of generating a stable flow of investments in the economy, and it was turning its forward-looking vision and growing resources into a more aggressive foreign policy. In addition, the region faced some long-standing security challenges, such as the nuclear ambitions of North Korea and China's relations with Taiwan.

Russia's first interest was in increasing its role in solving vital security issues in East Asia. For years, Russia's officials argued for the development of a multilateral security framework in the region and outside. The Kremlin insisted that security problems could only be solved through systematic coordination of state efforts, and not through use of force by ad hoc coalitions. For instance, it developed the Shanghai Cooperation Organization (SCO), with China and four central Asian states, for addressing threats from terrorism and the security vacuum in the area. In East Asia, Moscow advocated multilateral solutions to the nuclear crisis with North Korea and contributed considerably to creating the six-party format for dealing with the crisis.

Russia's most important priority remained economic modernization, and that required determination to win markets in arms and energy. China and India remained as Russia's largest buyers, purchasing more than 90 percent of Russia's annual arms exports. While promoting weapons sales in Asia, Putin did so mainly for commercial reasons, not out of desire to create some new strategic "axis" against the United States. Russia viewed itself as connected with Asia into an economically open region, in which Russia, due to richness of natural resources, occupies an appropriately important role and reaps considerable economic, as well as political, benefits. Although its energy markets remained primarily in Europe and accounted for about 50 percent of its foreign trade, Russia continued to aggressively promote itself as an energy pipeline hub connecting Asia, Europe, and North America. Russia's energy strategy estimated that by 2020, 30 percent of the country's oil exports would go to Asia, compared with 3 percent in 2005.

Russia's other priorities in the region include nuclear security and political stability. Seeking a non-nuclear status for North Korea, Moscow has worked to develop its ties with North Korea, and it stayed engaged with Pyongyang during nuclear crises. Close relationships with North Korea helped Russia to increase its participation in security negotiations, and it was ultimately Pyongyang that demanded that Moscow join the six-party format. It was critical for Russia that changes in the region, such as reunification of the two Koreas, were orderly and not destabilizing in nature. On several occasions, Putin extended his support for unification of the two Koreas if it takes place in an orderly fashion and on the basis of inter-Korean dialogue. Russian analysts considered a unified Korea a potential strategic partner, provided that the shape of unification was not overly determined by the United States. For these reasons, Russia insisted on preserving special and evenhanded relations with both Koreas.

Of course, none of this meant that Russia faced no constraints on advancing its greater influence in the region. One such constraint had to do with progressive power differentials. As Russia continued to supply China with energy and weapons and China continued to grow at a considerably higher rate than its northern neighbor, the risk of Moscow's becoming a junior partner in a Beijing-led coalition increased. However, a way out of this "relative gains" dilemma was not to reduce bilateral interactions, but rather to continue strengthening multilateral security institutions in the region. In addition, it was important to be versatile in developing economic relations by strengthening relations with the United States and promoting trilateral cooperation with South Korea and North Korea in anticipation of a future unification of Korea. Russia could only reap economic and security benefits through development of multiple ties in the region with all the sides involved—China, South Korea, North Korea, the United States, and Japan.[57]

6.5. THE FORMER SOVIET WORLD

The same commitment to economic development, political stability, and security delivered in assertive style was visible in Russia's foreign policy toward the former Soviet world.

"No More Energy Subsidies"

Consistently with the new vision, Russia moved to strengthen its energy position in world markets. In addition to increasing Russian shares in foreign companies abroad and coordinating its activities with other energy producers, Russia's energy strategy included building pipelines in all geographic directions, raising energy prices for its oil- and gas-dependent neighbors, and moving to control transportation networks in the former USSR. Although many interpreted Gazprom's energy dispute with Ukraine in December 2005 as an attempt by the Kremlin to punish the new leadership of Ukraine for the Orange Revolution, the dispute also aimed to economically normalize relations with Kiev by moving in the direction of establishing market-based prices for energy supplies. Moscow worked to reduce the amount of subsidies to the Ukrainian economy, and Kiev, understandably, resisted the effort. Russia's decision reflected the Kremlin's long-articulated pragmatic modernization approach in the former Soviet region. Already in February 2001, then secretary of the Security Council, Sergei Ivanov, announced that previous attempts to integrate the region of the CIS had come at a very high price and that Russia had to abandon the integration project in favor of a "pragmatic" course of bilateral relations. By the time this announcement was made, the CIS states' debt to Russia had reached $5.5 billion.[58]

Russia's decision also reflected a policy adjustment in the post-Soviet world following the colored revolutions. As Ukraine, Georgia, and Moldova moved to challenge Moscow by questioning the Russia-controlled CIS, the Kremlin was determined to secure economic gains in the region. As explained by Putin, "Over the last fifteen years Russia subsidized the Ukrainian economy by a sum that amounted to $3 to 5 billion each year," and "each year we raised the issue of whether we should change to the European regime for determining prices."[59] The fact that Russia's close allies in the region, such as Armenia and Belarus, were also presented with the same deal of tripled gas prices further indicated that the Kremlin's energy strategy reflected imperatives of economic modernization. In an energy dispute with Belarus during late 2006–early 2007, Russia's Gazprom canceled a preferential price, doubling it to $100 per 1,000 cubic meters and acquiring a 50 percent stake in the Belarusian state gas pipeline company, Beltransgaz. On oil, Russia imposed a new export duty, increasing domestic revenue and reducing Belarus's chances of re-exporting Russian oil. The net gain from both deals for Russia, according to some calculations, amounted to around $4 billion, or over 2 percent of the overall budget.[60]

Importantly, the Kremlin also renegotiated price arrangements with the oil- and gas-rich Turkmenistan and Kazakhstan, leaving them with less incentive to sell to Europe and China.[61] With attractive prices and an energy transportation system in place, the Caspian states would be less likely to construct new pipelines that are favored by non-Russian nations. In addition, the autocratic regimes in central Asia appreciate that Russia does not aim to "democratize" them.

Russia's energy policy was pursued against objections from various directions. Western countries expressed concerns over the Kremlin's use of energy as a "political weapon" against its neighbors. Belarusian president Aleksandr Lukashenka accused Moscow of trying to incorporate his country into Russia.[62] At home, Russia's Civilizationists attacked Putin's policies as betraying the notion of "Slavic unity" and pushing Belarus into the arms of the "hostile" West.[63] Yet the Kremlin remained firm, insisting that its policies of ending energy subsidies were perfectly legitimate and indeed necessary to join the WTO and remain a reliable energy supplier to European markets. If anything, the story reaffirmed that Russia remained pragmatically focused on selfish considerations of national recovery, not empire.

In Search of Stability and Security

As Russia's economic recovery required preservation of the international status quo, the Kremlin sought to insulate the region from what it saw as politically destabilizing activities. It took different approaches to different parts of the region. In central Asia, the Kremlin chose to work independently from the West and in partnership with China to address a challenge of destabilization from local and foreign Islamic radicals. This was a departure from the original policy of working with the West and allowing U.S. and NATO troops' presence in the central Asian states in order to launch a counterterrorist operation in Afghanistan. In Ukraine, it signaled a desire to move beyond the Orange Revolution and work with a broad range of political forces in the country.[64] In Georgia, the Kremlin took a hard-line approach, imposing sanctions, strengthening ties with separatist territories, and practicing containment toward Tbilisi. After President Mikhail Saakashvili's arrests of Russia's four intelligence officers in September 2006, Moscow reacted with a heavy package of economic and political sanctions that stayed in place even after the officers had returned to Russia.

Even this hard-line approach did not work, and on August 8, 2008, Georgia attacked the South Ossetian capital Tskhinvali in attempting to restore control over the rebellious province. Georgian troops killed ten Russian peacekeepers and, by attacking the city with heavy artillery, Georgia inflicted heavy civilian casualties on South Ossetia. Russia responded with overwhelming force that included several armored battalions, air power, and marines, defeating and destroying much of the Georgian military. Russia also recognized the independence of South Ossetia and Abkhazia and imposed areas of security control throughout Georgia. Despite Saakashvili's efforts to present his offensive as a response to Russia's aggression, sources as diverse as intelligence agencies, human rights organizations, the Georgian exiled leader Irakli Okruashvili and various government analysts agreed that the aggression came from Tbilisi, not Moscow.[65]

Much of Russia's reaction can be explained by its perception of threat stemming from the expansion of NATO. The West's geopolitical advances into what Russia has traditionally viewed as its sphere of interests and the desire expressed by the postrevolutionary Georgia and Ukraine to join NATO exacerbated Russia's sense of vulnerability and isolation by the West. Following the summit of NATO in Bucharest, Russia reiterated that it would do everything in its power to prevent expansion of the alliance and extension of its membership to Georgia and Ukraine.[66] The so-called frozen conflicts were merely leverage in the Kremlin's hands, and until the war in the Caucasus in August 2008, the Kremlin had planned to keep them frozen until NATO bore out its plans to continue its march to the East. In the aftermath of the summit, to signal its dissatisfaction to Georgia, the Kremlin extended additional assistance to the secessionist South Ossetia and Abkhazia.[67] Some Russian analysts argued that if membership in NATO is the most important to Georgia, then Tbilisi is likely to obtain it at the cost of its territorial integrity.[68] South Ossetia and Abkhazia continued to oppose Georgia's membership in the Western alliance and to press for integrating with Russia. Such integration came a few steps closer after the United States' recognition of the independence of Kosovo and the Kremlin's recognition of South Ossetia and Abkhazia's independence in the wake of the Caucasus crisis. At the same time, Moscow expedited negotiations with Moldova over incorporation of Transdniestr provided that Kishinev stays a neutral state and does not join NATO.[69] Moscow may be signaling that the "no NATO membership in exchange for territorial integrity" deal may still be possible to conclude with other republics outside Georgia, such as Ukraine and Azerbaijan.

6.6. EVALUATION OF GREAT POWER ASSERTIVENESS

Balance Sheet

On balance, the shift toward foreign policy assertiveness has been successful in defending Russia's objectives. Apart from the conflict with Georgia, Russia did not experience any major threats to its security, from either terrorist attacks or elsewhere. While pressing for preserving and strengthening security ties with Western countries, Russia managed to sustain good relations with Iran and other Middle Eastern nations. The latter often had complicated relationships with the United States and the EU and, no less importantly, had a potential to undermine Russia's security through funding religious extremist activities. The Kremlin's effort to reach out to the Muslim world by initiating contacts with its multilateral organizations and developing bilateral ties served Russia well. The overall situation improved in Chechnya, although terrorism in the Caucasus remained an important issue. In the former USSR, Russia strengthened its security standing by maintaining evenhanded relations with other states in central Asia and the Caucasus. The exception was Georgia, against which the Kremlin applied sanctions and then military force.

Russia's foreign policy was also relatively successful in meeting the objective of economic development. The Kremlin's strategy of capitalizing on the country's energy reserves added revenue without alienating potential foreign investors. Russia's drastic decisions to cut energy supplies for some of its neighbors, as well as some other components of its energy strategy, raised concerns among Western countries and former Soviet republics but on balance did not do any irreparable damage. More importantly, Russians themselves were strongly behind the course of foreign policy assertiveness. For example, in March 2007, 61 percent of respondents evaluated the Kremlin's international actions as well considered and well balanced. Indeed, 16 percent felt that the foreign policy course was too pro-Western for their taste, relative to only 8 percent of those who believed it was hard-line and uncompromising with regard to the West.[70]

Table 6.5 summarizes the record of Assertive Pragmatism.

Challenges

This assessment, of course, is subject to how well Russia is going to meet future foreign policy challenges. One can identify at least two groups of such challenges—external and internal.

Russia's main external challenge is to preserve the international status quo in order to continue with the vital program of domestic economic and social modernization. Major economic disturbances, such as world economic recession or a sharp decline in oil prices, are bound to complicate the process. The international financial crisis has made itself felt in Russia and may continue to negatively affect its economic development. If those experts who project growing demand for energy among both developed and developing nations, such as China and India, are correct, then in the midterm perspective Russia should still be able to take advantage of the situation if it is successful in developing its own reserves. Another danger might be related to further destabilization of the Middle East and continued expansion of the Western military presence to Russia's borders. The U.S. withdrawal of its troops from Iraq without leaving an adequate security framework in place or a military confrontation with Iran would be sure to create a large flow of refugees, in which case the region will be destabilized further. The effects of such destabilization are likely to be felt in the Caucasus and central Asia and therefore, at least indirectly, in Russia. No less dangerous could be NATO's decision to extend membership to Georgia and Ukraine, or American attempts to deliver elements of an antimissile defense system in close proximity to Russia. These kinds of international disturbances may provide ammunition to those inside Russia's political class who resent Putin's Great Power Pragmatism and want to push the assertive style to the edge of radically anti-Western policies.

The internal challenge remains to overcome the split within the political class over how to deal with Western pressures. Too many in Russia have become emboldened by its recent economic recovery to the point of forgetting the coun-

Table 6.5.   The Record of Assertive Pragmatism

Security	Remaining problems with terrorism in the Caucasus
Welfare	Improved economic and social standards
Autonomy	Increased ability to influence international affairs
Identity	Continued efforts to bridge Westernist and Statist values

try's lingering problems. Yet Russia, as the old saying goes, while never as weak as it seems, is also never as strong as it says. The country is strong in its growing international presence and energy power, yet it remains weak in such critical respects as population health, demographic dynamics, and the size of its middle class. Indicators of poverty, HIV infection, and demographic crisis are plentiful enough to make a convincing case for the nation's continuing weakness. Despite all the trumpets of great power revival, Russia remains a vulnerable country in an increasingly volatile environment. At least for the next ten to fifteen years, Russia will do well to think hard about the linkage between external war and internal instability. Its own experience speaks volumes about the linkage.

NOTES

1. "Speech at the Munich Conference on Security Policy," Munich, February 10, 2007, at www.kremlin.ru.

2. Charles Recknagel, "Iraq: U.S. Plans to Take In 7,000 Refugees," *RFE/RL Research Report*, February 15, 2007, at www.rferl.org.

3. Seymour M. Hersh, "The Next Act," *New Yorker*, November 27, 2006, www.newyorker.com/archive/2006/11/27/061127fa_fact?printable=true.

4. Vladimir Putin, "Press Statement and Answers to Journalists' Questions Following a Meeting of the Russia-NATO Council," Bucharest, April 4, 2008, at www.kremlin.ru.

5. "Poll Shows Russians See NATO Membership for Ukraine, Georgia as Threat," *Interfax*, April 1, 2008.

6. "Russia's Economy under Vladimir Putin: Achievements and Failures," *RIA Novosti*, March 1, 2008.

7. "Middle Class Grows Atop," *Kommersant*, February 27, 2008.

8. Andrea Crandall, "Invest in China? Invest in Russia," *Johnson's Russia List*, no. 22, April 19, 2006, at www.cdi.org/russia/johnson.

9. "Russia Is Most Attractive Emerging Economy for Investors," *Kommersant*, February 14, 2008.

10. Paul Abelsky, "Russia Industrial Output Rises 9.2%, Nine-Month High," Bloomberg, May 20, 2008.

11. "Russians Think Chosen Development Course Correct—Poll," *Interfax*, June 18, 2008.

12. Both Russian and Western analysts speculated that the security class became omnipresent in policymaking. See, for example, O. Kryshtanovskaya and S. White, "Putin's Militocracy," *Post-Soviet Affairs* 19, no. 4 (2003); Daniel Treisman, "Putin's Silovarchs," *Orbis* (Winter 2007).

13. See, for example, "A Potemkin Election," Editorial, *Washington Post*, January 30, 2008; "Kicking Democracy's Corpse in Russia," *New York Times*, Editorial, January 30, 2008; Alvaro Vargas Llosa, "Eternal Putin," *New Republic*, March 5, 2008; "Putin's Mini-Me (or Not?)," *New York Times*, Editorial, March 4, 2008.

14. Dmitri Medvedev, "Dlya protsvetaniya vsekh nado uchityvat' interesy kazh-dogo," *Ekspert* 28, no. 522 (July 24, 2006), http://expert.ru.

15. Vladimir Putin, "Rossiya na rubezhe tysyacheletiy," *Nezavisimaya gazeta*, December 1999.

16. Vladimir Putin, "Poslaniye Federal'nomu Sobraniyu Rossiyskoy Federatsiyi," March 2005, at www.kremlin.ru.

17. Putin, "Poslaniye," March 2005.

18. Vladimir Putin, "Poslaniye Federal'nomu Sobraniyu Rossiyskoy Federatsiyi," May 10, 2006, April 26, 2007, at www.kremlin.ru.

19. For development of this comparison, see Andrei P. Tsygankov, "Finding a Civilizational Idea: 'West,' 'Eurasia' and 'Euro-East' in Russia's Foreign Policy," *Geopolitics* 12, no. 3 (2007).

20. Gleb Pavlovski, "O politike Rossiyi na postsovetskom prostranstve," *America-Russia.net*, April 28, 2005, at www.america-russia.net; "Zapad—eto antiyevropeyskoye ponyatiye," *Izvestiya*, July 14, 2006.

21. Vladislav Surkov, "Suverenitet—eto politicheski sinonim konkurentnosposob-nosti," *Moscow News*, March 3, 2006; Aleksandr Tsipko, "Obratno puti net," *Literaturnaya Gazeta*, no. 19 (May 2006).

22. Not all in the Kremlin shared the concept of "sovereign democracy." For a different view, see Medvedev, "Dlya protsvetaniya vsekh nado uchityvat' interesy kazh-dogo."

23. Putin, "Speech at the Munich Conference."

24. Vlad Sobel, "A Resurgent Russia, or Triumphalist West?" *Johnson's Russia List*, no. 249 (November 6, 2006). In attempting to emphasize Europe's independence, Pavlovski has criticized the concepts of "West," viewing it as "anti-European" and only relevant for understanding of the Cold War ("Zapad—eto antiyevropeyskoye ponyatiye").

25. "Obzor vneshnei politiki Rossiyskoi federatsiyi," March 27, 2007, at www.mid.ru.

26. Dmitriy Medvedev, speech at the meeting with Russian Ambassadors and Permanent Representatives to International Organizations, Russian Foreign Ministry, Moscow, July 15, 2008; speech at World Policy Conference, Evian, France, October 8, 2008, at www.kremlin.ru. Also see the article by Russia's foreign minister Sergei Lavrov, "A Strategic Relationship: From Rivalry to Partnership," *Russia Beyond the Headlines*, May 28, 2008, at www.rbth.rg.ru/.

27. Dmitry Medvedev, speech at the Twelfth Petersburg International Economic Forum, St. Petersburg, June 7, 2008, at www.kremlin.ru.

28. For analyses of Russia's liberal currents, see especially G. Fisher, *Russian Liberalism: From Gentry to Intelligensia* (Cambridge, MA: Harvard University Press, 1958); Andrzej Walicki, *Legal Philosophies of Russian Liberalism* (Notre Dame, IN: University of Notre Dame Press, 1992); Marsha Wiedle, *Russia's Liberal Project* (University Park: Pennsylvania State University Press, 2000).

29. Sergei Ivanov, "Triada natsional'nykh tsennostei," *Izvestia*, July 14, 2006.

30. See, for example, Sergei Pereslegin, "Rossiya sosredorochilas'," *Russki zhurnal*, February 1, 2007, at www.russ.ru.

31. Moscow Mayor Yuri Luzhkov and a number of State Duma deputies, in particular, have been active in advancing this kind of goal.

32. Putin's special representative to the European Union Sergei Yastrzhembsky suggested that Putin's Munich speech was a "cold shower [and not a return] to a Cold War." Yastrzhembsky added that Putin's remarks were aimed primarily at a European public and also sought to draw attention to a variety of world issues. Pointing out that Putin challenged the concept of what he called a U.S.-dominated "unipolar world," the aide said that an unspecified recent poll showed that at least 60 percent of German respondents agreed with Putin's remarks (*RFE/RL Newsline*, February 23, 2007). In a different interview, Yastrzhembsky drew attention to Russia's desire to integrate with Europe economically. "The Russian business elite wants to go into a massive investment offensive, shall I say, in the best meaning of this word, in European market. One of the goals of the state is to create conditions for such activities of Russian entrepreneurs" (press conference with presidential aid Sergei Yastrzhembsky on RF-EU Relations, January 30, 2007, at www.fednews.ru).

33. For an early statement of this viewpoint, see Zbigniew Brzezinski, "The Premature Partnership," *Foreign Affairs* 73, no. 2 (March/April 1994).

34. Liliya Shevstova, "Rossiya-2007: Vlast' gotova k samovosproizvodstvu, ili ob opredelennosti neopredelennosti," *Carnegie Moscow Center Briefing* 1 (January 2007), at www.carnegie.ru.

35. Shevstova, "Rossiya-2007." For similar statements by Russian liberals, see Vladimir Milov, "Bratya imperialisty," *Vedomosti*, February 7, 2007; Grigori Yavlinski, "Present-Day Russia in an Autocracy," *Gazeta*, March 16–18, 2007, at www.gazeta.ru.

36. Mikhail Yuryev, *Tretya imperiya* (St. Petersburg: Limbus Press, 2007).

37. Den'ga Khalidov, "Myunkhen: rasstavaniye s illuziyami," *Russki zhurnal*, February 27, 2007, at www.russ.ru.

38. Oleg Matveychev, "Dukhovkyi suverenitet," *Russki zhurnal*, February 17, 2006, at www.russ.ru.

39. Aleksandr Prokhanov, "Belarus, ty prava!" *Zavtra* 3, no. 687 (January 17, 2007).

40. See, for example, Vladislav Inozemtsev, "Rossiya i mirovyye tsentry sily," Publichnyie lektsiyi "Polit.ru," at www.polit.ru.

41. Pereslegin, "Rossiya sosredorochilas.'"

42. *Nezavisimaya gazeta*, April 7, 2006.

43. "Poll Suggests Russians Unimpressed by 'Imperialist Ambitions,'" *RFE/RL Newsline*, January 24, 2007.

44. "Russians Like Order and Justice," *RosBusinessConsulting*, March 28, 2007.

45. "Russian Interests to Move to Asia in Future—Poll," *Interfax*, March 17, 2007.

46. "Poll Suggests Russians Favor Tough Foreign Policy," *RFE/RL Newsline*, March 14, 2007.

47. "Moscow Warns U.S. Iran Policy May Spark 'Clash of Civilizations,'" *RIA Novosti*, March 27, 2007.

48. "Russian Arms Business Breaks New Records," *RFE/RL Newsline*, March 22, 2007.

49. Kristin Roberts, "Gates Gets Cool Russian Welcome over Missile Plan," Reuters, April 23, 2007.

50. ITAR-TASS, "Medvedev Doubts Effectiveness of OSCE/NATO-Based Security System," June 11, 2008; Dmitry Rogozin, "Global Security and Propaganda," *International Herald Tribune*, July 1, 2008.

51. Henry Meyer and Sebastian Alison, "Medvedev Says Russia to Respond to U.S. Missile Deal," Bloomberg, July 9, 2008.

52. "Russia to Re-equip Its New Mobile ICBMs with Multiple Warheads," *RIA Novosti*, December 15, 2007.

53. "Iskander Plans If U.S. Scraps Missile Shield," *RIA Novosti*, March 3, 2009.

54. Andrew E. Kramer, "New Pipeline Will Bypass the Bosporus but Involve Russia," *New York Times*, March 16, 2007.

55. "Putin Wants 'Deeper Friendship' with Islamic World," *RFE/RL*, March 14, 2008.

56. ITAR-TASS, "Russia Ready to Contribute to Alliance of Civilizations Potential," January 16, 2008; "Minister Hails Ties to Muslim World," *RFE/RL*, January 11, 2008.

57. For development of these points, see Gil Rozman, Kazuhiko Togo, and Joseph Ferguson, eds., *Russian Strategic Thought toward Asia* (New York: Palgrave, 2006), especially the chapter by Aleksandr Lukin.

58. *Nezavisimaya gazeta*, February 7, 2001.

59. Vladimir Putin, transcript of meeting with the leaders of the news agencies of G-8 member countries, June 2, 2006, Novo-Ogaryovo, at www.kremlin.ru.

60. Andrei P. Tsygankov, "The Test of Belarus," *Johnson's Russia List*, no. 14 (January 19, 2007).

61. Max Delany, "Energy Ties Take Medvedev Eastward," *Moscow Times*, July 2, 2008.

62. "Belarusian President Rejects Russia's 'Imperial' Approach . . . ," *RFE/RL Newsline*, February 6, 2007.

63. Prokhanov, "Belarus', ty prava!"

64. However, in August 2009, President Medvedev delayed sending a new Russian ambassador to Ukraine, blaming Ukrainian president Viktor Yushchenko for conducting anti-Russian policies. Medvedev's letter to the Ukrainian president was widely interpreted as Russia's attempt to influence Ukrainian presidential elections by undermining the position of Yushchenko and his political supporters (for Medvedev's letter, see Dmitri Medvedev, "Address to the President of Ukraine Victor Yushchenko," August 11, 2009, at www.kremlin.ru).

65. See, for example, *A Month after the War: Violations of Human Rights and Norms of Humanitarian Law in the Conflict Zone in South Ossetia*, special press release by Memorial Human Rights Center, September 16, 2008; Patrick Armstrong, "The War He Actually Got," *Johnson's Russia List*, September 17, 2008; Brian Rohan, "Saakashvili 'Planned S. Ossetia Invasion': Ex-minister," Reuters, September 15, 2008; "Did Saakashvili Lie?" *Der Spiegel*, September 15, 2008.

66. "Russia Again Vows to Block NATO Enlargement," *RFE/RL Newsline*, April 9, 2008.

67. C. J. Chivers, "Russia Expands Support for Breakaway Regions in Georgia," *New York Times*, April 17, 2008.

68. Anatoly Tsyganok, "On the Consequences of Georgia's NATO Entry," *Fondsk.ru*, January 2, 2008, www.fondsk.ru/article.php?id=1148.

69. "Moldovan President, Transdniester Leader Hold Landmark Talks," *RFE/RL Newsline*, April 14, 2008.

70. Leonti Byzov, "Narodnyye imperialisty," *Vremya Novostei*, March 13, 2007.

7

The Post-Western World and Russia's Search for a New Direction

> As regards the content of the new stage in humankind's development, there are two basic approaches to it among countries. The first one holds that the world must gradually become a Greater West through the adoption of Western values. . . . The other approach—advocated by Russia—holds that competition is becoming truly global and acquiring a civilizational dimension; that is, the subject of competition now includes values and development models.
>
> —Sergei Lavrov[1]

The fall of 2008 changed the international context in which Russia had defended its interests. The West's ability to project global power was challenged in two principal ways. The Russia-Georgia war undermined the United States' and Europe's monopoly for use of force in world politics; and the global financial meltdown revealed the West's economic vulnerability. Although Russia, too, was hit hard by the global economic crisis, it is the altered position of the Western nations in the international system that is likely to affect the world for many years to come. If the West is indeed in a relative decline and the great power shift defined as "the rise of the rest"[2] is approaching, it has important implications for Russia's foreign policy. The shift puts limitations on the Kremlin's strategy of becoming a "normal great power" or gaining recognition of its interests through development of economic and political ties with the Western world. This chapter describes the challenge of the emerging post-Western world, Russia's new identity debate, and its potential to act as a post-Western great power. It concludes by briefly reflecting on the West's choices regarding Russia's search for a new direction.

201

7.1. THE POST-WESTERN WORLD

International Conditions

The second half of 2008 revealed that the world is entering a principally new stage of development. The end of the Cold War produced the new expectation of increasing economic and political convergence across nations around the notion of West-centered globalization.[3] Today these expectations are frequently criticized as ethnocentric and unrealistic, and many observers are increasingly aware that the West-centered world is beginning to unravel. Structurally, it is still the familiar world of American primacy[4] with the Western—especially American—military predominance and the West's global superiority in political, economic, and cultural dimensions. But dynamically the world is moving away from its West-centeredness,[5] even though the exact direction and result of the identified trajectory remains unclear. In sum, the world is entering its post-American[6] and—to the extent that the United States has shaped the West—a post-Western stage.[7]

At least four emerging features of the new world can be identified. The first feature has to do with declining hard power of the West. Its military decline is now evident in the growing proliferation of nuclear weapons and emerged incidents of unsanctioned use of conventional weapons in non-Western regions. Its economic decline is no less obvious with the rise of China and the Asia-Pacific region as new centers of the world's gravity. Instead of relying on the protection and welfare of Western hegemony, nations increasingly seek refuge in reformulating their interests to better protect their societies and readjusting to their regional environments.[8] Instead of promising egalitarian trends in response to the West-centered globalization, critics point to new socioeconomic divisions.[9] Failure of the United States to successfully complete its military operations in Afghanistan and Iraq prevents Iran and Russia from developing their nuclear cooperation; and the failure to maintain a viable international economic order also indicates that the world is departing from its politically unipolar state of the 1990s.

The second feature points to the West's growing difficulties with projecting its soft power across the globe. Here, the George W. Bush era, too, serves as an important threshold, with America's prestige greatly declining in the world.[10] The idea of Western-style democracy, while still attractive, no longer commands the same attention. In part, decline of the idea's attractiveness is related to the fact that democratization and democracy promotion outside the West are not infrequently accompanied by state weakness, lawlessness, and ethnic violence.[11]

The third and the forth features point to the rise of alternative hard and soft power projects. In response to the decline of the West's hard power, attempts to dominate others by using tools of military and economic coercion are going to be increasingly decentralized and undertaken without consultation with Western nations. Two events in the second half of 2008 are of importance here—the beginning of the global economic crisis and the Russia-Georgia war in August. While the former has severely undermined the West-centered model of global economic expansion, the latter ended the West's monopoly for unilateral use of force previously demonstrated by NATO's military attacks on Yugoslavia and the United States' invasion of Iraq. That Russia has chosen to use force in the Caucasus in defiance of the West implies decentralization of hard power usage and promises serious difficulties for Western nations with continuous expansion of NATO's geopolitical responsibilities at the expense of political arrangements, such as the Shanghai Cooperation Organization and Collective Security Treaty Organization.[12] Observers have also noted intensification of processes of cultural reformulations[13] and the rise of alternative soft power projects[14] that develop both within and outside the legitimizing language of democracy.[15]

Russia's New Conditions: Weakness or Strength?

Is Russia prepared to face the new post-Western world? The answer partly depends on whether Russia has emerged as sufficiently strong in terms of its domestic material capabilities, human capital, and institutional capacity. A strong and competitive Russia would be in a position to successfully address the most pressing problems of its security and development. Depending on its leadership's preferences, the nation may then try to tackle its problems unilaterally or in concert with other powers. As a result, it may become a center of material power in the future multipolar world and a model of cultural gravitation.

If, however, a nation is relatively weak, it is hardly in a position to solve critical issues of its development and serve as a model of attraction for the outside world. In that case, Russia has to choose among at least three strategies. In an increasingly multipolar and/or multicultural world, it may choose to side with one of the more powerful states, thereby engaging in hard or soft balancing against other powers. For example, a considerable part of Russia's experience with the European international system of the second half of the nineteenth century and the first half of the twentieth century can be described as the experience of participating in alliances with and against powerful states. Another strategy might be to respond to potentially unfavorable external conditions by engaging in an internal balancing and disengaging from making explicit international choices (back-passing).[16] In the late twentieth and the early twentiy-first century, this strategy has been generally followed by China, yet it may not be available to Russia. The latter is too large and too central in its geographic location between Europe and Asia to delegate solution of critical issues of world politics to other powers.

Perhaps more appropriate for Russia is to consider a revised version of its nineteenth-century *recuiellement* following the defeat in the Crimean War. The two key principles of the *recuiellement*, as introduced by Russia's new chancellor, Prince Alexander Gorchakov, after his predecessor, Count Karl Nesselrode, were relative isolation from European affairs and flexible alliances with other states. While the former was deemed necessary for conducting internal reforms after defeat in the war, the latter was designed to provide the required international calm for domestic recovery. "The circumstances have given us back a full freedom of action," wrote Gorchakov referring to the collapsed Holy Alliance and the perceived betrayal of Austria.[17] To the outside world, the chancellor sought to clarify that Russia adopted a new policy out of domestic needs and not anger at European powers: "La Russie ne boude pas—elle se recueille."[18] Scholars characterized the *recueillement* as moderate and defensive yet aiming at revising the status quo established by the Paris treaty.[19]

7.2. THE NEW IDENTITY DEBATE

The Official View

In the perception by Russia's officials, the nation has regained its strength and fully recovered from the material and institutional problems of the 1990s. Until the global economic crisis, and especially immediately following the crisis in the Caucasus, the dominant narrative in Russia had been that of a strong and rising power. Such rhetoric was supported by the official declarations that projected Russia to become the world's fifth-largest economy, free from dependence on exports of oil and a full-fledged member in a multipolar international order, by 2020. The released "National Security Strategy of the Russian Federation until 2020" opens with the statement that Russia has overcome the consequences of the systemic political and socioeconomic crisis at end of the twentieth century and has restored its capacity to "defend national interests as a subject of multipolar international relations."[20]

As a result of such self-perception, the Kremlin has advocated the strategy of great power normalization. The strategy assumed an increasing cooperation with the world's economic and political system, but not at the expense of Russia's traditional security interests and preservation of statehood.[21] Around 2005—partly in response to Russia's dissatisfaction with the United States' policy of regime change in Iraq and the former Soviet region, and partly to reflect Russia's new economic confidence—the Kremlin adopted a more assertive stance to defend its vision. The Kremlin also introduced the concept of energy superpower to capitalize on Russia's natural resource advantage and position the country as a global player and a maker of new global rules. Russia's new president, Dmitri Medvedev, built on the vision of his predecessor, proposing a new pan-European treaty to establish a new security architecture beyond NATO expansion[22] and to overhaul the international economic order.[23] Russia did not become anti-American and did not call for any concerted effort to undermine the U.S. global position. Instead, it defended the notion of collective leadership and multilateral diplomacy as the alternative to unilateralism and hegemony in international relations.[24] Medvedev also emphasized that Russia and the West shared the same values, although they had to assure that the "values [were] understood in the same way."[25]

The deep economic crisis has not altered the generally optimistic assessment by Russia's officials. Russia's new National Security Strategy to the year 2020 has provided a long list of potential threats to the country's security, but it has stated in its preamble confidence in the country's ability "to reliably prevent internal and external threats to national security and to dynamically develop the Russian Federation and to turn it into a leading power in terms of technological progress, people's quality of life and influence on global processes."[26] In Medvedev's own words, "Russia is totally different now and it has gone through a transitional period, it is developing confidently and steadily, and it has reached a qualitatively new level of long-term, strategic development."[27] Although the global economic crisis created a divide within the Kremlin—with some advocating a sharper diversification of the economy and others a continuing support for energy corporations[28]—the officials are yet to revise their initial assessments and draw more fundamental lessons from the crisis.

Westernizers

Liberal Westernizers within the Russian foreign policy community have been critical of the country's domestic conditions and its ability to become a great power. According to this group, Russia's principal problem has been the chosen model of economic and political development under Vladimir Putin. Excessively centralized and energy oriented, the model is blocking the country's modernization and integration with Western institutions. Politicians and experts such as Boris Nemtsov, Vladimir Milov, Yevgeni Gontmakher, and Igor' Yurgens have challenged the government Strategy until 2020 as misguided and unrealistic.[29] They have criticized Russia's involvement in the war with Georgia and offered a bleak assessment of the country's prospects of recovering from the economic crisis without dismantling the existing model of development.

Externally, Westernizers have positioned Russia as a country of Western identity. They have blamed the government for being in denial about the nation's internal weakness and the rising China problem.[30] In the words of one commentator, "We do not discuss our 'China problem' at all because . . . that makes it too frightening to even bring up the subject."[31] The group has recognized the West's relative decline, but argued that both culturally and politically Russia's choice in addressing its principal economic and security problems should be with Europe and the United States. As Fyodor Lukyanov stated, "the world without the West" may be "even more dangerous a place than the hateful 'mono-polar world.'"[32] Director of the Moscow Carnegie Center Dmitri Trenin made an even more pronounced cultural argument in favor of Russia choosing the Western orientation.[33] According to him, "Russia is not a distinct civilization or a world unto itself" and therefore "it cannot seriously expect to be a power center on par with China—or the United States for that matter. Thus, Russia's non-inclusion into the European security architecture is a problem, while China's absence from the U.S.-led system of security arrangements in Asia is not." Trenin has been among a few in the Westernist group who have granted Russia the right to intervene in the Caucasus in August 2008, but not the right to recognize the independence of South Ossetia and Abkhasia—partly because of the risk of Russia's being isolated by the West.[34]

The Rise of Civilizational Discourse

Perhaps the most interesting intellectual response to the West's relative decline is the revival of Russia's Civilizational discourse. Formerly marginalized, the discourse of Russia as a distinct cultural entity, not just a great power as in the official description, is gaining currency in political circles. The Kremlin, too, is increasingly aware of Russia's soft power potential that includes historical, ethnic, and religious characteristics shared by the nation with its neighbors. As Vladimir Putin stated on one occasion, "The historical credits of trust and friendship, the close ties that link the peoples of our countries" continue to present the "existing potential of influence" for Russia.[35]

Civilizationists, however, go beyond merely recognizing Russia's soft power as a foreign policy potential and argue for a distinct cultural way of living. Since the decline of the USSR, intellectuals have argued that the former Soviet region is united by a historical destiny and Russian language. In 1990, Alexander Solzhenitsyn defended the revival of a Slavic community that includes Russia, Ukraine, Belarus, and northern Kazakhstan.[36] More recently, Russian commentators such as Vitali Tretyakov advocated the idea of Russia as a politically divided nation that is waiting for its unification in the manner of German unification at the end of the Cold War.[37] Unlike those who emphasized

Russia's security interests in the war with Georgia, Civilizationists have high-lighted the cultural obligation to protect those who have historically gravi-tated to Russia. As were Slavophiles in the past, the contemporary Civiliza-tionists are eager to advance Russia's distinct cultural values, rather than merely state foreign policy interests. In response to the economic crisis, they have insisted that socioeconomic bases are not sufficient for recovering and that the emphasis on the middle class as the principal target of Russia's trans-formation is misguided. As Sergei Kara-Murza argued, "overcoming the crisis can be achieved only within the framework of a civilizational project."[38]

Civilizationists can be broken into two main groups, mobilizers and expan-sionists. While sharing the belief in Russia's civilizational distinctiveness, they disagree in assessing the strength of the nation's material and cultural capa-bilities and propose different ways of promoting Russian cultural objectives. Mobilizers tend to view the former Soviet region as open to various influ-ences. They have assumed that Russia is not strong enough to unite the region unilaterally, let alone by force, but have expressed confidence in Russia's ability to mobilize economic and cultural influences by taking advantage of the country's "intersection" position in the middle of Eurasia and linking its southern, western, and eastern peripheries through the development of trans-portation routes across Russian and ex-Soviet states' territories.[39] At least some within the group have been in favor of stronger ties with China and viewed the economic crisis as an opportunity to rebuild Russia's cultural influ-ence in the region without necessarily breaking existing ties with the West.[40]

Expansionists, however, have advanced the notion of a Russian Orthodox empire capable of resisting the West and becoming self-sufficient.[41] They have pursued a more entrenched vision of Russia as sufficiently powerful to deploy its soft power resources coercively and without regard for the ex-republics' possible desire to develop relationships with the European Union and the United States. In the words of Vitali Tretyakov, the official recognition of the independence of South Ossetia and Abkhazia has been "the most important event at this time in the Russian history of the twenty-first century" because it implies "a real start to the practical recreation of the Soviet Union, which is to say of the state-civilization which in various periods of its life was called the Grand Duchy of Moscow, the Kingdom of Muscovy, the Russian Empire, and the Soviet Union."[42] According to this group, a forceful imposition of a Rus-sian "ideological and geopolitical project" is also partly warranted by the West's decline and possible subsequent disintegration in response to the global economic crisis.[43]

The division between the two groups is somewhat reminiscent of the nineteenth-century divide between the old Slavophiles and Pan-Slavists exem-plified by the disagreement of the Aksakov brothers. Both of them thought of

Russia as a unique cultural and religious community, rather than merely an offspring of the European civilization. However, Konstantin defended the notion of the *obshchina* as a truly Christian social organism and was not concerned about the fate of the Slavs residing under the Ottoman Empire, whereas Ivan grew under the influence of the Polish revolt of 1863 into an expansionist and advocate of a forceful policy of liberating Balkan Slavs.[44] Slavs had to choose whether they wished to remain Slavs, wrote Ivan Aksakov in 1867, "either the road to the West or the road to the East, the road to Latinity or the road of Orthodoxy, union either with the destinies of the Western European world or the destinies of the Greco-Slavic world."[45]

As the soft power argument is finding its way to the Kremlin, the foreign policy debate is increasingly framed in cultural categories. So far, the Kremlin has not embraced the autarchic vision of the region, but it warned Western nations against attempts to destabilize its political and cultural environment,[46] and it called for a revival of Russia's historical and cultural capital in the region.

Table 7.1 summarizes Russia's new debate on foreign policy.

The Larger Society

The larger society has been aware of Russia's cultural distinctness, viewing its culture as different from that of the West. In 2008, 60 percent of Russians denied that Western society was a good model for them to follow, and only 7.2 percent agreed.[47] At the same time, Russians think that their country exerts a positive influence in the world. According to a recent BBC World Service poll, 82 percent of Russians believe that they exert such an influence, up from 69 percent in 2005.[48] In addition, more than 30 percent of Russians support conservative traditional values and independence in international politics, relative to about 13 percent sharing liberal ideas and 40 percent not holding clear ideological views.[49] The public, however, offers no support for extensive civilizational projects and is well aware of the considerable financial and political costs of embarking on imperial projects. Instead, the public favors multilateral

Table 7.1.   Russia's New Debate on Foreign Policy

	State	Westernizers	Civilizationists	
			Mobilizers	Expansionists
Relative Strength	Strong	Weak	Weak	Strong
Favored Strategy	Partnership with the West on equal terms	Partnership with the West on Western terms	Flexible alliances	Balance against the West alone or in alliance with China and others

solutions in world politics. The BBC poll found that 50 percent of Russians think that their country should use its power and influence to cooperate with other nations in solving international problems.[50]

7.3. ACTING AS A POST-WESTERN POWER

Between West and China

From Russia's perspective, the most important international challenges are the projection of Western power, the rise of China, and the ability of the two to undermine Russia's own position and interests.

Until the five-day war in the Caucasus, an especially tense issue had been the expansion of the West's military infrastructure closer to the Russian borders. At the Bucharest summit in April 2008, Russia managed to block Georgia and Ukraine from receiving Membership Action Plans (MAPs) for NATO, and Moscow expressed strong opposition to Washington's plans to deploy elements of a missile defense system in Eastern Europe. Nevertheless, there remains a broad support for both developments in the United States. Concerned about the reassertion of Russia in the Caucasus and Ukraine, Washington has signed bilateral agreements of strategic partnership with the two nations and pledged assistance for their security.[51] The U.S. Navy has preserved its presence in the Black Sea since August, and the United States has expressed interest in expanding its military cooperation with states in central Asia.[52] In May 2009, NATO also conducted a military exercise in Georgia despite vehement protests from Russia.

Another aspect of the West's expansion has been the efforts by the United States and Europe to undermine Russia's energy-based modernization and exploit central Asian resources without regard for Russia's interests. Rather than looking for ways to work with Russia as an energy partner, Western leaders engaged in denouncing the Kremlin for energy imperialism[53] and building alternative pipelines from the Caspian area. In May 2009, Brussels and Washington sought to expedite the ambitious Nabucco pipeline and tie the non-Russian countries in the region into a broad southern infrastructure project. The project assumes participation of Kazakhstan and Turkmenistan, the key suppliers of natural gas in the region.

Russia has been also concerned about advancement of Western soft power projects in the former Soviet region. Since 2003, the United States, in line with its democracy promotion strategy, pushed the region toward transforming its political institutions. It provided funds for the opposition and supported revolutions in Georgia, Ukraine, and Kyrgyzstan.[54] Influential elites in the United States also maintained contacts with some radical organizations in Russia, such as the National Bolshevik Party, while increasing pressures on the Kremlin to "democratize" and respect political freedoms. The U.S. State Department continued to issue reports highly critical of Russia's political system, pledging various assistance to "democratic organizations" inside the country. More recently, the European Union has acted on a Polish-Swedish initiative to launch the Eastern Partnership project and pull the six countries between the EU and Russia—Ukraine, Moldova, Belarus, Georgia, Armenia, and Azerbaijan—into the EU's orbit of influence.[55] The Kremlin expressed concerns at both developments, viewing them as politically destabilizing and as disrespectful of Russia.[56]

The rising China presents Russia with another challenge. Although the two's relations are good and continue to improve, there are signs of Russia's growing dependence on China and of the latter's increasing assertiveness. Beijing has been working to acquire Russian energy assets, obtain favorable deals, and make Russia more dependent on its growing sales market. For example, in 2002, China's National Petroleum Company tried to purchase Slavneft.[57] China is also known for its aggressive efforts to negotiate energy supplies below market prices,[58] and it has recently signed a twenty-year oil agreement with its neighbor in the amount of $90 billion in exchange for lending Russian oil companies $25 billion.[59] Even routine domestic economic decisions in Russia are increasingly made with a consideration for China.[60] In recognition of the growing need for China's investments, credits, and the sales market, Russia was unwilling to press environmental claims against its neighbor when China polluted the Amur River, and the Kremlin also demarcated borders with several territories going to China.[61] Given its broadening power, it is only a matter of time before China demands a greater role in shaping the region. Russian officials are wary of the rise of China and are keenly interested in preserving the existing balance of power and the status of an equal partner in relations with the Asian giant. As Medvedev openly stated in 2008, Russia could lose the Far East if it failed to develop the region.[62]

Russia's Capabilities

Assessment of Russia's capabilities does not warrant the above-quoted conclusion by the nation's officials about its fully restored ability to "defend national interests as a subject of multipolar international relations" and become "a leading power in terms of technological progress, people's quality of life and influence on global processes." Although Russia has largely recovered from the chronic illnesses of the 1990s by gaining a greater confidence and preserving important attributes of a great power, in a foreseeable future it cannot act on par with the West and China. Despite the occasionally heard rhetoric of

Russia's resurgence, Russia has not become and is not in a position to become a *rising* great power relative to growing international challenges, such as the continued expansion of the Western and Chinese influences in Eurasia. The fact that Russia continues to muddle through is not a guarantee that such will be the case in the future, and the economic crisis narrows the Kremlin's options further.

Russia's constraints on acting as a great power in the post-Western world are multiple. Securing its long geographic borders and providing the necessary protection for conducting domestic reforms remains Russia's critical challenge. Russia's material capabilities are also limited. Although it has recovered from the longest economic depression in its history, much of Russia's recovery has been due to high oil prices, which slowed down the government's work to reduce reliance on energy exports.[63] Russia's overall growth during the seven years preceding the recent financial crisis was impressive, but its share of global GDP is a mere 2.3 percent and will only rise to 3.5 percent by 2020.[64] In terms of GDP size, Russia's gap with the United States during the next ten to fifteen years is not likely to be narrowed in any meaningful way and will continue to widen relative to China and India (see table 7.2). Russia's military expenditures, too, are not matching those of China, France, and some other nations, not to mention the United States.

Table 7.2. GDP Based on PPP, Share of the World*

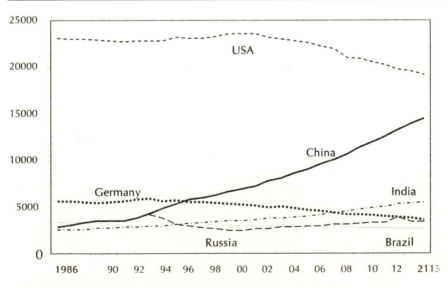

*Individual countries' share of total world GDP at purchasing power parities.
Source: IMF Data Mapper, www.imf.org/external/datamapper/index.php.

In addition, Russia continues to suffer from serious demographic, administrative, and ideological problems. The country has an aging and rapidly declining population, which can only be reversed by massive state intervention and years of sustained economic growth. Russia's indicators of life expectancy and infant mortality have been deteriorating since the late 1980s. These indicators have begun to improve since 2005, but only marginally so relative to the late 1980s. Similar dynamics of insufficient improvements can be demonstrated by referring to Russia's human development index, which has yet to reach the level of 1990—in contrast to the steady improvement in neighboring Poland.[65]

Administratively, the current state is not sufficiently consolidated, lacking both the legitimacy and capacity to isolate pressures of special interests. Although Putin and Medvedev are popular with the general public, they have yet to translate their political capital into effective administrative reforms. For example, the available statistics indicate state weakness in curbing crime, corruption, and suicides.[66] Finally, after the disintegration of the communist system, Russians live in an ideological vacuum and are yet to formulate their historical values, which affect their ability to successfully tackle problems of crime and corruption as well as offer attractive soft power projects for Russia's neighbors.

Choosing a Strategic Direction: A Middle Power or a Great Power?

The analysis of Russia's international capabilities suggests that within the next twenty years the country is not likely to emerge as an independent center of power and cultural influence and therefore should set more realistic objectives. Despite the officially upbeat assessment of the nation's great power capabilities, Russia continues to suffer from a number of economic, social, and ideological problems that will further hinder its full-fledged international engagement.

Bandwagoning or back-passing as strategies of acting from a relative weakness are also hardly good options for Russia. Siding with Western states, as recommended by liberal Westernizers, has already proven too costly after the end of the Cold War. The option of becoming a junior partner in the China-led coalition of states is no more attractive and also is likely to come at the expense of Russia's interests and influence in the world. It is not at all assured that firmly established coalitions with more powerful players will assist Russia in solving its problems of an unstable society, dwindling population, and truncated sovereignty. Back-passing, too, is hardly an appropriate strategy for the geographically expansive Russia.

This leaves Russia with some version of the above-mentioned strategy of *recuiellement*.[67] The country has already tried it unsuccessfully under its second foreign minister, Yevgeni Primakov. The course failed because the *recuiel-lement* can work only under conditions of multipolarity, while the post–Cold War world is the closest to being unipolar. Today, the situation is noticeably changing, as the United States' hard and soft power is being increasingly challenged by other international actors. The transition to a full-fledged multipolarity is likely to take a considerable time—probably twenty years or so—and it requires a strategy of adaptation to the new international condition. During the era of transition, Russia will be in a group of the tipping-point states that will be determining the balance of power among the world's largest states—the United States, the European Union, and China.[68] While remaining assertive in defending its core interests, Russia will do well to design a long-term strategy of flexible cross-cultural alliances and domestic concentration.

Although a full assessment of the new *recuiellement*'s chances to succeed in the post-Western world deserves a more extended treatment, the strategy may draw some lessons from Gorchakov's response to Russia's defeat in the Crimean War. The *recueillement* succeeded in meeting Russia's objectives of neutralizing the Paris Treaty and denouncing the Black Sea clauses. The success was achieved by diplomatic means and not at the expense of Russia's domestic transformation largely because Russia's objectives were narrow and because Gorchakov skillfully exploited a lack of unity among Western powers. Prussia was supportive; France and Austria were too weak to resist the move by Russia; and Britain was isolated in its opposition. Due to lack of Western unity and activist foreign policy, Russia managed not to isolate itself from the international scene. However, the price of success was the emergence of the unified Germany on Russia's western borders—the lesson that the Kremlin ought to learn if the nineteenth-century Germany bears any resemblance to the twenty-first century China. Today's policy may be more successful if China does not show strong expansionist tendencies and if the United Nations Security Council or a regionally developed collective security system is effective in preserving the existing international boundaries. But perhaps the most important lesson is the *recueillement*'s winning of international calm for domestic recovery. As in the nineteenth century, Russia again needs a twenty-year period of stable and broad-based internal growth.

Sustaining the New *Recuiellement*

Although a strategy of becoming an independent political and cultural pole in the post-Western world is not currently applicable for Russia, other foreign policy options may preclude its decline and put it on the track of becoming a post-Western great power in a more distant future. Russia's success requires that the Kremlin realistically assess its capabilities, act on some existing opportunities, and become more creative in explaining Russia's objectives to the outside world.

Russia's opportunities include the largely favorable geopolitical environment, or the relatively low likelihood of a major war in the regions adjacent to its territory. Following the policy of flexible coalitions, Russia should seek to devise collective security systems in Europe and Eurasia by minimizing a unilateral use of force. As a member of several important organizations, Russia may take full advantage of being an international participant. In a post-Western world, security alliances increasingly lose their traditional significance, making it imperative to rely on soft balancing tactics. Issue-specific international engagement is a way to make such tactics more effective, and Russia ought to become more active in regional institution building. For example, unable on its own to effectively respond to security challenges from NATO, Russia should continue to develop soft balancing coalitions with selected European countries, China, and Iran. However, Russia should also continue to build ties with the European Union, United States, India, South Korea, and Japan as soft balancing tactics to address the issue of rising China. Additional coalitions that Russia has already explored include BRIC (Brazil, Russia, India, and China) and the Customs Union in the former Soviet region. The former may assist Russia in consolidating its global niche as an emerging economic power, while the latter may get it closer to creating a viable regional arrangement. Similar flexible engagements may be relevant for addressing issues of weapons proliferation, terrorism, energy, and drug trafficking.

Another important opportunity for building soft alliances may still be available from exploiting the energy markets. Although the global economic recession has seriously affected Russia, energy experts project recovery of the markets within the next several years. Energy remains the country's important comparative advantage, and Moscow hardly has a choice of not developing its capacity as a global middleman by coordinating its production with other key energy producers and offering its expertise in building energy infrastructure across the world. A realistic outlook also requires that the Kremlin be more aggressive in investing in non-energy areas, such as administrative reform, demography, and human infrastructure.

Finally, Russia's soft power in the former Soviet world is also an opportunity if it is successfully exploited. This remains largely the Russia-influenced world, and the Kremlin can benefit greatly from exploiting shared historical legacies, institutions, and cultural ties in the region by offsetting Western and Chinese power. If the Kremlin articulates a vision that taps into these legacies and institutions, Russia may be able to reduce its reliance on unilateralist tactics and a tough confrontational rhetoric in defending its international economic and security objectives.

7.4. WESTERN OPTIONS

Arrival of the new post-Western world has important implications for the United States and European nations. It also contains challenges and opportunities for international actors across the globe. For the West, the message of the new world is that, rather than trying to secure the twenty-first century as another American or Western century, Washington and Brussels will do well to acknowledge the irreversible—albeit gradual—nature of Western decline and prepare for an honorable retreat from the position of global hegemony. If the Western nations continue to act on unilateral and imperial temptations, new challenges will inevitably arise, as the Bush era has demonstrated all too well.[69] In this case, the non-Western nations beginning with Russia will continue to act in defiance by unilaterally asserting what they see as their strategic and economic interests. In the absence of sufficiently strong international institutions, such interaction is likely to facilitate new conflicts, not peace and stability in the world.

On the other hand, the post-Western world promises new opportunities to those who are willing and able to seize them. A gradual retreat of the West does not have to be accompanied by growing destabilization across the globe, but instead may create an international environment for reducing arsenals of deadly weapons, devising more socially egalitarian and politically responsive institutions, and developing greater cultural sensitivity in the world. The still predominant West would then need to lead by example, showing the way not to the new "Western century" but to controlled disarmament, establishment of a new economic order, assistance with regional political institutions, and initiation of innovative cross-cultural learning programs around the world.

In application to U.S.-Russia relations, the latter attitude means the need to act in concert and consultation with the Kremlin, rather than out of the expectation of its being helpful in executing the West's grand plans. Although many in the United States and Russia are skeptical of a serious improvement in the two countries' relations in the near future, their interests are compatible in a number of critical areas. Depending on how ambitious they become, the United States and Russia may considerably improve their trust and cooperation or even become strategic partners in developing nuclear, energy, and regional security ties. Although the coming post-Western world makes a strong alliance with Russia exceeding unlikely, a considerable progress may still be achieved. For example, Russia and the Western nations may agree on a greater security cooperation and deployment of a shared missile defense system even though Russia is not likely to side with the West against Iran. Russia and the Western nations may also manage to reduce their energy competition and learn to jointly exploit the existing pipelines even though the Kremlin's dream of becoming a vehicle for reducing the West's dependence on Middle Eastern oil doesn't have a strong chance to be realized. The two sides may also establish a greater security dialogue in the Eurasian region without becoming full-fledged allies.

In terms of the three strategic options for Russia—pro-Western, pro-Chinese, and the flexible option—the West should prepare to live with the flexible Kremlin and work not so much to encourage Russia to becoming pro-Western, but to discourage it from being pro-Chinese at the expense of ties with the Western nations. The objective should be not to marginalize or isolate China, but rather to strengthen Russia's ability to choose its future partners in the post-Western world. As one pundit wrote, "The West has made little secret of its efforts to displace Russia in Europe's East, but should it want Russia to be dismembered in its own east? . . . Today the United States and the EU might need to rescue Russia from its politically suicidal embrace of China in order to remain in the heartland."[70] Although the Western nations should not expect Russia to be a strategic partner, they would benefit from the Kremlin's decision not to undermine the already declining position of the West in the world. Overall, the sooner the United States and Russia are able to see themselves as normal post-Western powers, the more likely they are to productively cooperate in the future.

NOTES

1. Sergei Lavrov, "Russia and the World in the 21st Century," *Russia in Global Affairs*, no. 3 (July–September 2008).

2. Fareed Zakaria, *The Post-American World* (New York: W. W. Norton, 2008), 2.

3. Francis Fukuyama, "The End of History?" *National Interest* 16 (Summer 1989); Michael Mandelbaum, *The Ideas That Conquered the World* (New York: Public Affairs, 2005).

4. Stephen G. Brooks and William C. Wohlforth, *World out of Balance : International Relations and the Challenge of American Primacy* (Princeton: Princeton University Press, 2008).

5. I follow here a conventional institutional definition of the West as an area that includes the United States and European nations. These nations share pluralistic political institutions, market economies, and basic geopolitical objectives of advancing their values and institutions across the globe and defeating their ideological and politicoeconomic opponents.

6. Zakaria, *The Post-American World*. For similar earlier descriptions of the world's emerging political structure, see Samuel Huntington, "The Lonely Superpower," *Foreign Affairs* 78: 2 (1999). Russian analysts, too, have envisioned a relative decline of the U.S. position in the new international system, describing it as "pluralistic" rather than as a one-state "unipolarity" and presenting Russia as a

member of the unipolar center or a group of states (Aleksei D. Bogaturov, "Sovremennyi mezhdunarodnyi poryadok," *Mezhdunarodnyye protsessy* 1, no. 1 (2003), at www.intertrends.ru).

7. For analysis of politicoeconomic aspects of this world, see Naazneen Barma, Ely Ratner, and Steven Weber, "The World without West," *National Interest* 90, no. 4 (2007).

8. Eric Helleiner and Andeas Pickel, eds., *Economic Nationalism in a Globalizing World* (Ithaca, NY: Cornell University Press, 2005).

9. Craig N. Murphy, "Political Consequences of the New Inequality," *International Studies Quarterly* 45, no. 3 (September 2001).

10. Joseph Nye, "The Decline of America's Soft Power," *Foreign Affairs* 83, no. 3 (2004).

11. Edward D. Mansfield and Jack Snyder, *Electing to Fight: Why Emerging Democracies Go to War* (Cambridge: Cambridge University Press, 2007).

12. This does not mean emergence of West-balancing coalitions—at least not yet—and non-Western countries are merely developing their own rules and arrangements in world politics (Barma, Ratner, and Weber, "The World without West"). At best, countries such as Russia, China, and India are involved in soft balancing against the United States (R. A. Pipe, "Soft Balancing against the United States," *International Security* 30, no. 1 (2005); T. V. Paul, "Soft Balancing in the Age of U.S. Primacy," *International Security* 30, no. 1 (2005).

13. Douglas Blum, "Contested National Identities and Weak State Structures in Eurasia," in *Limiting Institutions? The Challenge of Eurasian Security and Governance*, ed. James Sperling, Sean Kay, and S. Victor Papacosma (Manchester: Manchester University Press, 2003).

14. On China, see, for example, William A. Callahan, "Chinese Visions of World Order: Post-hegemonic or a New Hegemony?" *International Studies Review* 10, no. 4 (2008). For Russia's attempts to move in this direction, see Andrei P. Tsygankov, "Finding a Civilizational Idea: 'West,' 'Eurasia,' and 'Euro-East' in Russia's Foreign Policy," *Geopolitics* 12 (2007); Valentina Feklunina, "Battle for Perceptions: Projecting Russia in the West," *Europe-Asia Studies* 60, no. 4 (2008).

15. For example, despite their differences from the West, both Russia and China present their grand visions as consistent with the idea of democracy. Islamists, however, do not hide their despisement for secular democratic ideals and promote the notion of Islamic world order.

16. For a description of back-passing, see John Mearsheimer, *The Tragedy of Great Powers* (New York: W. W. Norton, 2001), 139.

17. S. K. Bushuyev, *A. M. Gorchakov* (Moscow: 1961), 82.

18. Yevgeni V. Tarle, "Napoleon III i Yevropa," in *Istoriya diplomatiyi*, Vol. 1, ed. V. P. Potemkin (Moscow: Izdatel'stvo akademiyi nauk, 1945), 471.

19. William C. Fuller, Jr. *Strategy and Power in Russia, 1600–1914* (New York: Free Press, 1992), 266; Flemming Splidsboel-Hansen, "Past and Future Meet: Aleksandr Gorchakov and Russian Foreign Policy," *Europe-Asia Studies* 54, no. 3 (2002).

20. *Kommersant*, December 25, 2008.

21. See chapter 5 for details.

22. ITAR-TASS, June 11, 2008. See also the articles by Russia's foreign minister Sergei Lavrov, "A Strategic Relationship: From Rivalry to Partnership," *Russia Beyond the Headlines*, May 28, 2008, at www.rbth.rg.ru/, and "Shake Loose the Cold War," *Guardian*, January 30, 2009.

23. Dmitry Medvedev, speech at the 12th Petersburg International Economic Forum, St. Petersburg, June 7, 2008, at www.kremlin.ru.

24. The vision is reflected in the Foreign Ministry report entitled "A Review of the Russian Federation's Foreign Policy," commissioned by the Kremlin (*Obzor vneshnei politiki Rossiyskoi federatsiyi*, March 27, 2007, at www.mid.ru).

25. ITAR-TASS, December 5, 2008.

26. *Interfax-AVN*, May 13, 2009. The full Russian text of the strategy is published on the website of the Russian Security Council at www.scrf.gov.ru.

27. *Interfax*, March 24, 2009.

28. Commentators noted a divide between Igor Sechin and Igor' Shuvalov within the government, as well as one between Deputy Head of Presidential Administration Vladislav Surkov, on the one hand, and Presidential Advisers Arkadi Dvorkovich and Igor' Yurgens, on the other (Boris Mezhuyev, "Russki spor o politicheskoi sisteme," *Russki zhurnal*, March 18, 2009, http://russ.ru/pole/Russkij-spor-o-politicheskoj-sisteme; Brian Whitmore, "The Battle of the Igors," *RFE/RL*, April 24, 2009, www.rferl.org/archive/The_Power_Vertical/latest/884/884.html).

29. Boris Nemtsov and Vladimir Milov, "Putin i krizis," *Nezavisimaya gazeta*, March 20, 2009; Yevgeniy Gontmakher, "Who Will Take Power?" *New Times*, March 2, 2009; Andrew E. Kramer, "Political Aide Says Kremlin May Need to Ease Control," *New York Times*, February 10, 2009.

30. Aleksandr Khramchikhin, "Sovbez ozabotilsya natsional'noi bezopasnostyu," *Nezavisimoye voyennoye obozreniye*, January 16, 2009.

31. Yulia Latynina, "The Problem: China and Caucasus," *Moscow Times*, December 18, 2008.

32. Fyodor Lukyanov, "Rossiya mezhdu Kitayem i Zapadom," *Novoye Vremya*, no. 22 (June 2, 2008).

33. Dmitri Trenin, "Blowing Both Hot and Cold," *Moscow Times*, March 24, 2009. Based on power measurements, however, Trenin has acknowledged the futility of the Kremlin's attempts to have equal relations with the United States (Dmitri Trenin, "Nepraktichnyi pragmatizm," *Pro et Contra* 12, no. 5–6 [2008]).

34. Trenin, "Nepraktichnyi pragmatizm."

35. Vladimir Putin, address at the Plenary Session of the Russian Federation Ambassadors, Moscow, Foreign Ministry, July 12, 2004, at www.kremlin.ru.

36. Alexander Solzhenitsyn, *Kak nam obustroyit' Rossiyu* (Moscow: Izvestiya, 1990).

37. Vitali Tretyakov, "Krusheniye SSSR i vozrozhdeniye Rossiyi," *Politicheski klass*, no. 12 (December 2006) www.politklass.ru/cgi-bin/issue.pl?id=688.

38. Sergei Kara-Murza, "Trebuyetsya gegemon," *Izvestiya*, May 6, 2009.

39. For an earlier analysis of this group's views, see Andrei P. Tsygankov, "Mastering Space in Eurasia: Russian Geopolitical Thinking after the Soviet Break-Up," *Communist and Post-Communist Studies* 35, no. 1 (2003).

40. Anna Kaledina, "Drugoye delo—Aziya," *Izvestiya*, May 13, 2009; Stanislav Kha-tuntsev, "O sovremennom miroporyadke i ego geopoliticheskom karkase," *Russki zhurnal*, March 17, 2009, http://russ.ru/pole/O-sovremennom -miroporyadke-i-ego-geoekonomicheskom-karkase.

41. *Russkaya doktrina* (Moscow: Yauza, 2007). Similarly, a recent popular volume identifies two cultural poles—the material, profit-driven United States, and a Russia that is viewed as the last stronghold of Christianity (*Proyekt Rossiya* [Moscow: Eksmo, 2008], 42–45).

42. Irina Pavlova, "Down, Profil!" *Grani.ru*, September 23, 2008.

43. For example, see recent statements by commentators such as Igor' Panarin (2009) about the United States' approaching disintegration.

44. Andrzej Walicki, *A History of Russian Thought from Enlightenment to Marxism* (Stanford: Stanford University Press, 1979), 112–114.

45. Michael Boro Petrovich, *The Emergence of Russian Panslavism, 1856–1870* (New York: Columbia University Press, 1956), 90.

46. The motive of noninterference in the region's developments from outside only became stronger since 2005 and was clearly reflected in Putin's addresses to the Federation Council in May 2006 and April 2007, www.kremlin.ru.

47. Susan Richards, "Russians Don't Much Like the West," www.opendemocracy. net, February 25, 2009.

48. BBC World Service, April 22, 2009.

49. *Interfax*, February 4, 2009.

50. BBC World Service, April 22, 2009.

51. Desmond Butler, "US, Ukraine Look to Strengthen Ties," Associated Press, December 19, 2008; Vladimir Socor, "U.S. and Georgia Sign Strategic Partnership Charter," *Jamestown Eurasian Daily Monitor*, January 12, 2009.

52. *Interfax-AVN*, December 16, 2008.

53. See, for example, the remarks by Assistant Secretary of State for European and Eurasian Affairs Daniel Fried before the U.S. Senate Foreign Relations Committee (Fried 2007).

54. For details and background, see, for example, Mark MacKinnon, *The New Cold War: Revolutions, Rigged Elections and Pipeline Politics in the Former Soviet Union* (New York: Random House, 2007).

55. Andrew Wilson and Nicu Popescu, "Creating Good Neighbors in Russia's Backyard," *Moscow Times*, May 7, 2009.

56. AFP, April 28, 2009.

57. The deal was approved by Putin but blocked by the Duma (Nicklas Norling, "China and Russia: Partners with Tensions," *Policy Perspectives* [2007]: 44).

58. *Kommersant*, July 22, 2008. For the divergence of Russia's and China's energy policies in central Asia, see Geir Flikke and Julie Wilhelmsen, *Central Asia: A Testing Ground for New Great Power Relations* (Oslo: Norwegian Institute of International Affairs, 2008).

59. This and other previous agreements with China were criticized by Russian media as disproportionate concessions on the part of the Kremlin (*Nezavisimaya gazeta*, October 10 and October 29, 2008; *Novaya gazeta*, July 2009).

60. In July 2009, Beijing sent a delegation to Moscow to negotiate conditions of a large group of ethnic Chinese affected by the Moscow government's decision to close the large Cherkizovski trading area due to multiple violations. Headed by the deputy trade minister, the delegation negotiated restoration of the trading area on condition of a Chinese $1 billion investment (*Kommersant*, July 30, 2009).

61. Some Russian economists estimated the damage of transferring territories for Russia at $3 billion (*Kommersant*, July 22, 2008).

62. "Medvedev: Far East Ignored Too Long," *RIA RosBusinessConsulting*, September 26, 2008.

63. According to World Bank estimates, energy has accounted for about 25 percent of the Russian economy and for about 50 percent of its GDP growth (Peter Rutland, "Putin's Economic Record: Is the Oil Boom Sustainable?" *Europe-Asia Studies* 60, no. 6: 1063–1064.

64. Andrew Kuchins and Robert Weitz, *Russia's Place in an Unsettled Order—Calculations in the Kremlin* (Washington, DC: Stanley Foundation, 2008), 6.

65. *Russia Analytical Digest*, October 17, 2008.

66. *Russia Analytical Digest*, October 17, 2008: 19; *Russia Analytical Digest*, April 2, 2008: 24.

67. Russia's foreign minister, Sergei Lavrov, instead views the *recueillement* period first heralded by Yevgeni Primakov in 1996 as "largely completed" (*Kommersant*, January 19, 2009).

68. Parag Khanna, *The Second World: Empires and Influence in the New Global Order* (New York: Random House, 2008).

69. For an argument about the demise of liberal internationalism in the United States, see Charles A. Kupchan and Peter L. Trubowitz, "Dead Center: The Demise of Liberal Internationalism in the United States," *International Security* 32, no. 2 (2007).

70. Khanna, *The Second World*, 74.

8

Conclusions and Lessons

> All healthy human action . . . must establish a balance between utopia and reality, between free will and determinism.
>
> —E. H. Carr[1]

This final chapter summarizes the approach taken in this book to understanding change and continuity in Russian foreign policy. It also suggests several lessons that Russian and Western policymakers can learn from the past twenty years of their interaction if they wish to improve their communication and security in the world.

8.1. CHANGE AND CONTINUITY IN RUSSIA'S FOREIGN POLICY

Five Visions of National Interest

Despite what realists and liberals often assume, nations rarely have once and forever established visions of their fundamental external interests. More typically, national interests fluctuate with changes on the domestic and international political scene. This book identifies four distinct visions of national interest that Russia has developed and pursued throughout the past twenty years.

Mikhail Gorbachev's vision of his country's interest, New Thinking, was a part of his perestroika project, which meant to revive socialist values at home and achieve a fundamentally new level of cooperation abroad. New Thinking saw the world as socially diverse and yet united by common human values, as well as by fundamental threats. In particular, the new leadership pointed to threats of nuclear catastrophe, ecological devastation, and poverty. It saw as the solution establishing a new level of cross-national and cross-cultural understanding, acknowledging the primacy of values "common to all humankind," and reenergizing common efforts to achieve a better international security. National interests were to be pursued in close coordination with other members of the global society, and, for the Soviet Union, this meant the need to give up the old ideological vision and to acknowledge positive contributions by the West to the world's development.

Despite growing resistance from various domestic opponents, the leader of New Thinking acted consistently with his beliefs. He made a number of significant foreign policy overtures to the West, hoping for reciprocal measures. He made disproportionately large cuts in conventional and nuclear arsenals and proposed to eliminate all nuclear weapons by 2000. He also withdrew from Afghanistan and other third world countries. Furthermore, Gorbachev abandoned the "Brezhnev doctrine" of limited sovereignty in Eastern Europe and made it possible to tear down the Berlin Wall. Finally, the new Soviet leader committed himself to the idea of principally reforming the United Nations and supporting it with greater resources so that the organization would be capable of meeting new world challenges. At home, Gorbachev—admittedly belatedly—recognized the need to give up the old imperial principles of maintaining Soviet unity, and he offered a vision that combined elements of federation and confederation. The new union treaty was to be renegotiated and approved through a people's referendum. This approach, too, was a part of New Thinking's commitment to the declared principle of "freedom of choice," according to which people themselves were to choose their way of participating in the global society.

For various domestic and international reasons, the New Thinking vision could not be sustained and was soon replaced by the idea of Integration with the West. The new domestic coalition undermined Gorbachev's standing by insisting that Russia had been a country with a suppressed Western identity and that it now had to give up its socialist system in favor of a Western-style market democracy. Unlike New Thinkers, who sought to engage the West by developing the notions of global threats and common responsibility for their emergence, the new Russian leaders—Boris Yeltsin and his foreign minister Andrei Kozyrev—saw no major flaws in the West. Instead, they argued that the world had exhausted the list of alternative development projects, and Russia simply had to follow the already-established pattern of modernization. They planned to rapidly gain membership in Western international organizations and to minimize relationships with the former Soviet states. These steps meant to soon bring Russia to the front-rank status of advanced European countries and the United States.

Like Gorbachev, the new Russian leaders were hoping to receive adequate recognition and resources from Western nations in response to their commitment to the new vision. They quickly joined the IMF and World Bank and announced their intentions to acquire memberships in G-7, NATO, and the EU. They also loyally supported the Western international security agenda by accepting sanctions against Yugoslavia, Libya, and Iraq. Similarly to Gorbachev, Yeltsin and Kozyrev made major concessions to the United States in reducing the size of strategic nuclear weapons. Furthermore, they initially displayed little interest in developing relationships with non-Western nations, whether in Asia or in the Muslim world. That, too, corresponded with their perception of the West as the leading civilization that merited their prime foreign policy attention.

In the former Soviet region, consistent with their vision, Yeltsin and Kozyrev pursued policies of isolationism in economic and security matters. Despite the earlier negotiated agreement, they did not coordinate their economic reform with their neighbors. Eager to integrate with the West directly, they announced their openness to Western economic activities, but placed considerable commercial restrictions on relations with the ex-republics. Politically, this eagerness expressed itself in consolidating Russia's sovereignty and minimizing responsibilities for maintaining order and security in the region through mechanisms of multilateral cooperation. The new transnational organization in the region, the CIS, was understood to facilitate the process of acquiring independence, rather than to serve other common cross-regional objectives. Accordingly, Moscow saw little need to maintain its military in the former republics, and it did not see itself as responsible for the political and cultural well-being of Russian minorities in the region.

Opposition to the course of integration with the West was formidable, and the course began to unravel soon after attempts at its implementation. When a leading critic of this course, Yevgeni Primakov, was appointed the new foreign minister, the vision of national interest changed yet again. By selecting him, Yeltsin, to a degree, committed himself to a new perception of external threats and foreign policy objectives. Rather than proposing modernization and Westernization as Russia's key national interests, Primakov pointed to the dangers of a concentration of world power associated with the unipolar status of the United States. A realist rather than an economic liberal, Primakov proposed the vision of Great Power Balancing for the purpose of gradually turning the existing unipolar world into a multipolar one. The vision required integration of the former Soviet region under Russian leadership and seeking assistance from other powerful states, such as China and India, in order to balance the American hegemony.

Unlike his predecessors, Primakov held no illusions about Russian integration with Western economic and security institutions. Viewing these institutions in power terms, he saw his task, instead, as minimizing their encroachment on Russia. In particular, the new minister sought to prevent, or at least slow down, the announced expansion of NATO toward Russia's western borders. Establishing the Permanent Joint Council for consultations with NATO members was also meant to serve this objective. Being a pragmatist, Primakov was careful not to be seen as confrontational. On some issues, he disagreed with domestic hard-liners and argued, for instance, for the ratification of START II. On other issues, however, he was tough, as he was on U.S. military strikes in Iraq and on NATO's military air campaign in Yugoslavia over Kosovo. In addition, the minister placed a fundamentally new emphasis on relations with non-Western nations, particularly China. Under him, Russia and China became considerably closer. Their vision of world politics and threats to a "multipolar world" was a shared one, and their trade and arms sales improved greatly. Finally, Primakov was active in developing Russia's rapprochement with Iran and India. On a couple of occasions, he even spoke openly of the desirability of a Russia-India-China coalition as a "new pole in world politics."

In the former Soviet region, Primakov's strategy of reintegrating the ex-republics into a tighter union became the official one. He was willing to commit considerable state resources to the project of integration, partly because he saw it as important in responding to the enlargement of NATO. Economically, Russia was to capitalize on its resources and intensify relations within the former Soviet Union, particularly with Belarus, Kazakhstan, and Ukraine. In terms of security, the "integration" meant to consolidate the Russian military presence in the region. Russia also became more active in maintaining peace in the republics, especially in the Caucasus and central Asia. The end of the Tajik civil war in June 1997 was a part of this new activism in the region. In addition, Russia signed the "Big Treaty" by formally normalizing political relations with Ukraine, and it took new steps to form a union with Belarus. Finally, the new vision of integration linked the fate of the Russians in the region directly to the survival and prosperity of Russia.

Too many of Primakov's initiatives remained on paper only, and that contributed to the replacement of his vision with a new one. Vladimir Putin's vision was in many ways completely different. Instead of capitalizing on the unipolarity threat, the new Russian leader drew attention to the world's instabilities, such as terrorism, as well as some new economic opportunities. Unlike Primakov and similar to Gorbachev, Putin saw the need to engage the West in an ambitious joint project. However, unlike Gorbachev and Kozyrev, he visualized Russia as a great power and sought Western recognition of this.

Putin redefined national interest as that of Great Power Pragmatism. Rather than balancing the United States' power, the key objective was now pronounced as an economic modernization for the sake of preserving the great power status.

In attempting to reengage the West, Putin showed himself to be extremely active in developing relations with the United States, particularly after the September 11, 2001, terrorist attacks on that country. He offered a far-reaching intelligence cooperation and proposed new ways to develop Russian-U.S. energy ties. Putin was even more energetic when it came to activating economic and political ties with Europe. In some areas, such as visa relations with European countries, the president demonstrated his readiness to go much further than European leaders themselves. Yet Putin was no Gorbachev—his activism was pragmatic and driven by calculations of state power. On issues where Russian state autonomy was at stake, he was firm in limiting cooperation with foreign nations. Thus, despite his support of U.S. actions in Afghanistan, Putin sided with a number of European nations in condemning American intervention in Iraq without a United Nations mandate. And in his relations with Europe, he placed the emphasis on economic and energy cooperation, while restricting cooperation on security issues, such as Chechnya or peacemaking activities in the former Soviet region. In this, as in actively pursuing commercial sales of weapons abroad, Putin continued traditions of Primakov's diplomacy.

In the former Soviet Union, the vision of Great Power Pragmatism implied an abandonment of Primakov's integration project in favor of less costly and mutually advantageous bilateral relations. In reestablishing bilateral ties consistent with his belief in economic modernization, Putin reasserted control over many of the ex-republics' strategic property and transportation, particularly electricity and energy pipeline facilities. He concluded a number of partnership and strategic partnership agreements in the Caucasus and central Asia, as well with Ukraine and Belarus. The Russian leader also took a different approach to security issues by emphasizing cooperation in counterterrorism and seeking to assemble on that basis his own coalition of the willing. He strengthened Russia's military presence in central Asia and the Caucasus by signing appropriate bilateral and multilateral agreements. Finally, Putin promoted new energy and transportation projects to further implement his vision of geoeconomically based and state-driven modernization.

Around 2005, Putin's vision changed in the direction of assertiveness. The Kremlin no longer believed in defensive cooperation with Western nations and insisted on greater acceptance of Russia's interests. Russia's leadership sharply criticized what it viewed as the United States' "unilateralism" in world politics and pursued more independent economic and security policies in the world. Following Putin's speech at the Munich Conference in January, the Kremlin was busy signaling its frustration with its inability to develop more equitable relations with the United States. Russia felt humiliated that it had to swallow the war in the Balkans, two rounds of NATO expansion, the U.S. withdrawal from the ABM Treaty, military presence in central Asia, the invasion of Iraq, and plans to deploy elements of nuclear missile defense in Eastern Europe. In the wake of the Russia-Georgia conflict, Dmitri Medvedev stated, "We will not tolerate any more humiliation, and we are not joking."[2]

Table 8.1 summarizes Russia's five visions of the world and its national interest.

Understanding National Interest Formation

Liberal and realist theories of international relations are too simplistic for understanding the described process and outcomes of national interest formation. Each of them emphasizes either modernization or the need to maintain power as shaping foreign policy choices. Yet in reality both of these forces figure prominently in how nations determine their interests. In order to understand the formation of Russia's national interests, this book employed a complex framework that incorporates both types of influence. In the first chapter, I hypothesized that the vision of national interest is a product of the nation's interaction with the world, and Russia's strategic choices can be viewed as reactions to the behavior of the Western powers. At least since Peter the Great, the West has played a special role in Russian development, and much of the country's international behavior has meant efforts of the Russian Self to win recognition by its significant Other. Western actions are contested domestically, and local conditions are no less important in shaping a dominant vision of national identity and foreign policy. A closer analysis of Russia's foreign policy developments throughout the book has revealed three local factors that clarify the process of Russian interpretation of Western actions. These three—national tradition, cur-

Table 8.1.   Russia's Five Visions of the World and National Interest

	Perceived World	National Interest
Gorbachev	Cold War crisis	New Thinking and cross-cultural dialogue
Yeltsin/Kozyrev	Western institutional dominance	Integration with the West
Primakov	U.S. power hegemony	Balancing against the U.S.
Putin I	Terrorism and economic competition	Pragmatic cooperation with the West
Putin II	U.S. unilateralism	Assertiveness

rent concerns, and state capacity—specify, rather than distort, the general causal mechanism of national interest formation.

Gorbachev's New Thinking originated, in part, from the hostilities of the Cold War and unrealized opportunities presented by the brief period of dé-tente. In contrast to the realists' emphasis on the West's economic and military strength, Gorbachev responded to social democratic ideas of détente's European supporters and the domestic tradition of reform socialism, which was associated with the late Lenin, Bukharin, and Khrushchev. In putting forth his vision, the leader of New Thinking was hoping to garner and maintain a sufficient support among elites and within the broader society. It is no accident that his project contained elements of Westernism, Statism, and Civilization-ism—the three main schools of foreign policy thinking in the Soviet Union.

Yet the task of keeping the unstable coalition together proved to be unten-able. Soon, conservative Civilizationists and Statists, on the one hand, and radical Westernizers, on the other, were attacking New Thinking. The conservative and radical opponents wanted principally different—in fact, mutually exclusive—outcomes, and Gorbachev could have made progress only if he were to deliver on his promises to improve people's lives. Instead, busy persuading the West of the authenticity of his intentions and not getting as much as he expected in return, the leader of perestroika was rapidly losing the initiative and support at home. Increasingly, people saw the reforms as a "talking shop." The perception was strengthening that the Russians were living through an unavoidable political disintegration and economic deterioration, and that was radicalizing the society and improving the political standing of Gorbachev's opponents. After 1989, it was the vision of radical Westernizers, expressed by Boris Yeltsin, that was receiving growing social recognition. Yeltsin's argument, that the West could not extend the expected material support to Russia unless it abandoned its socialist vision, undermined Gorbachev.

What was also hardly helpful to Gorbachev was that, by his own design and contrary to his own expectations, he had been increasingly losing the power to continue with the policy course. State capacity, which includes the legitimacy and ability to withstand various domestic pressures in staying the course, was next to nonexistent. Canceling state orders cost Gorbachev control over the economy, and not getting himself elected by popular vote greatly contributed to his loss of political legitimacy. In the meantime, the Westernist opposition skillfully exploited the newly emerged opportunities to challenge the ruling center. Unlike Gorbachev, Yeltsin was elected president of Russia by popular vote, and he continued to argue that economic deterioration could be stopped only by radical Western-style reforms. Yeltsin also entered a coalition with other republican nationalists and insisted that the efforts to preserve the union were doomed. In sum, what ultimately destroyed Gorbachev's coalition were three factors. First, what was missing was the reciprocal support from the West that could have boosted support for New Thinking at home. Second, a gap between concerns of the West and ordinary Russians was growing. As the West was celebrating its triumph in ending the Cold War, Russians were worried about the deterioration of their living standards and security of their state. Finally, the severely undermined capacity of the state allowed the Westernist opposition to seize the moment and, after the failed August 1991 coup, to claim power and legitimacy.

However, the new Westernist coalition was hardly a stable one. It consisted of pragmatic members of the former Communist *nomenklatura*, such as Yeltsin himself, and idealistic liberal reformers, such as Gaidar and Kozyrev. The new ruling coalition, therefore, tried to synthesize the influences of Westernizers and former Soviet Statists, but the majority of the elites—military industrialists, the army, and the security services—remained excluded. The challenge that came from that majority was formidable, and the Westernist foreign policy course soon began to fade under powerful attacks from both Statists and conservative Civilizationists. The opposition took advantage of the attitude the Western nations had adopted toward the new Russia. Despite some considerable financial assistance given to the new Russian government, the West was clearly not eager to integrate Russia into its midst. NATO's decision to expand brushed aside Russia's hopes for transforming the alliance into a nonmilitary one or for being admitted as a full member of the organization. This came as a major blow to the reformers. Along with the West's slowness to recognize Russia as one of its own in other matters, NATO's expansion provided the anti-Western opposition with the required ammunition to construct an image of an external threat and question the objectives of the new government.

Additional factors that undermined the course of integration with the West were the power of the national tradition of Statist thinking, new local concerns of ordinary Russians, and the aforementioned weakness of the state. First, as the most influential school in Russian foreign policy thinking, Statism had a cultural appeal. It therefore had some discursive advantages in emphasizing the values of stability and sovereignty over those of freedom and democracy. Once the proclaimed freedom proved to be accompanied by growing disorder, corruption, and poverty, many Russians were inclined to trust the Statist opposition more than ruling Westernizers. Second, Russia's local concerns had changed dramatically and for the worse. Shock therapy brought additional misery, and the isolationist policies in the former Soviet region contributed to the rise of military conflicts in a number of the ex-republics. With the Soviet disintegration, Russia found itself in an entirely different geopolitical situation. Overall, the people's preoccupation with loss of international prestige, poverty, crime, and corruption was the shift in status from a country that, under Gorbachev, had hopes of catching up with the world of industrialized nations to that of a more peripheral developing country. Finally, just as Westernizers exploited the state's weakness in order to challenge Gorbachev, Statists used various institutional advantages presented by the weakly centralized political system. Statists argued their case publicly—in the national parliament, media, and various conferences—and through informal and nonpublic channels, such as Russia's Security Council, presidential administration, and nongovernmental organizations. A combination of these three influences helped to shape the Western Other's lack of support into an entirely different vision of national interest.

The new foreign minister, Yevgeni Primakov, articulated the new vision of Great Power Balancing and attempted to put it into practice. Working with the much less cooperative West, he sought to consolidate Russia's position as a great power and to resituate it into the center of the former Soviet region. The new minister—who subsequently became prime minister—also attempted to limit the power of the oligarchs in Russian economic and political life. The new course was not successful in delivering improved social and economic standards, and it unnecessarily alienated pro-Western forces, pushing them into opposition. The course was also quite expensive because it sought to restore the ties among the former Soviet republics primarily through subsidies by the Russian state. The vision therefore was not attractive to Russian business elites, and it also had little appeal to some isolationist-minded nationalists, who were formerly supportive members of Primakov's coalition.

As a result, when Yeltsin appointed Vladimir Putin prime minister and, subsequently, acting president, the new leader had a considerably different coalition of support behind him. In particular, he drew support from pro-Western commercial groups, formerly neglected by Primakov, and from state-oriented security services. Changed international conditions and Western attitudes assisted the new leadership in keeping the coalition together. Both the Russian economic recovery and the renewed threat of international terrorism made Russia important in the eyes of Western leaders. Russia's energy supplies were becoming critical in European economies, and Russian intelligence was now available to assist in American efforts to crush terrorism in Afghanistan and other areas of central Asia.

In addition to the changed international context, several domestic factors aided in maintaining Putin's rule. First, like Primakov, Putin relied heavily on the national tradition of Statist thinking. Even while reshaping Primakov's vision into a more inclusive and West-friendly philosophy, the new leader remained committed to the notion of great power and Russia's national interest as distinct from that of the West. Putin's philosophy was a departure from the older version of Statism, but not from Statism as the nationally recognized tradition. It is thanks to this tradition that Putin's regime, widely supported by the general public, ultimately succeeded in suppressing the oligarchs' independent economic and political ambitions. In addition, Russia's local concerns became somewhat more compatible with those of Western nations. What the United States experienced on September 11, 2001, and Spain experienced in March 2003, Russians had already known from their own recent history of explosions in residential buildings and various public places. Although the war in Chechnya had its own unique characteristics and the Chechen rebels made their own demands on Russia that differed from those of Al Qaeda on the West, many Russians saw parallels between Chechnya and Al Qaeda. So did the Western leaders, who softened their rhetoric regarding Russian violations of human rights in Chechnya and acknowledged the significance of Russia in fighting the threat of international terrorism. The compatibility of Russian and Western concerns greatly assisted Putin in boosting his credibility at home and abroad. Finally, Putin was far more successful than Primakov in restoring the state's capacity to govern and impose order. With his high public approval, he set out to meticulously control major sources of opposition to his vision of national interest. The new leader made it clear to the oligarchs that he expected them to pay taxes and cooperate in restoring Russia's status as a great power. He initiated a far-reaching military reform with the intention of reducing the power of the general chief of staff and creating a more dynamic army. Finally, he reformed the system of relationships between the Kremlin and the regions, and he shut down highly critical media—all with the idea of reestablishing the state as the central governing institution and promoting the new vision of Russia's interests.

Putin's ratings remained high throughout his second presidential term as he adopted the more assertive version of Great Power Pragmatism. The West, too, has an important role to play. As Russia continues to be influenced by Western ideas and practices, Western policymakers and public-opinion leaders ought to be sensitive to the perception of these influences in Russia. A better appreciation of Russia's cultural distinctness and foreign policy concerns may encourage Putin and his successors to move further toward long-term cooperation with Europe and the United States. On the other hand, a more unilateral and isolationist approach is more likely to push the new regime in the direction of suppressing opposition at home.

Such were some of the key foreign policy challenges confronted by the Russian leaders. Each of the leaders sought to creatively respond to various external developments, particularly those initiated in the West. Some, like Gorbachev and Kozyrev, wanted to engage the West in essentially liberal projects and to demonstrate their willingness to bring Russia into the family of Western nations. These leaders expressed Russia's eagerness to be recognized by the West as one of its own, and they saw the West as driven by essentially liberal motivations to spread justice and freedom in the world. Others, like Primakov and Putin, while avoiding confrontation with the West, sought to reassert Russia's power. Unlike their liberal predecessors, they were suspicious of the West's power motivations—both geopolitical and geoeconomic—and wanted to restore Russian national pride and independence. Russia faced multiple foreign challenges and opportunities—dangers of arms races, promises of post–Cold War economic and security cooperation, NATO expansion, and threats of global terrorism. Confronted with those challenges and opportunities, some leaders, in Albert Sorel's memorable formulation, arranged "their policy to suit the realities of the world," while others imagined "the world to suit their policy."[3] There will certainly be many other external challenges ahead of Russia, and they are likely to lead to other creative visions of national interest and foreign policy strategy. It is, as the same thinker put it some century ago, "the eternal dispute."

8.2. LESSONS FOR RUSSIA

What lessons can Russia learn from the past twenty years of its foreign policy? Are there particular steps it should take, or abstain from taking, that would preserve and enhance its status in the world?

Staying Engaged

First and foremost, it is important that in adjusting to new external challenges and solving its more specific domestic problems, Russia stay engaged with the world in general, and the West in particular. Lack of acceptance by the West should not prompt Russian leaders to take an isolationist path; rather, it should encourage them to double their efforts to explain their international policies as consistent with their vision of a global world. Isolationism cannot be practical in a world that has grown increasingly global in terms of both new opportunities and new threats. Russia should not deprive itself of new opportunities to participate in global flows of information, capital, and labor. Nor can it fully shield itself against new diseases or types of violence, or other crises of a transnational nature.

Isolationism, particularly an anti-Western one, remains strong in Russia. Hard-line Civilizationists, as well as some Statists, continue to argue that Russia is destined to oppose the West's civilizational and political influences across the globe. These forces insist on viewing the world in black and white terms and refuse to acknowledge that many of Russia's interests are best accomplished through participation in international organizations and joint activities. They continue to practice the old maxim "the enemy of my enemy is my friend" by recommending that Russia support anti-Western forces and work against those who are supportive of the West. In the post-Western world, these forces may become more powerful, especially if this world proves to be more unstable and dangerous than the world of the U.S. unipolarity. The former Soviet region has emerged as an especially contested area in this respect, and the Russia-Georgia war should serve as the historically confirmed failure of international law to preserve peace in the area. No viable institutions exist in the Caucasus, and additional provocations may further encourage nationalist policies, thereby exacerbating relations with the Western nations.

Despite all the flawed policies of New Thinking and Integration with the West, the general effort of these philosophies to move away from anti-Western isolationism must be recognized. One should remember that before their failures, each of these courses had had a broad social appeal and expressed some deep Russian aspirations. These aspirations must not be neglected in the future, and they can be assessed based on the criteria of security, welfare, and identity. Russians supported the vision of New Thinking because it promised to prevent a threat of nuclear war and to reform the heavily militarized economy. The society was eager to replace the rigid economic and political system with one that would be more open to the world. In addition, a considerable part of Soviet society identified itself with the West culturally. Many in the post-Stalin generation saw the need to move beyond the discourse of "irreconcilable contradictions" between socialism and capitalism, and were open to ideas and cultural products from Europe and the United States. Just as many Russians had initially supported New Thinking, they did not initially oppose the strategy of Integration with the West. That strategy, too, was appealing for its openness to the world. It was no accident that in being hard on Gorbachev for his lack of domestic economic reforms, Yeltsin and Kozyrev took the New Thinking as their point of departure in building relationships with the West.

The post-Kozyrev Great Power Balancing did not mean to return to the Soviet-like isolationism. Indeed, its principal architect, Yevgeni Primakov, had been a New Thinking supporter and a member of Gorbachev's close circle of trusted advisers. Yet the strategy of balancing the United States and building a multipolar world proved to contain elements of isolationism, some of which were unnecessary and did not serve Russia well. Brought up in the tradition of Soviet class-based geopolitics, the father of Great Power Balancing continued to be a geopolitical thinker and thought more about defending his country's political independence and security perimeter than about Russia's economic opportunities. Condemning NATO's enlargement decision was one thing, but attempting to integrate the former Soviet region at the expense of Russia's scarce resources in response to the enlargement was an entirely different matter. The post-Soviet integration was almost explicitly geopolitically driven and was viewed by many as an isolationist-minded project rather than an engagement-minded one. Along the same lines, developing closer economic and political cooperation with non-Western nations in Asia and the Muslim world was fully justified and appropriate, but inviting them into an essentially anti-American balancing coalition was misleading and counterproductive. Resisting American and Western influences in world politics was not merely impractical given Russia's then-poor state of economic and security capabilities. It was also fundamentally misguided conceptually because it was based on the outdated nineteenth-century vision of balance-of-power politics. The strategy was a flawed one because within the increasingly globalized world, staying engaged is not just an option, but a foreign policy imperative.

The vision of Russia as Eurasia, so long as it had a geostrategic balancing component to it, was also a flawed one. It is not surprising that many hard-line nationalists in Russia had been supportive of the vision. To them, the theme of Eurasia was merely a new cloth for the same old geopolitical projection of power and values across the globe at the expense of those in the West. This insistence on Eurasia as anti-American and anti-European did a disservice to Primakov. Even if his own approach was more refined and pragmatic than that of the hard-liners, embracing Eurasia as a traditionally geopolitical notion added to Western perceptions of Russia's new foreign policy as essentially isolationist. Understood in zero-sum terms—if not West, then Eurasia, and vice versa—the vision also could not resonate with the majority of the Russian public. Although many Russians differentiate themselves from the West culturally, few do so in the zero-sum way. Rather, "Western" and "Eurasian" coexist and overlap within the Russian psyche. Russia continues to be a multicultural, multiethnic, and multireligious community that has coexisted and interacted with the Asian and Middle Eastern region. That alone qualifies it to be a "Eurasian power." At the same time, Russia's European-rich experience is no less significant to its cultural identity. In an increasingly global world, Russia and many other national cultures face the challenge of incorporating parts of the West into their own fabric without losing their cultural uniqueness.

Following a National Path

It is no less important that in staying engaged with the world, Russian leaders do not lose sight of what has historically made Russia a special cultural community. Historically, Russia has played a vital role in European developments, while preserving special relations with Asia and the Muslim world. This special geopolitical and geocultural location has not harmed Russia's own identity development—the Russians have learned from their neighbors, while remaining a community with a distinct culture and history.

Globalization, too, is unlikely to erase Russia's distinctiveness, yet it does present the great challenge of finding an appropriate national niche in the new world. Russia must take advantage of the increased global flow of knowledge, goods, and capital. At the same time it must avoid some highly divisive social, economic, and political consequences of globalization, and that requires a considerable national creativity and imagination. The negative consequences of globalization are now visible everywhere. Instead of the earlier expected convergence of cultures and state policies in the world, scholars have observed new cleavages and divergences. Globalization has brought new poverty and socioeconomic divisions. It has created new areas of violence and lawlessness. It has reactivated arms races. And it has enacted new and intensified some old processes of cultural reformulations. Instead of relying on the protection and welfare of Western hegemony, nations often seek refuge in reformulating their interests to better protect their societies and readjust to their regional environments.[4] The new regional and global arrangements therefore emerge as a way of highlighting and accentuating national differences, rather than as a way of reducing their significance. In the process of adjustment to new global challenges, institutional and cultural advantages are no less important than comparative and competitive economic advantages.

Russia's foreign policy, too, needs to reflect the realities of the increasingly global and yet persistently diverse world. Global adjustment can be successful if it is selective and does not come at the expense of vital national institutions and values. Properly applied, such institutions and values should assist Russia in successfully responding to some new security, economic, and cultural challenges during the era of globalization. In security matters, Russia is confronted with threats of terrorism, weapons proliferation, ethnic conflicts, and drug trafficking in the highly volatile Eurasian region. In economic matters, Russia is presented with the new challenges of transnationalization of capital, labor, and energy. And in cultural affairs, Russia has to preserve its identity as it faces a sharply intensified inflow of Western movies, literature, and other cultural products. In responding to these challenges, Russians are likely to empower their state with sufficient capabilities to formulate a strategy of global adjustment. While the state's areas of responsibility must be clearly defined, a strong state has been a part of national history and is likely to remain as such. It is through state leadership that a nation, like Russia, has a chance to successfully respond to the above-noted political, economic, and cultural challenges.

Russia's experience of the past twenty years suggests some errors, as well as accomplishments, in constructing a national path to a globalizing world. New Thinking and, especially, Integration with the West did not withstand the test of time partly because their proponents overestimated the liberal nature of globalization and underestimated the forces of divisiveness and conflict in the world. While advocating global engagement, they neglected the significance of national history and identity. As a result, their international engagement was not sufficiently supported at home, and it came at a very high price of domestic political, social, and economic disintegration. Both New Thinkers and Integrationists sought to solve their domestic problems by obtaining external material and institutional recognition. Both lost control over the economy—Gorbachev as a result of destroying the old centralized system of state orders without having a new one in place, and Yeltsin as a result of introducing price liberalization under the monopolistic structural environment. Both leaders had been stripped of some of their political power—Gorbachev ceded power to radical Westernizers, and Yeltsin made serious concessions to Statists and incorporated them into the ruling establishment. Most importantly, both had little faith in the ability of the state to lead the process of global adjustment. This, too, was a consequence of placing a much higher premium on transnational and global developments than on searching for a national formula of adaptation to these developments. Integrationism was especially guilty of holding an inflexible interpretation of some fundamental phenomena of the contemporary world, such as state power, regional economic differentiation, and cultural diversity. Rather than trying to rethink these phenomena and their role under contemporary conditions, Integrationists often denied their significance altogether under the pretext of the new era of the West-controlled global convergence.

Today, partly as the result of this earlier national amnesia, Westernist proponents of Russian foreign policy have considerably lost their domestic influence. Westernist parties lost the last parliamentary elections, having failed to pass the required 5 percent threshold in order to be represented in the State Duma. In domestic foreign policy discourse, Westernizers continue to be active and visible, partly because they are in a position to draw public attention to impressive developments in the West, and partly because of the West's material support of their efforts. Western institutions, such as the Carnegie Endowment for International Peace, are particularly active in promoting the Westernizers' vision in Russia, and their experts in Moscow are influential participants in all major foreign policy discussions. The past failures have signaled, however, that the vision of Integration with the West is unlikely to succeed as long as it continues to view national tradition as a liability, rather than as an asset in global adjustment.

Great Power Balancing and Great Power Pragmatism showed greater sensitivity to the national tradition in searching for a path to globalization. Primakov's major accomplishment had to do with restoring some important attributes of foreign policy autonomy. Working under the conditions of Russia's continuous economic decline and under a president committed to the previously articulated Westernist vision, the father of Great Power Balancing was able to take and sustain a considerably more independent line in Russia's relations with Yugoslavia, Iraq, and the former Soviet region. He also showed that Russia was in a position to improve its security environment in the former Soviet Union, once it had been willing to invest important diplomatic resources in it. Continuing to be engaged in the tough defense of what Primakov saw as Russia's national interest, while maintaining dialogue with the West, became an important example for Putin to follow. While softening Primakov's preoccupation with geopolitics and strengthening the emphasis on globalization and economic modernization, Putin followed the line of defending national interests as different from those of Western nations. Sensitive to the national tradition, the initiator of Great Power Pragmatism differentiated himself and his strategy of globalization sharply from those associated with New Thinking and Integration with the West.

Overall, Russia confirms the old wisdom that foreign policy is as much a science of revealing some patterns of behavior as it is an art of following them by creatively synthesizing national and global imperatives. Both vision and power are critical here—vision for a reality-grounded strategy formulation, and power for its implementation. Or, if we are to apply Carr's terms, both utopia and reality, free will and determinism, are essential in successful foreign policymaking.

8.3. LESSONS FOR THE WEST

Russia is sufficiently big and powerful, and that limits Western ability to influence its developments. Vast territory, enormous natural resources and military capabilities, and a significant political and diplomatic weight in the world have allowed and will continue to allow Russia considerable room for foreign policy maneuvering. It is hard to believe that the West will ever possess enough power to fully determine the shape and direction of Russia's developments. Yet, as this book has argued, one should not take lightly the role of Western ideas. When united, the West has been and will be influencing Russia in important ways. It is only when divided over issues, such as military intervention in Iraq, that the West would be unlikely to exercise this influence. The West remains Russia's significant Other, and it should act with this in mind by avoiding serious disagreements and sending Russia a unified, rather than conflicted, message. One lesson we can learn from the past twenty years is that engagement, reciprocity, and patience should be the main principles guiding Western actions toward this nation. Carefully applied, these principles in time can bring more security and stability to the world.

Staying Engaged

The first principle that should guide Western actions toward Russia is engagement. A number of Western policymakers, particularly within the Clinton administration, well understood the significance of engaging Russia. For instance, Strobe Talbott, the principal architect of American strategy toward Russia, argued appropriately that reform in Russia was not just about this country, but about the very shape of the new international order waiting to be born in the wake of the Cold War. This was the view of Clinton himself, who felt "if Russia goes bad . . . we'll be back here talking about reversing our defense cuts and spending really big money to wage a new cold war."[5] In the late 1980s–early 1990s, many in Russia, too, believed in Western engagement and even predicated Russia's success on it. This attitude was far from a purely selfish expectation. A genuine Russia-West engagement is critical for making progress in arms control, counterterrorism, and the establishment of regional security arrangements in Eurasia. It is equally critical for developing cooperation in economic and energy matters.

Yet, the West's engagement with Russia has been modest. The majority of the political class in Western nations continued to mistrust Russia well after the Soviet disintegration and showed interest mainly in reducing nuclear threats coming from the region. Despite Gorbachev's and Yeltin's expectations, the West never introduced anything remotely similar to the post–World War II Marshall Plan. Many in Russia and the West evaluated the absence of such a plan as a lack of engagement and a flaw of strategic significance on the West's part. In some ways, the West used Russia's ideological and psychological dependence on its approval and recognition, promising Moscow consistent engagement but limiting such engagement to the bare minimum. The Western leaders went only as far as to extend Russia some symbolic forms of recognition, such as membership in the G-7, while abstaining from more serious commitments to transforming the postcommunist economic and political institutions. The involvement of international organizations, too, proved to be limited and of little assistance in Russia's economic recovery. The IMF, for instance, was late to acknowledge the need for institutional reform in Russia, and it was hardly in a position to stimulate such reform. The more recent efforts by President Barack Obama to "reset" relations with Russia suggest a new promising way of engaging it directly and bilaterally, thereby recognizing the country's importance in the world.

Opponents of engagement with Russia in the West continue to be strong. Criticism of Western, particularly American, policy toward Russia was especially loud under President Bush.[6] Some see problems with Russia's human rights record under Putin. Others charge that Russia presents a threat to the West's strategic interests and collaborates with dangerous regimes. Still others point to Russia's recent activism in the former Soviet region, seeing in it expressions of the Kremlin's new imperialism and attempts to muscle its way with the newly independent states at the expense of their sovereignty. This rhetoric became especially prominent in the wake of the Russia-Georgia war. Suffice it to recall the White House's initial reaction to the recent crisis in the South Caucasus, with U.S. Secretary of State Condoleezza Rice comparing Russia's role to the Soviet Union's invasion of Czechoslovakia in 1968 and Vice President Dick Cheney vowing to punish Russia for its "aggression." Several NATO vessels have also entered the Black Sea—officially to distribute humanitarian aid, but in reality to intimidate Russia. With the latter's determination to secure its presence in the Caucasus by recognizing independence of Abkhasia and South Ossetia, the former Soviet region became a cordon sanitaire separating Russia and Western powers. Events were developing in a direction similar to what happened after World War II, when the two sides found themselves locked in a race to secure Europe on their own terms. If Western leaders continued to push for NATO membership for Georgia and Ukraine by offering them Membership Action Plans (MAPs), confrontation with Russia was sure to escalate.

Punishing or ignoring Russia is not likely to discipline it, however. Russia continues to be in a position not to yield to the pressure of tough rhetoric and isolationist actions from the West. Against expectations, such policies are likely to strengthen anti-Western Russian nationalists and push Russia further away from the Western nations. Nationalists need an image of the West as a threat—they are dependent on it for their own survival. They will only be grateful to Western politicians, like Cheney, for assisting them in constructing such an image. Until the West becomes a key reference point for Russia, Western isolationism will be counterproductive in influencing the Kremlin. The examples of NATO's expansion and military interventions in Kosovo and Iraq teach us that ignoring Russia or viewing it as a threat is likely to lead to a more defiant, not a more cooperative, Russia. Continuing along these lines risks missing important opportunities in economic and security areas in Eurasia. It is also sure to get Russia off track politically by improving the position of authoritarian nationalist forces and providing "proof" that the West is really interested in stripping Russia of its international status, not in strengthening its currently weak democratic institutions.

Engaging on Mutually Acceptable Terms

Engagement will be especially effective when conducted on a reciprocal or mutually acceptable basis. Anything short of reciprocity might result in cheating by the sides involved. Hegemonic engagement on Western terms will come at the price of Russia's own interests and perceptions. As Thomas Graham wrote, "It is not Russia's strength that generates and feeds the fear of it, it is weakness of the West and its lack of confidence."[7] Rather than trying to dictate policies, the United States should acknowledge a strong and confident Russia that acts as a responsible protector of its interests in the world. On the other hand, attempts to appease Russia by jeopardizing the West's own interests are not likely to last either, because of a lack of sufficient support within Western societies. Former Cold War enemies will develop the required trust only when they openly engage in direct negotiations of mutually acceptable forms of cooperation.

Unfortunately, the support in the West for hegemonic engagement with Russia is stronger than for reciprocal engagement. Many in the West are convinced that they are doing Russia a great favor by insisting on the universal applicability of Western market democracy and pressing ahead with making Russia in their own image. Russia's insistence on its own interests and cultural specifics often gets dismissed as reflecting the views of remnants of the Soviet "totalitarianism" and anti-Western nationalism. The dominant policy community in the West believes that Western civilization is in a position to teach the rest of the world about economic and political institutions as well as moral standards. Possessing enormous power and resources, the West has a tendency to perceive non-Western nations as passive and backward followers, rather than equal participants in world development. This attitude remains a serious obstacle to the mutual understanding required for reciprocal engagement.

Examples of this kind of hegemonic attitude are multiple. Francis Fukuyama, an ardent proponent of Western triumphalism in the world and the author of the popular "end of history" thesis, once famously denied Russia the need to have its own national interests. In the context of Russia's new geopolitical boundaries and ethnic conflicts after the Soviet breakup, he recommended that Russia concentrate on its "internal" problems of modernization and let the West deal with external challenges.[8] To Russia, this was hardly an attractive proposition. Both the elites and the larger society soon rediscovered Russia's geopolitical identity and distinct national interests. Partly as a result of the described hegemonic attitude visible in Western actions, many Russians also chose to blame the West, overwhelmingly, for their poverty and insecurity. For example, in 2001, according to the respected polling agency Public Opinion, about 50 percent of Russians agreed with the statement, "In today's world, the United States plays a negative, rather than positive, role."[9] This attitude has become even more pronounced over time, as the U.S.-Russia relations have progressed following the war in Iraq and the colored revolutions in the former Soviet region.

A practical illustration of this sentiment is the fact that U.S.-Russia relations over the past ten years often displayed the noted hegemonic attitude. Not listening to what Russians themselves—across the political spectrum—identified as their national interests and acting against such identification was, unfortunately, all too common. Russia's insistence on the need to provide security and stability in the former Soviet Union was often labeled as "neoimperial" temptations. Russia also wanted to fully participate in European security institutions, not to be isolated from them. It therefore opposed the plan to expand NATO. However, many in the West dismissed Russia's opposition as pure paranoia, and few seriously thought there was a need to accommodate Russia's desire to be a member of the Western world. The Russia-Georgia conflict, too, became possible in part because the balance of power in the region has long ago been violated by NATO's decision to expand its military infrastructure at the expense of Russia's interests. International law was silent in the Caucasus because it had been silent when Yugoslavia and Iraq were attacked by Western powers without approval of the United Nations, of which Russia is a member. Russia's recognition of South Ossetia and Abkhazia also followed the West's recognition of Kosovo, which had established dangerous precedent for redrawing the political map of the world.

In economic reform, many in Russia preferred a gradual pace and strong role reserved for the state. Yet U.S. officials forcefully communicated to their Russian counterparts that they believed in shock therapy, or fast solutions, not gradualism. This made a difference in how Yeltsin proceeded with economic reform, but also set the terms for his confrontation with the opposition. These were hardly the best terms for engagement with Russia. American officials wanted to participate in changes in Russia and Eurasia, but often were unprepared to compromise on their policy vision.

In addition, U.S. attitudes were occasionally plagued by inconsistencies and double standards, which also did not strengthen the American engagement with Russia. Different standards were applied to the United States and Russia in world affairs: in some cases, Russian actions were found to be "unacceptable," whereas similar behavior by the United States was understood to reflect that country's national interests. Thus, American officials at first unequivocally supported Yeltsin's decision to invade Chechnya, but withdrew their support at later stages. Furthermore, beginning in 1995, various representatives of the Clinton administration started to raise concerns over Russian military bases in the former Soviet region, but did not make a connection to the United States' extensive military presence around the world. Finally, there was serious criticism of growing sales of Russian arms abroad, despite the fact that the United States consistently ranked as the top seller of weapons in international markets.

The mutually acceptable engagement also means a respectful treatment by both sides. While indicating a willingness to engage Russia in equal relationships, it is important to avoid rhetoric and lecturing—the model of which was set by President Obama during the U.S.-Russia summit in Moscow in July 2009. However, Obama's efforts were then undermined at home with Vice President Joseph Biden's public statement about Russia. "The reality is, the Russians are where they are," Biden said, implying that Russia will have no choice but to agree to work with the United States. "They have a shrinking population base, they have a withering economy, they have a banking sector and structure that is not likely to be able to withstand the next fifteen years, they're in a situation where the world is changing before them and they're clinging to something in the past that is not sustainable."[10] Biden's remarks immediately provoked questions from the Kremlin about the seriousness of the White House intentions. Calling the criticism "perplexing," Sergei Prikhodko, the chief foreign policy adviser to President Medvedev, asked, "The question is: who is shaping the U.S. foreign policy, the president or respectable members of his team? . . . If some members of Obama's team and government . . . disagree with the course of their president, we just need to know this."[11]

A genuinely successful engagement is therefore difficult to design and maintain. Given the history of hostilities between Russia and the West and divergent current interests, there will always be differences in the two nations' approaches to solving existing problems. Nevertheless, in light of the alternatives, engagement on mutually acceptable terms is worth a serious effort. The alternatives are likely to be similar to those resulting from Western attempts to isolate Russia as a meaningful world politics player. A resentful Russia is hardly a reliable partner. Faced with powerful Western pressures, Russia may not always be able to defend its vision of national interest. However, it is sure to have sufficient resources to make it difficult for the West to pursue its own interests in the post-Soviet region. Russian leaders will be likely to shirk obligations into which they have been coerced. Reciprocal actions, honest communication over existing approaches, and explicit agreements—written ones, if necessary—are a better way to solidify trust and cooperation.

Tempering Expectations

In addition to engagement and reciprocity in relations with Russia, the West ought to be patient and not expect miracles. Unreasonable expectations about

Russia have not been uncommon in the past and should not be a guide in the future. After the fall of the Berlin Wall, many hoped for Russia to quickly leave its past behind and to emerge as a market democracy with special relationships to Western nations. The reality proved different, and Russia's modernization so far has not really entailed Westernization. In the economic realm, Russia has built not a free-market model of capitalism, but rather an oligarchical capitalism, with the economy largely controlled by and divided among former high-ranking state and Communist Party officials. In the area of political and legal institutions, Russia developed a superpresidential system with few effective checks and balances. Utilizing this system, Putin tightened his grip over the legislature, party building, regions, and electronic media. As far as the relationship with the West is concerned, many polls indicate that many Russians see the West as a potential threat, rather than as a friend or strategic partner.

The West bears a share of the responsibility for these unattractive outcomes. After all, Western officials pushed aggressively for shock therapy as a model for economic reform in Russia. They also deepened their relationships with Yeltsin beyond a reasonable level and supported him even when he relied on military force in relations with parliament and the rebellious republic of Chechnya. In the long run, the perception of Yeltsin as a "good guy" fighting "bad guys" or the "red-brown" opposition did a great disservice to Russia, and it worsened the image of the West. Finally, the choice to expand NATO by excluding Russia from it, despite available alternative ways to provide security in Europe, did not and could not improve Western credibility in the Russians' eyes.

The new efforts by the United States to "reset" relations with Russia will also require time and persistence. While it is encouraging to see a serious attempt to change the relationship on the part of the United States, there are serious issues that divide the two sides—NATO expansion, missile defense system, and exploitation of energy reserves in the former Soviet region—and it remains to be seen how they are going to be addressed and resolved. Framework for their resolution is yet to be put in place.

To change the skeptical attitudes by Russians and the Kremlin, it is important to formulate some long-term objectives and to organize relationships with Russia with these objectives in mind. First, nations should select the bilateral relationships' most vital and pressing issues that would reflect broad social needs and the interests of whole societies. For example, the issue of economic transformation should be put on the agenda only if it reflects the desires of both Russian and Western societies. In the past, there have been gaps in preferences between Western ruling elites and larger societies. Thus, in the United States, the willingness of President Clinton to put together a massive package of financial assistance to support Yeltsin's economic reform was only partially backed by the U.S. Congress. Although this willingness generated inflated expectations in Russia, many in the West simply did not see the economic assistance as a basis for a long-term relationship; instead, they emphasized the significance of security issues, such as nuclear arms reduction. The second and related point is that Western policymakers must avoid developing exclusive relationships with the ruling elite, much less with the president and his entourage. While negotiating with the official leadership, it is important to keep track of political attitudes across the entire social and political spectrum. It is with an eye on issues that are important to society as a whole, rather than the ruling elite only, that the negotiation agenda should be set. The personalization of relationships with Russian presidents may contribute to the emergence of a regime that will be only rhetorically democratic and pro-Western, but in reality will alienate the majority of Russians and serve the interests of very narrow political circles. Foreign policy that is blind to developments outside the ruling regime has no balance and is likely to fail as soon as the leadership in the Kremlin changes. Finally, once both sides determine and agree on the most important issues, they should commit appropriate resources and stay focused on solving the issues.

This way of determining a Western-Russian agenda is likely to take time, but it may produce more robust and predictable relationships in the future. Over time, realistic expectations about Russia, attentiveness to attitudes across Russian society, and a willingness to be true to assumed commitment should help to erase the current image of the West as overly pushy and opportunistic. Western policymakers ought to remember: the West continues to be Russia's significant Other. So long as Russia's leaders carefully study and seek to learn from Western thinking and actions, the West will continue to make important contributions to how Russia progresses into its future.

NOTES

1. Edward Hallett Carr, *The Twenty Years' Crisis, 1919–1939* (New York: Harper & Row, 1964), 11.

2. As quoted in Andrew Kuchins's notes from a meeting with Medvedev at the Valdai Discussion Club in September 2008 (Georgie Anne Geyer, "Russia First to Test New President," *Chicago Tribune*, November 14, 2008, www.chicagotribune.com/news/nationworld/chi-oped1114geyernov14,0,7013815.story).

3. Carr, *Twenty Years' Crisis*, 11.

4. On national searches for strategies of adaptation to global economy, see Erik Helleiner and Andreas Pickel, eds., *Economic Nationalism in a Globalizing World* (Ithaca, NY: Cornell University Press, 2005).

5. Strobe Talbott, *The Russia House* (New York: Random House, 2002), 58.

6. Andrei P. Tsygankov, *Russophobia: Anti-Russian Lobby and American Foreign Policy* (New York: Palgrave, 2009).

7. Thomas Graham, "Dialektika sily i slabosti," *Vedomosti*, June 29, 2007.

8. Francis Fukuyama, "Ambiguities of National Interest," in *Rethinking Russia's National Interests*, ed. Stephen Sestanovich (Washington, DC: Center for Strategic and International Studies, 1994).

9. *Amerika: Vzglyad iz Rossiyi* (Moscow: Institut fonda "Obschestvennoye mneniye," 2001), 137, 215.

10. Vice President Joe Biden's interview with Peter Spiegel, *Wall Street Journal*, July 23, 2009, http://online.wsj.com/article/SB124846217750479721.html.

11. Andrew E. Kramer, "New Biden Criticism Surprises Russia," *New York Times*, July 26, 2009.

Essential Reading

OFFICIAL VIEWS

Kozyrev, A. V. "Russia: A Chance for Survival." *Foreign Affairs* 71, no. 2, 1992.

Lavrov, Sergei. "Russia and the World in the 21st Century." *Russia in Global Affairs*, no. 3, July–September, 2008.

Medvedev, Dmitri. Presidential Address to the Federal Assembly. Moscow, November 5, 2008, www.kremlin.ru.

Putin, Vladimir. "Rossiya na rubezhe tysyacheletiy." *Nezavisimaya gazeta*, December 30, 1999.

Putin, Vladimir. Speech at the Munich Conference on Security Policy. Munich, February 10, 2007, www.kremlin.ru.

Primakov, Ye. *Russian Crossroads: Toward the New Millennium*. Yale University Press, 2004.

BOOKS

Allison, R., M. Light, and S. White. *Putin's Russia and the Enlarged Europe*. Wiley-Blackwell, 2006.

Antonenko, O., and K. Pinnick. *Russia and the European Union: Prospects for a New Relationship*. Routledge, 2008.

Baev, P. *Russian Energy Policy and Military Power: Putin's Quest for Greatness*. Routledge, 2008.

Bowker, M. 2007. *Russia, America and the Islamic World*. Ashgate, 2007.

Clunan, Anne L. *The Social Construction of Russia's Resurgence: Aspirations, Identity and Security Interests*. Johns Hopkins University Press, 2009.

Danilovich, A. *Russian-Belarus Integration: Playing Games behind the Kremlin Walls*. Ashgate, 2006.

Donaldson, R. H., and J. L. Nogee. *The Foreign Policy of Russia: Changing Systems, Enduring Interests*. M. E. Sharpe, 2009.

Goldgeier, J., and M. McFaul. *Power and Purpose: US Policy toward Russia after the Cold War*. Washington, DC, 2003.

Kreutz, A. *Russia in the Middle East. Friend or Foe?* Greenwood, 2006.

Kuhrt, Natasha, and N. Kuhrt. *Russian Policy towards China and Japan: The Yeltsin and Putin Periods*. Routledge, 2007.

Legvold, Robert, ed. *Russian Foreign Policy in the 21st Century and the Shadow of the Past*. Columbia University Press, 2007.

Lo, Bobo. *Axis of Convenience: Moscow, Beijing and the New Geopolitics*. Brookings Institution, 2008.

Malcolm, N., A. Pravda, R. Allison, and M. Light. *Internal Factors in Russian Foreign Policy*. Oxford University Press, 1996.

Mankoff, Jeffrey. *Russian Foreign Policy: The Return of Great Power Politics*. Rowman & Littlefield, 2009.

Nygren, Bertil. *The Rebuilding of Greater Russia: Putin's Foreign Policy towards the CIS Countries*. Routledge, 2007.

Shakleyina, T. A., ed. *Vneshnyaya politika i bezopasnost' sovremennoi Rossiyi, 1991– 2002*. 4 vols. ROSSPEN, 2002.

Tsygankov, Andrei P. *Whose World Order? Russia's Perception of American Ideas after the Cold War*. University of Notre Dame Press, 2004.

Wishnick, E. *Mending Fences: The Evolution of Moscow's China Policy from Brezhnev to Yeltsin*. University of Washington Press, 2001.

Zimmerman, W. *The Russian People and Foreign Policy: Russian Elite and Mass Perspectives, 1993–2000*. Princeton University Press, 2002.

ARTICLES

Allison, R. "Russia Resurgent? Moscow's Campaign to 'Coerce Georgia to Peace.'" *International Affairs* 6, 2008.

Averre, D. "Russia's Foreign Policy and the Global Political Environment." *Problems of Post-Communism* 55, no. 5, 2008.

Bukkvoll, T. "Putin's Strategic Partnership with the West: The Domestic Politics of Russian Foreign Policy." *Comparative Strategy* 22, no. 3, 2003.

Charap, S. "The Petersburg Experience: Putin's Political Career and Russian Foreign Policy." *Problems of Post-Communism* 51, no. 1, 2004.

Feklyunina, Valentina. "Battle for Perceptions: Projecting Russia in the West." *Europe-Asia Studies*, 60, no. 4, 2008.

Lynch, A. "Realism of Russian Foreign Policy." *Europe-Asia Studies* 53, 2001.

O'Loughlin, J., G. O Tuathail, and V. Kolossov. "A 'Risky Westward Turn'? Putin's 9-11 Script and Ordinary Russians." *Europe-Asia Studies* 56, no. 1, 2004.

Renz, Bettina. "Putin's Militocracy? An Alternative Interpretation of *Siloviki* in Russian Politics." *Europe-Asia Studies* 58, no. 6, 2006.

Splidsboel-Hansen, F. "Past and Future Meet: Alexandr Gorchakov and Russian Foreign Policy." *Europe-Asia Studies* 54, no. 3, 2002.

Stent, Angela. "Revolution and Restoration in Putin's Foreign Policy." *Europe-Asia Studies* 60, no. 6, 2008.

Rose, Richard, and Neil Munro. "Do Russians See Their Future in Europe or the CIS?" *Europe-Asia Studies*, 60, no. 1, 2008.

Trenin, D. "Russia Leaves the West." *Foreign Affairs*, 2007.

Tsygankov, Andrei P. "If Not by Tanks, Then by Banks? The Role of Soft Power in Putin's Foreign Policy." *Europe-Asia Studies*, 58, no. 7, 2006.

INTERNET SITES

Eurasia Daily Monitor, Jamestown Foundation, http://jamestown.org/edm.

Foreign Ministry of Russian Federation, www.mid.ru.

Johnson's Russia List, Center for Defense Information, www.cdi.org/russia/johnson/default.cfm.

Radio Free Europe/Radio Liberty, www.rferl.org.

Russia in Global Affairs, http://eng.globalaffairs.ru.

Russia's President, www.kremlin.ru.

Russia Profile, www.russiaprofile.org.

Russian & Eurasian Program, Carnegie Endowment for International Peace or Moscow Center, www.carnegieendowment.org/programs/russia/.

Index

About the Author

Andrei P. Tsygankov is professor of international relations and political science at San Francisco State University. He is the author of many books, including *Russophobia: Anti-Russian Lobby and American Foreign Policy* (2009), *Whose World Order? Russia's Perception of American Ideas after the Cold War* (2004), and *Pathways after Empire: National Identity and Foreign Economic Policy in the Post-Soviet World* (2001). He has also published dozens of book chapters, journal articles, and academic papers on Russia, foreign policy, and international relations.